Kids and branding in a digital world

MANCHESTER
1824
Manchester University Press

Kids and branding in a digital world

Barrie Gunter

Manchester University Press

The right of Barrie Gunter to be identified as the author of this work has been asserted by him in accordance with the Copyright, Designs and Patents Act 1988.

Published by Manchester University Press
Altrincham Street, Manchester M1 7JA

www.manchesteruniversitypress.co.uk

British Library Cataloguing-in-Publication Data
A catalogue record for this book is available from the British Library

Library of Congress Cataloging-in-Publication Data applied for

ISBN 978 0 7190 9787 4 hardback
ISBN 978 1 7849 9245 3 paperback

First published 2016

The publisher has no responsibility for the persistence or accuracy of URLs for any external or third-party internet websites referred to in this book, and does not guarantee that any content on such websites is, or will remain, accurate or appropriate.

Typeset in Bembo and Helvetica by
Servis Filmsetting Ltd, Stockport, Cheshire
Printed in Great Britain by
Bell & Bain Ltd, Glasgow

Contents

Introduction

Children are born into a world surrounded by commodities and services that cater to their every need. This world of consumerism plies them with multiple choices in terms of what to eat and drink, things they can play with, how to look after their well-being, how to fit in with others, how to define their identity and present it to the world, how to improve their abilities and skills, and how to grow and develop as individuals. Much of what children do in their early years is about learning and having fun. Acquiring rules about how to behave in socially acceptable ways across a range of settings, and developing physical and mental skills, through formal education and informal play, pre-occupy their lives. This is how it has always been. The key feature today is that much of this developmental activity takes place against a backdrop of 'consumerism'.

Children have needs, and products or services have functions that are directed towards need fulfilment. If a child is hungry, he or she eats. If they are thirsty, they take a drink. To cover their bodies they wear clothes. To establish their territory, they get their own room which they furnish to their own taste. To alleviate boredom, they play with toys or games. None of these behaviours has just surfaced. Today, however, children are confronted with a multitude of choices. When deciding what to eat for breakfast, supermarkets may offer a range of 200+ cereals to choose from. Enter the search phrase, 'clothing brands for children' into Google, and it delivers 179 million results. Do the same for 'toy brands for children' and it delivers over 43 million results.

As consumers, we are all confronted with choices of this kind; we have had to learn how to cope with this overload of information and make choices from diverse selections across a multitude of product types. An important aspect of this choice process is the concept of the 'brand'. A brand is a distinguishing mark that separates one version of a product from others. In physical terms it takes the form of a label or name that is often accompanied by other distinguishing attributes such as logos or symbols that have distinctive designs and colours. At a psychological level, brands comprise much more than these physical attributes. They convey meanings to us about what makes the brand special compared with other rival products in the same category. Our own experiences with the brand might then confirm the impression of itself the brand conveys to us through its symbolism or they might even add to the manufacturer's self-promotions. The meaning of a brand can often derive from the kind of identity we can create for ourselves through using or being associated with it.

As part of their growing up, children learn about consumerism and about branding. They learn not only what are the functions of different commodities but also whether and why a product variant with one distinguishing mark or 'brand' can be deemed superior to another (Gunter & Furnham, 1998). This process of development or 'consumer socialisation' among children evolves gradually over time. Children's abilities in this context can be driven forward at varying pace by the richness and diversity of their own consumer experiences, but they are also underpinned by the level of cognitive development they have attained (John, 1999). As we will see in this book, there have been running debates about whether children's cognitive development can be articulated as a series of distinct stages that generally appear at specific ages or whether it is a fluid process that evolves gradually rather than in a stepwise process.

What is now widely established through a range of sources is that, regardless of their level of psychological complexity, children display some brand consciousness not only by the time they reach their teens but long before this during their 'tweens' (ages 8 to 12) and in some cases even in their 'pre-tweens' (ages 2 to 7). Furthermore, brand developers and advertisers are well aware of this phenomenon and devise marketing strategies to target children (or their parents) from the earliest stages of their lives. Hence, we live in a world in which kids are converted into consumers at the earliest opportunity. As young people who are also young 'consumers', kids display an awareness of brands that might initially take the form of brand name identification or product requests to parents using these names. A major young consumer study sponsored by industry magazine, *Marketing Week*, that was carried out in the UK among 6–11-year-olds found that these kids were able to match brand logos to brand names for soft drinks' brands such as Coca-Cola, Pepsi, Tropicana, Ribena, Sprite, Fanta; for sports' brands such as Adidas and Nike; and for an entertainment brand such as Disney and a technology brand such as Apple, with extremely high levels (90%) of accuracy (Costa, 2010).

As they get older and become capable of seeing the world in more sophisticated and reflective ways, they attach special meanings to brand names, and choices are made not just because they desire a particular product – which is usually the level at which 'pre-tweens' operate – but because they want a specific variant of a product identified by its brand name. In this case, the brand name signals something more than the type of product or its distinctive core product-related functionalities but also carries meaning about spin-off effects of consumption, often manifest in terms of self-identity or social status.

Similarly with advertising, researchers have observed and traced specific patterns of child development that provide an important backdrop to the emergence of young people as informed and discerning consumers. At first, children cannot differentiate advertising from surrounding media content within which it is embedded, but gradually they do notice the distinctive qualities of advertisements. Initially, very simple perceptual distinctions are drawn, with the observation that advertisements on television, for example, are noticeably shorter in duration than are programmes (Ward & Wackman, 1973; Ward, Wackman & Wartella, 1977). As they grow older, children come to recognise that advertisements have a different purpose from programmes; they develop an understanding of what that purpose is, the ways in which it can be achieved, and eventually, they can evaluate the quality and truthfulness of advertisers' claims (Kunkel, 2010).

Over time, as children's comprehension of advertising grows, so their ideas and perceptions concerning brands become more sophisticated. The *Marketing Week* survey mentioned earlier found that even kids under the age of 9 could rank brands by their 'coolness', although tastes were also found to change with age, and the 'coolest' brands for the under-9s were not the same as those named by older children. Once they advance in their 'tweenage' years (8 to 12), kids already begin to demonstrate a stronger interest in more adult-oriented brands. They also object to any brand advertising that adopts what they perceive to be a 'childish' tone in its promotions (Costa, 2010).

Teachers have also observed that kids are influenced by brands and brand logos. One survey of teaching support staff across England found that an overwhelming proportion of those interviewed (90%+) rated brands and logos as being as important to children's choices as were their friends. These school support staff had observed children denigrating 'cheap' goods and preferring more expensive brands, even when the children were known to come from economically poorer households. Choosing the right brand to be associated with was a critical factor underpinning personal taste and social standing (ATL, 2008).

Such findings do not, of course, tell us how brand awareness became established, whether branding per se determined product choices and consumption levels, or the degree to which brand preferences can be separated from the recommendations or choices of friends or wider peer groups. This is a topic that we will examine in this book. As we will see later, all these variables can be important to brand choices among kids, and more complex research methodologies than survey interviews with witnesses are needed to establish how these variables are inter-connected. Nonetheless, this evidence does serve to underline that brands are talked about a lot by children from an early age, and kids seem able to articulate brand-related opinions almost as soon as their language abilities provide them with the tools to do so.

Much of the early thinking about children, advertising, and branding tended to give much emphasis to the vulnerability of young people to the persuasive influences of marketing professionals and their commercial messages. A lack of understanding of what brands are and how advertising works was thought to place children at a disadvantage, compared with adults, in terms of being able to protect themselves against the influences of commercial promotions. Not surprisingly, such observations led to calls for tighter controls over advertising directed at children and over advertising that appeared in media outputs known to be popular among children (Roberts, 1983). Such concerns were especially pronounced in relation to product domains such as alcohol and food (Page & Brewster, 2007; Warren, Wicks, Fosu & Chung, 2008; Gunter, Hansen & Touri, 2010).

As a counterpoint to these understandable concerns, some evidence – though not much initially – emerged that children could be helped to cope better with attractive persuasive appeals by being better informed about advertising, branding, and the activities of marketing professionals. Training programmes could be developed, for instance, that could educate children about marketing and persuasion, and through this type of activity, young and immature consumers could be taught to internalise cognitive defences of their own against the influences of advertising and branding (Rogers, 2002). Some empirical evidence even emerged that such defences could help to protect children and render them less vulnerable to these influences (Robertson & Rossiter, 1974).

A lot of early thinking about children's developing comprehension of advertising and branding was underpinned by a specific model of child development originally created by French psychologist, Jean Piaget. Piaget identified a number of distinct stages to children's cognitive development that were tied closely to specific age ranges. As children passed from one stage to the next, their abilities to interpret events in the world around them became more sophisticated. Until they had reached a given stage of development, however, they might be incapable of engaging in certain kinds of thought processes which in turn limited the complexity of their judgements about objects and events in their every day environments. This model was widely adopted by scholars interested in finding a model to explain the nature of children's developing comprehension of advertising. Using this model, the simplistic nature of young children's descriptions and explanations of advertising was ascribed to their stage of cognitive development which delimited the quality and complexity of judgements they were capable of making.

Just as Piaget's model of children's cognitive development has been challenged by developmental psychologists, and was later modified, a shift was also noted in the value attached to his model in the child consumer context. An alternative viewpoint was presented that accepted that while there may be some truth in Piaget's articulations of different kinds of thought processes, their emergence was more fluid and less age-dependent than he had allowed. Newer models of children's cognitive maturation recognised that some children could acquire advanced cognitive skills sooner than others and that the types of skills that defined a specific Piagetian stage of development did not always develop at the same pace among different children (John, 1999; Moses & Baldwin, 2005). These newer models of children's cognitive development have provided fresh explanations of young consumers' understanding of the sales purpose and persuasive intent of brand advertising and of their growing abilities to recognise deception and bias in promotional messages (Mills & Keil, 2005).

Subsequently, theoretical thinking about child development and consumerism developed still further with the observation that responses to advertisements and brands can occur not only at a cognitive level but also at an emotional level. The latter type of response can create conditions that preempt cognitive interpretation and mediate the nature of a consumer's engagement with advertising messages. Much can depend here also on the importance of the advertised product for the consumer. With important – often high cost items – consumers tend to give more careful thought to purchases because making the wrong decision can be costly (Gunter, Oates & Blades, 2005).

With low cost items that are often purchased more regularly, such weighing up of product attributes is less likely to occur. With 'important' items, consumers become more involved in assessing brands and associated advertisements and seek out factual information about quality and performance. With less important items, decisions can be swayed more by the stylistic features of the advertising itself. Thus, any educational packages designed to enhance children's knowledge and understanding of advertising, branding and persuasion need to take into account different levels of cognitive processing and emotional responding for different product types to ensure that any programmes designed to enhance cognitive defences take these different levels of processing into account (Rozendaal, Lapierre, van Reijmersdal & Buijzen, 2013).

The mode of processing of advertisements and brands – and whether this is primarily cognitive or emotional – can also be triggered by specific characteristics of advertising. These triggers work best when they can be clearly discerned. The ability of children in the first instance to differentiate advertising from surrounding media content therefore remains an important element even in this new model of child development (Brucks, Armstrong & Goldberg, 1988).

In the digital era, as consumers have become more empowered in terms of their reception of media content, advertisers have responded by developing more subtle forms of promotion and persuasion that are not always clearly discernible from the surrounding media content in which they are embedded. Such marketing developments pose fresh concerns about the vulnerability of children to marketing campaigns and new tests for the efficacy of models of analysis of children's consumer development (Winkler & Buckner, 2006; Lee, Choi, Quilliam & Cole, 2009).

The twenty-first century has witnessed dramatic changes in the way people can communicate with each other. The emergence of wired and wireless communications networks in the form of the internet and associated online social media have transformed our private lives and the world of business. Through these technologies, consumers have been empowered, not just because they have more choices but also because more brand-related information is available to them. Furthermore, a lot of this brand information now comes from other consumers, not just from brand manufacturers and their agents. At the same time, brand promotion techniques have evolved and adopted these technologies for their own purposes (Deal, 2005; Dean, Digrande, Field et al., 2012). One outcome has been the emergence of more subtle forms of brand promotion that have moved away from more obvious forms of advertising that experienced consumers readily recognise and often develop scepticism about (Moore & Rideout, 2007).

Brand developers are keenly aware that they need to capture the attention of children from as soon as they are cognitively capable of even the crudest forms of brand recognition. However, even with these young and unformed consumers, new techniques are needed to cultivate brand loyalty. The best way to get children's attention might mean using formats that are known to be effective outside the world of marketing. This can take the form of merging a product brand with an established entertainment brand such as an animated cartoon character. It might also take the form of integrating the product brand with an entertainment environment such as an electronic game or virtual world (Bergstrom 2000; Costa, 2010; Dredge, 2012).

Some of these new promotional activities can serve a parallel, socially constructive purpose such as the promotion of healthy or positive social behaviour among children. One interesting example of this phenomenon is the children's television series *Lazy Town* in which the hero Sportacus encourages the fictional kids in Lazy Town to be more active, take exercise and eat a healthy diet. As well as being a successful entertainment brand in its own right, *Lazy Town* has spawned spin-off merchandise and attracted partnerships from other established brands. Partner brands are selected with care and must convey symbolic messages that are socially positive and consistent with the ethos of the television brand (Costa, 2010). Nevertheless, an entertainment format that attracts children is permeated with brand promotions.

As we will see, the use of social media, electronic games, and online virtual environments or 'advergames' and 'adverworlds' to promote brands is a rapidly growing phenomenon and raises important questions for marketers about their effectiveness as advertising techniques, as well as for society about their ethics in targeting children (Harris, Speers, Schwartz & Brownell, 2012). Although consumerism is a central aspect of children's lives, as with all other consumers they are entitled to know when they are confronted with material that is designed to influence them in terms of the commodity preferences and purchase decisions. With overt forms of advertising that are openly identified in terms of purpose, inexperienced consumers gradually learn to discern promotional messages. With disguised forms of brand promotion, their subtlety can mean that even adult consumers may not always be aware that an apparent entertainment experience is also a marketing activity (Quilliam, Lee, Cole & Kim, 2011).

In this book we will examine the way children become brand conscious, how this process develops, and the different ways in which brand engagement is manifest among young consumers. With the dramatic changes that have occurred in communications media since the turn of the twenty-first century, we will consider how these have been adopted by brands and whether our understanding of brand socialisation that derives from the study of children and traditional forms of advertising can be translated to this new world of marketing. To begin this journey, we must first consider the meaning of 'brand' and 'branding' and examine some of their historical roots.

This book draws heavily on psychological research into cognitive development and its relevance to how consumers learn to handle marketing across childhood. Against this backdrop it focuses on newer developments in marketing that have accompanied the emergence of digital media technologies and the new forms of communications they have produced. These platforms have been enthusiastically adopted by marketers. Why? In part, the answer to this question is because they are there. In part, it is also because they know that many people, young and old, engage with these technologies and so provide a ready-made audience for promotions about brands that run through these new communications systems. There is also the fact that through technological modifications to mainstream mass media increasingly computer literate consumers have learned how to circumvent conventional advertising messages used by marketers to reach mass consumer markets and many niche markets.

It is in recognition and acknowledgement of the fact that most consumers learn to become critical in their dealings with marketing messages and brand presentations that marketers have been drawn to new media formats. These formats provide marketers with opportunities to engage with consumers in ways that are not always obvious to consumers. The 'obviousness' of marketing here refers to the traditional advertising formats to which consumers became accustomed over several generations.

Marketers have witnessed deterioration in effectiveness of conventional forms of advertising because digital media systems have equipped consumers to take control over media consumption in ways that were not previously available to them. Such developments have empowered consumers so that they can no longer be spoon-fed advertising and other branding promotions via mainstream media in ways that are difficult for them to avoid. Nowadays consumers can edit out advertisements from their TV diets and this has forced advertisers to seek new methods that consumers can less easily avoid. One solution here is to integrate the marketing content more tightly into other media (entertainment and information) content. Another aspect of this development has been the emergence of more disguised forms of brand promotions in new media – especially within social media and computer games – where there is less distinction between the 'brand promotion' and other content.

Consumers do learn to become informed about marketing practices in the traditional sense and skilled at coping with them. This learning process – usually subsumed under the broad heading of 'consumer socialisation' – is an integral aspect of child development these days. Children learn about brands. They learn about standard forms of advertising. Initially they learn to distinguish physically between promotional messages and surrounding media content and then later to make judgments about advertising based on an understanding of what the message is designed for.

Children learn from early on about the subtle production techniques used by advertisers and make comparisons between what advertisers tell them and what their own brand experiences have revealed to them. The problem is that this learning is attached to traditional forms of advertising and other types of brand promotion. Where new forms of promotion occur that are less clearly differentiated from the surrounding media environment, then problems can occur in terms of knowing that there is 'marketing' taking place. Nevertheless, consumer literacy skills can still be imparted to young consumers even in relation to these new marketing forms. This requires a new form of learning and that is in part what this book makes reference to.

In addition, the regulators of marketing as well as advertisers themselves have duties of responsibility in this context. There are comprehensive mandatory regulations and codes of practices drawn up and implemented by advertising regulators, and others voluntarily developed by different industry trade bodies and by some large corporations. Often the latter reflect the mandated codes. The important point here is that the regulators and their codes have not kept pace with new marketing developments catalysed by digital media developments. Hence, there are some forms of subtle brand promotions now in place that are not yet recognised as 'advertising' and so are not covered by any regulations. This, of course, is a matter than could be fixed; advertising regulators are not insensitive to these issues and are beginning to act.

It is acknowledged in this book that advertisers will always try to find new methods to reach consumers and that they will be more strongly motivated to do so as older advertising methods become less effective. The critical point is that when this happens, it should do so within a legal framework designed to protect the interests of consumers and within the spirit of any related regulations and codes of practice as well as within the word of the law. Often, advertisers will try to stretch a point and find ways of avoiding compliance, and then regulators must act. The work of advertisers has become more challenging as consumers have become more marketing savvy, and also as media developments have reduced the effectiveness of traditional forms of advertising.

There are critics of digital marketing developments who have claimed there is a massive complacency on the part of governments and their regulators because of the way brand advertisers have adapted to changing media land-scapes. This is perhaps an unfair assessment, although it is probably accurate to state that marketing regulations and the procedures adopted to implement them have been outpaced by the digital media evolution in the twenty-first century. Regulators have been caught napping by the speed of technological change and the pace at which the marketing profession has adopted platforms such as social media sites, computer games, and virtual worlds to reach and influence consumers.

Consumers are gaining more literacy of relevance in coping with a diversified brand marketing environment. There is no doubt that consumers are bombarded with brand promotions across a wide range of settings. There is also little doubt that there has been a diversification of marketing practices as new technology platforms for brand promoting activity have penetrated far into the consumer marketplace. People as consumers need product and service information, but deserve it to be accurate and not to mislead them. Children are especially important here because their consumer literacy faculties are not fully formed and therefore need more legislative protection.

People as citizens as well as consumers have a right to expect that advertising will not harm them or their children and so there must be an overriding leg-islative framework that sets parameters within which advertisers are permitted to operate. The world is a constantly changing place, however. The pace of change has increased in the twenty-first century with the rapid developments that have occurred in computer technology and wired and wireless communi-cations systems. Understandably marketers have witnessed opportunities here. In taking up these opportunities, however, some advertisers have pushed at the boundaries of what is permitted legally and what ought to happen ethically. This has created tensions in that in a free market economy, advertisers expect to be able openly to market their goods and services. Yet they must not be tempted to do so in ways that mislead or harm the people they target.

Regulators have a protection role to play here but there will always be some advertising methods that are potentially harmful and yet cannot be deemed illegal. There is also a need therefore for consumers to be able to protect themselves. This is something that has happened in the past through consumer socialisation in childhood. As digital media developments have brought on board a number of new forms of brand promotion, old consumer literacy skills retain some relevance but are no longer sufficient to provide complete protection. Hence, both regulators and consumers (and, where children are concerned, parents/carers) are stakeholders here and have their parts to play, as do advertisers and the industries they are part of.

The thesis of this book is that all is not lost. The advance of communications technology platforms will continue and in many ways is something we should all welcome. If marketers can find new ways of giving people the information they need, and want to help people make purchase choices in increasingly crowded brand markets, this is not something anyone should be fearful about. At the same time, complacency must be avoided in terms of open acceptance of these developments divorced from the recognition that marketers have their own agenda and that this is not invariably one that holds the best interests of consumers as sacrosanct.

New marketing methods that take on more disguised forms can leave consumers off guard. This is a state of affairs that might be tackled through consumer literacy education in childhood, but it is also a matter for marketing and advertising regulators to address. Regulators are waking up to this fact but have been left at the starting gate. They are playing catch-up. They do need to think carefully about expanding their definitions of 'advertising' so that they can revise their codes of practice. Parents need to know also that their children may not use the consumer literacy skills learned in relation to televised advertising when confronted with brands trying to 'friend' them on Facebook.

1

What is a brand?

What is a brand? The term has been defined in various ways over time. According to the American Marketing Association Dictionary, a brand is the 'name, term, design, symbol, or any other feature that identifies one seller's product distinct from those of other sellers' (American Marketing Association Dictionary, 2013). The Merriam-Webster Dictionary adopted a more historical perspective in its collection of definitions of 'brand', which traced its etymological roots to the idea of something being burned into something else as an identifying mark or sign of source of origin or ownership. Hence, one definition of brand was 'a mark made by burning with a hot iron to attest manufacture or quality or to designate ownership'. Linked to this is the concept of 'trademark' which is 'a printed mark made for similar purposes'. There was also the use of brands to mark out criminals, with the 'brand' again taking the form of a mark that was burned into the skin by a hot iron. Then, there is a definition provided that is more consistent with the modern day idea of a brand, namely 'a class of goods identified by name as the product of a single firm or manufacturer' (Merriam-Webster, no date).

Historically, the term brand has been traced to the Old Norse word *brandr*, which means 'to burn'. Producers would literally burn their mark into their merchandise to differentiate it from similar commodities marketed by other producers (*Marketing Magazine*, 2006). Thousands of years ago, ancient craftsmen in societies in the Far East and Middle East not only marked their products, but also used other markers on signs and, when it became available, early forms of paper such as papyrus, to make announcements about their wares. Thus branding, from early on, became inter-twined with promotional messages or advertisements. It would be over simplifying 'branding', however, as a cultural phenomenon to claim that it is defined principally by advertising. These communications can be used to spread brand familiarity, but the meanings of brands reside in the minds of consumers and derive from different experiences they have had or reports of others' experiences with specific products they have heard.

A well-known brand such as Coca-Cola or McDonald's comprises more than just a familiar name. That name signals to people other attributes or features that have derived from personal experiences or stories they have heard about these suppliers and their products or services. Advertising represents one source of such story-telling, but does not operate on its own (Holt, 2003).

In the earliest days of commerce, advertising emerged in what today would be seen as crude forms of promotions, but which nonetheless had the same overall objectives as modern day multi-modal, 'integrated' marketing campaigns. This was simply to draw to people's attention the availability of commodities or services and the names of their producers or suppliers. The earliest discovered formats have included tradesmen's signs or the signs outside taverns that date from ancient Egyptian, Mesopotamian, Greek and Roman eras (Nevitt, 1982).

Perhaps the best known examples of pre-industrialised branding were the marks used by farmers to identify their livestock and differentiate them from those owned by others. Cattle owners, for example, would burn a mark with a branding iron into the animal's skin. Many of us will be familiar with this form of branding from the old Hollywood westerns. In essence, branding signals where a product was made, who its producer is, and indicates its authenticity. These features became increasingly important with societal developments that saw more widespread transportation of goods to distant markets. In less complex societies, people were dependent on local produce with which they would be very familiar. They would often personally know the source of origin and would thus be in no need of additional information about its authenticity.

As societies developed through technology innovations, branding became closely linked to advertising, which in turn comprised a collection of techniques designed to promote commodities, services, or events. The term brand referred to the item being promoted, or to the manufacturer, supplier, or owner of the creative rights to the property or service being produced. Advertising as an activity has played a key part in defining the meaning of brands by presenting to brand consumers or users information about the product or service being provided; this eventually becomes an integral aspect of what the brand stands for or what makes it distinctive (McDonald & Scott, 2007).

While improvements in transportation meant that people travelled further and experienced commodities in markets they were less familiar with, and often returned with commodities they might then share with others, with word-of-mouth recommendations, the emergence of mass markets often meant that these more direct brand experiences would not be available. Manufacturers therefore needed to find ways of marking out their products from those of rivals and increasingly to incentivise consumers to choose their wares.

Branding and advertising became more widespread as mass product markets emerged following the period of industrial revolution in the eighteenth and nineteenth centuries (Kotler, 1965). Developments in production technologies and in forms of transportation meant that products could be produced in larger quantities and moved more swiftly from location to location. From a world in which people relied on local produce, people found more product choices opened up to them as commodities sourced from many miles away could be transported to them more quickly. Locally produced household products found that they faced competition from similar items sourced long distances away that were often competitive in terms of pricing and, with the early emergence of advertising, were accompanied with promotional messages claiming that these interlopers into the local market were superior to local products (O'Guinn, Allen & Semenik, 2009).

As commodity markets moved from being purely local to mass and geographically dispersed, so a need grew for more information to be provided to consumers about the expanded range of variants within a product class where familiarity with non-local producers was scant. Advertising, therefore, became important for consumers in relation to their decision making, and for producers and suppliers to enhance their credibility and distinctiveness as well as that of their own brands (Norris, 1981).

'Brands' that emerged during the industrialised era took the form of trademarks, which were also distinctive marks of ownership of products that became increasingly widely used as the technologies of mass production evolved in industrialised urban centres in the nineteenth century. Manufacturers would imprint company logos or other distinguishing marks onto their products as well as onto the packaging in which the products were transported.

There are competitive claims by different companies to have introduced the world's first trademark. Bass & Company made this claim in respect to their triangle brand. Lyle's made a similar claim for their Golden Syrup, which has hardly changed its green and gold packaging since 1885. Other early brands introduced during the nineteenth century that persist and remain prominent to the present day include Campbell's Soup, Coca-Cola, Pears Soap and Quaker Oats. Kellogg's also emerged during this period with their initial range of breakfast cereals (O'Guinn, Allen & Semenik, 2009).

Brands and their associated advertising also had to become increasingly mindful of the different needs of their consumers, and in particular the changes that occurred in the nature of key decision makers in respect of household purchases. During the nineteenth century and early twentieth century, there were numerous national, international, and global conflicts that resulted in men folk being away fighting wars. These events facilitated role changes in the home, with women adopting a more dominant role in making domestic purchases (O'Guinn, Allen & Semenik, 2009).

In some commodity fields where men and women may once have engaged in do-it-yourself solutions, the long absences of men away from home encouraged women consumers to seek more ready-made products – including food and clothes – rather than growing or making their own (Tellis, 1998). A demand grew for products that effectively made life easier – a trend that has continued to the present day where supermarkets provide one-stop shops for ready-made everything you can think of. This new kind of consumer demand created markets for more variants of specific types of products that in turn increased the importance of establishing product distinctiveness through branding.

Such social developments not only gave rise to the early mass consumer markets but also spawned specialist service industries to advise commodity manufacturers and suppliers on how to capture the attention of consumers in more crowded and competitive markets. By the end of the nineteenth century, the advertising industry had become established and the major agency of the time, J. Walter Thompson, represents another brand that has remained at the forefront of its business field ever since. The agency produced one of the first documents that attempted to explain to non-experts the meaning of trademarks and advertising. This treatise laid down foundations of modern branding activities engaged in by professional marketers. Over the early decades of the twentieth century, advertising emerged as a standard practice for virtually all product manufacturers and service suppliers when they wished to get a new product to market. It also became de rigour in terms of maintaining the market profiles of established brands as product marketplaces became increasingly crowded and competitive (McDonald & Scott, 2007).

Getting the right 'brand' became a primary objective for commercial organisations across all major sectors of production and major service industries. Marketing evolved as a discipline, defining and developing key concepts such as brand identity, brand personality, and brand equity and value. Product manufacturers came to realise that their customers were not just purchasing their commodities but more significantly they were buying their brands. Although a product might have functional value for consumers, in a marketplace that might offer a menu of more than ten or even more than twenty variants to choose from, market leaders were those items with the strongest or most appealing brand image. If a product's brand image took a tumble because of events that called its reputation into question, its volume of sales and market share could also plummet (Klein, 2000).

With these social changes taking place during the late nineteenth century and early twentieth centuries, so-called 'aspirational' brands began to emerge. Not only were these brands and their associated logos and symbols signifiers of origin and quality, they also conveyed other messages to consumers about social status or fashion sense and taste, which added value to products over and above their functionality, reliability, and performance. Some early brands of this kind, such as accessories brand Louis Vuitton, were so successful they triggered large counterfeiting markets that copied the style of Louis Vuitton originals and labelled them with the 'LV' monogram but which were nonetheless fakes. One estimate calculated that around 99% of all alleged Louis Vuitton goods in circulation were not originals (Brand Domain, 2013).

Brand importance

In the modern era of mass production, brands can represent commercial organisations' most valuable assets. The development, maintenance, and evolution of a brand is closely tied to a range of promotional activities broadly subsumed under marketing and advertising. A brand is not just a mark of differentiation in the sense of a distinctive physical identity, it also increasingly an indicator of quality or excellence.

Brands are therefore defined to a significant extent by their reputation among consumers. They are signifiers to consumers that this particular version of a product will deliver greater satisfaction than others (Keller & Ewards, 1998). In addition, consumers will be willing to pay more for a strong brand than a weak brand even though both belong to the same product category and may be functionally the same (Grassl, 1999).

The popularity of a brand in terms of the positive opinions that consumers hold about it underpin its value and its market share. The brand can cover a single product or extend across a range of product variants and can even evolve to be applied to the company responsible for its production or delivery and distribution. Children can begin to make produce requests using the names of brands while they are still infants (McNeal & Yeh, 1993). Very young children lack any spending power of their own. They can, however, ask others – most usually their parents – to make purchases for them. Once they have started school, and more especially as they enter their 'tweenage' (8–12) and teenage years, they acquire more spending capability of their own and an understanding of money and how to use it (Gunter & Furnham, 1998). Their early requests tend to centre on food and toys, later switching to clothes and communications and entertainment gadgets (McNeal, 1992).

As they get into their teens, young consumers spend money on going out with their friends. Their activities will include entertainment and sports, but shopping is also an important leisure pursuit. Brand requests can be triggered by seeing what other children have got and by talking to peer groups (Moschis & Churchill, 1978; Moschis & Moore, 1979, 1980). Peer groups become progressively more important to children as they get older and gradually more influential in relation to brand choices (Saunders, Samli & Tozier, 1973; Coleman & Hendry, 1990; Lee & Brown, 1995). Children's brand choices can also be influenced by advertising (Gorn & Goldberg, 1978; Prasad, Rao & Sheikh, 1978; Goldberg, Gorn & Gibson, 1987). The influences of advertising can also interact with and be mediated by parental and peer group effects (Galst, 1980; Stoneman & Brody, 1982).

As branding has become the norm in the sphere of product and service marketing its meaning has evolved from what it represented in its earliest forms. The initial brands were physical marks of distinction to signify ownership or the name of a product's creator and manufacturer. Over time, as commodity fields became swamped with brands, it has come to mean much more than this. The concept of 'brand' evolved as the practice of advertising grew and different models of advertising and its effectiveness were tried and tested.

During the first part of the twentieth century, the advertising industry realised it needed to understand more about consumer behaviour and the effectiveness of different media platforms as promotional vehicles, in order to offer better advice to clients about how to spend their advertising budgets. The agencies realised that this kind of value added service not only gave them a direction in which to develop their own services and the revenue streams they could earn, but that if they could produce better measurable impacts of benefit to their clients than rival agencies, this would strengthen their own brand.

It was during this period that agencies made closer study of behaviourist psychology to develop a better understanding of how consumer behaviour could be shaped. Furthermore, agencies hired marketing researchers to develop market research techniques that not only measured post campaign impact among consumers but also fed into the design of campaigns before they were launched (Naik, 2007).

The concept of the 'unique selling proposition' also emerged during this period, crystallising the idea that a brand would deliver some specific and unique benefit unlike that offered by any other brand in the same product range. The value attached to this benefit needed to be sufficient to persuade consumers to choose the brand so described in preference to all others, and then remain loyal to it (Reeves, 1960; Lavidge & Steiner, 1961). Hence, the concept of 'brand' developed over time from meaning a distinguishing mark of ownership or origin of production to a feature that was linked more closely with the needs of consumers (O'Guinn, Allen & Semenik, 2009).

In taking this thinking about consumer benefit even further, some of the big advertising gurus of the time, including leading agency heads Leo Burnett, David Ogilvy and Bill Bernbach, argued that the distinctiveness of a brand did not only have to be defined in functional terms (i.e. delivery of a specific gratification to those consumers who use it). It could also represent more abstract ideas about lifestyle, personality, and external social identity that resonate with the needs of consumers but go beyond them. In other words, a brand might make a statement about the social or cultural status of the person who chooses to be seen with it (Frank, 1997).

The idea thus surfaced of 'brand image', which comprised a set of beliefs that became attached to a product variant that in turn defined a human-like personality for it. This brand 'personality' was often further reinforced and overtly manifest in the form of a celebrity endorser, an original fictional character spokesperson, or a style of use. Hence, through repeat exposure in the mainstream media and on product packaging, brands and endorsers came to be conceived as one and the same, and the appearance of one would trigger thoughts about the other. One of the best examples of this phenomenon was the animated character Tony the Tiger and Kellogg's Frosted Flakes. For fifty years, Tony the Tiger was an iconic figure that appeared in advertisements for this breakfast cereal, telling consumers with his famous growl, which became a registered trade mark in its own right, 'They're gr-r-reat!'

Advertising techniques are used to attach a range of social and psychological meanings to brands. These associated attributes may be more prominent to consumers when they think about what a brand means to them than is the idea that the brand name signals who made it. A brand's 'image' therefore is built out of the reputation it has with its users for delivery on what it has promised. Hence, if it is a soap brand, it must be found to clean effectively. If it is a food brand, it must taste good or be easy to prepare.

Beyond this functionality, advertisers can also instil in us thoughts about what the use of the brand might mean in terms of how we are perceived by other consumers. If the use of a particular brand of shampoo is believed to make our hair healthier and look better and this in turn enhances our appeal to the opposite sex, the brand takes on a whole new meaning that extends far beyond its effectiveness as a cleaning substance.

Hence, the notion of brand has evolved over time from being simply a distinctive mark of ownership, through to a functional description of what it can do for those of us who use it, through to claims about its superiority over other brands defined usually in terms of performance or other functional qualities, to statements about how it can bring important changes to us as individuals in the form of enhanced social status or better quality lifestyles (Taylor, 1999).

With constant promotion of branding messages, a brand acquires a unique image or reputation over time that can become deeply embedded in our consumer consciousness. Sometimes a brand can become so salient and so powerful that it even takes on the mantle of a generic label for a whole product category such as Hoover did with vacuum cleaners and Google has done with online World Wide Web search. These brands spawn their own verbs – 'to Hoover' and 'to Google' – which respectively describe acts of carpet vacuum cleaning and internet searching.

In modern markets, if your products do not have a salient brand image they are unlikely to make much market impact. The Holy Grail of product manufacturers and service suppliers is to make their brands so well known that when consumers are prompted with the name of a product category, their brand is the one that people think of first (Tan, 2010). Some brands become 'top-of-the-mind' concepts that people immediately think of when their minds turn to specific types of behaviour. Examples of this type of brand effect are Kellogg's with breakfast cereals, Kraft with cheese, Kleenex with tissues and Uncle Ben's with rice.

The first aim of branding as an activity is to develop a distinctive identity for a brand. In the case of products, this identity is manifest in the outward appearance of the commodity. The product variant will have a distinctive name – and this is the name by which it will become known to consumers. The name is often associated with a logo or trademark which generally comprises some sort of visual shape combined with a verbal symbol or words that signify a specific corporate meaning or motto. The product and/or its packaging may have a distinctive physical shape and colour and there may be functional descriptive information and promotional messages that describe what the product can do, how it can be used, or the benefits it can bring. Together these verbal and non-verbal attributes combine to create an overall impression about this product variant that over time gives it a distinctive identity in the marketplace. Usually, this identity is one that the brand owner wishes to impart to consumers, both about this product and about the company that makes it (Underwood, 2003).

Brand names are important in this context because they are the most prominent feature that helps the brand to stand out from other brands competing with it. The name has to be distinctive, easy to recall, and seem relevant to the type of product. It must also try to avoid negative symbolic connotations that would damage the brand's reputation from the start (Pincott, 2009).

Brands are more than just a name, logo, and other design features. Although these elements single them out from competitors in the same product range, the identity of a brand also stems from the meanings that consumers attach to it (Bristow & Asquith, 1999). These meanings may convey symbolic messages to consumers about the quality of the brand, the social status it delivers to users, or other expectations that have become attached to the brand through the different stories that have been told about it by its producers, other consumers, the views of consumer opinion leaders, or media reports (Colapinto, 2011; Holt, 2003). The knowledge that a consumer develops about a brand is therefore characterised by multiple dimensions that include awareness of the physical features of a branded product, the kinds of functional and social benefits it can bring, the needs it can satisfy, judgements about its qualities and performance, feelings about what it means to the consumer, and memories of personal experiences with it (Keller, 2003).

In a way, a brand makes a promise to the consumer. It creates and imparts an impression about functionality, quality, performance, and value that it must then deliver. Insofar as brands deliver on their initial promises, their initial image will remain intact. If brands continue to deliver, their image will be reinforced and a positive reputation will grow up around them – this will serve further to enhance positive consumer sentiment that will in turn drive consumer loyalty (Pincott, 2009).

One important outcome of the building of a brand's reputation in this way is that the brand itself acquires equity or a value all of its own. Thus, while the variants within a product category may be priced over a limited range, brands that have the greatest 'brand equity' – that is, an added value associated specifically with the brand itself – can charge consumers premium rates and still retain custom. One of the main objectives of advertising is to establish brand equity (Zufryden, 1996). A brand's equity indicates the value it has to consumers, who may be willing to pay a great deal more for it than for rival brands in the same product range simply because of its reputation or standing in the marketplace or in wider social and cultural terms (Holt, 2003).

The benefits of this outcome work in two directions. Established and trusted brands command greater consumer loyalty. At the same time consumers will often display greater tolerance for repeat exposure to promotions for this brand. In contrast, repetitions of promotions for unknown or less highly rated brands can cause irritation to consumers and even result in such brands being rated even more poorly (Calder & Sternthal, 1980; Campbell & Keller, 2003).

By keeping customers satisfied, the hope is that they will return for more. Companies then become more competitive and as their brands become established they gain in value and add to their overall corporate capital value (Aaker, 1991). In the offline world, brands have played a significant part in helping specific companies' products to stand out from the rest. In the online world, brands remain important, but consumers have access both to more information about brands provided by their owners and producers and also by other consumers. Public opinion about brands can spread like wildfire on the internet and in particular through social media sites (Jarvis, 2005). This can be either a good thing or a bad thing for brands, depending upon what people are saying about them.

The growth of the internet as a platform for business transactions and window shopping has led increasingly to pressure on old and new businesses alike to establish a web presence. Failing to do this is regarded as missing out on an important opportunity to cultivate consumer markets. Going online requires some modification of marketing strategy because the online world does not mirror the offline world in terms of how people and organisations behave.

In both the offline and online worlds, consumers develop their own impressions and opinions about brands that can be influenced by talking to other consumers and seeing, hearing, or reading promotional messages distributed by brand owners. Personal experience with a brand is also a highly significant variable in this judgement. Consumers can then pass on their experiences of brand via word-of-mouth which has been known to play an important part in brand reputation building in the everyday world (Anderson, 1998; Keller, 2007). The big difference between offline and online word-of-mouth communications is that in the online world, these conversations about brands can spread much more rapidly and reach large numbers of consumers as fast as mass media advertising.

In the online world, on a social media site, for instance, each consumer potentially can achieve exposure to a much greater volume of public chit-chat about brands. Brand owners have also sought to capitalise on this phenomenon by getting directly involved in these conversations and even by instigating them (Winkler & Buckner, 2006; Cheyne, Dorfman, Bukofzer & Harris, 2013). This is a new direction in brand marketing that we will revisit in more detail in Chapter 5 where we will find that there are ethical as well as sales considerations that are invoked by the proactive engagement of consumers by brand managers to promote their brands, especially when this activity takes place among child consumers.

Used effectively, online word-of-mouth promotions that are generated through social media can facilitate the rapid spread of consumer-to-consumer brand recommendations that can benefit the image or sale of brands (Berger & Milkman, 2012). Whichever platform is used, however, the spread of positive opinions about brands remains dependent upon a specific brand's uniqueness and quality of performance for consumers (Cheema & Kaikati, 2010). A bad reputation for a poorly performing brand can spread as quickly as a good reputation for a brand that delivers high customer satisfaction (Anderson, 1998; Mudambi & Schuff, 2010).

Children and brands

We have long known that children represent a large and potentially lucrative consumer sector (McNeal, 1992). We should not be surprised that brand marketers target young consumers. They have tremendous spending power in their own right and they also have influence over their parents' brand choices. Lindstrom (2011) estimated that pre-teenage children aged 8–12 spent over US$121 billion. In the UK, kids aged 8–14 years were estimated to have a disposable income of US$2.7 billion a year. At different ages, kids get money from their parents, from other relatives, and by taking part-time jobs.

As we will see later, kids have long been known to exhibit distinctive brand preferences, but what a brand means to a child can vary a great deal from one child to the next and is linked to their cognitive and social development. Kids can bond with brands from early on and this is important for marketers in terms of ensuring brand loyalty and repeat business. Some companies also market a range of brands that are targeted at different age groups, and through brand extensions they seek to capture kids early on and retain them at a later age with age appropriate products with their brand imprint (Lindstrom, 2011).

Wherever branding activity occurs, however, it is crucial to understand how children's reactions to it can change as they grow older and they develop increasingly sophisticated views of the world around them. As we will see, children cannot be treated as a single demographic category, or as two distinct gender-defined categories. As children grow older, they change in terms of their cognitive and social skills. There have been debates about whether this development occurs in discrete stages or whether it is much more fluid and gradual, occurring at different paces for different skills and for different children. What is clear is that different levels of cognitive and social sophistication produce changes in the way children react to and relate to brands. The importance of brands – when conceived as being part of a broader orientation towards materialism – can fluctuate between children in different age groups, depending upon their psychological state at different points in their early life (Chaplin & John, 2007). In the next chapter, we turn our attention to children's emergent involvement with brands.

2

Kids and branding

Kids today are bombarded with branding messages. This activity represents an aspect of a wider campaign being waged by commercial organisations in capitalist economies to establish, maintain and grow their presence in specific product and service markets. Reaching out to consumers while they are still going through the early stages of their psychological development represents an exercise in conditioning not simply a consumer culture, but a branded one.

As we have already seen, historically, brands were originally markers of ownership, but in crowded and competitive consumer marketplaces they have evolved to assume the status of symbolic indicators of personal identity on behalf of people who buy them. Brands have 'personalities' that are carefully crafted by marketing professionals on behalf of product manufacturers or service suppliers. It is these 'personalities' that tend to be defined in relation to specific lifestyles, values, and iconic endorsers with celebrity status that consumers buy into. In effect, consumers seek self-definition through brands.

This type of appeal can work particularly well with young consumers whose personal identities are not yet fully formed and who proactively seek identity ideas to try out. Of course, sometimes, brands can be accused of selling themselves on the back of inappropriate 'identities', especially when children are their targets. This criticism has grown particularly acute in respect of the use of sexual themes to sell brands (Lamb & Brown, 2006; Levin & Kilbourne, 2008). Although this might be accepted for some products aimed at adult consumers, there is far less tolerance for its gratuitous application to brands where sexual themes are functionally irrelevant, or for any products targeted at pre-pubescent children (Papadopoulos, 2010).

Children are targeted by brands of all kinds. There are brands that are made especially for different children's markets. There are brands that are made for the whole family where it is known that kids often have considerable influence over brand choices. There are also brands targeted at adults that nevertheless are known to children because of their entertaining marketing campaigns. Although advertisers of adult-oriented brands may not deliberately target children, they do not mind the fact that children get to know of their brands because these youngsters could eventually become part of their future adult consumer base. Thus, marketers will target brand messages at kids for the obvious product categories such as toys and games. In addition, there are clothes and accessories targeted at very young consumers. Family products such as foods and soft drinks will include child products and other products that the whole family consume, where the kids in the household will know of brands and ask for products by brand name. There are also out-of-home eating brands represented by the best-known fast food chains such as Burger King, Kentucky Fried Chicken, and McDonald's, which children become familiar with from an early age (Gunter et al., 2005).

Once beyond infancy, both pre-teenagers ('tweens') and teenagers can name their favourite brands when asked (Hite & Hite, 1995; Dammler & Middelmann-Motz, 2002). Brand favourites can change with age however. The Kids Brand Index produced in the UK by agency Brand Republic found that there were many overlaps between younger and older kids in their brand favourites, but some shifting around in brand rankings. In 2011, the ten favourite brands among pre-teenagers (ages 7–11) were Walkers Crisps, Nintendo Wii, Nintendo DS, McDonald's, The Simpsons, Haribo, CBBC, Coca-Cola, Lego, and Kellogg's Coco Pops. Among teenagers (ages 12–15), the top ten brands were Facebook, YouTube, Coca-Cola, The Simpsons, Walkers Crisps, McDonald's, Game, iPod, Maltesers, and Cadbury Dairy Milk (*PR Week*, no date). The brands here reflect both eating habits and leisure activities of kids at different stages of life. Notable perhaps is the prominence of computer game brands among the tweens, and social media brands among the teens (Brand Republic, 2011).

Despite concerns that have grown about certain aspects of child-directed marketing, especially with regard to the so-called 'sexualisation of childhood', children and their parents are encouraged by product manufacturers and service suppliers – and the advisors, agencies, and consultants who work for these organisations – to think about brands, to choose and to own and use branded merchandise as an extension of their personal identities. This should not be a surprise to us given the growing spending power of children in developed societies and their influence also over the spending of their parents (Buckingham, 2009).

Children do not only have influence over the purchases that are made specifically for them, but can also have important input to more general household purchases decisions (Kuhn & Eischen, 1997). While there has been some debate about the degree of influence of this sort that children actually exert (Tinson & Nancarrow, 2007), there is evidence that children do develop an understanding of money and learn how to use it well before adolescence (Marshall, 1997; Gunter & Furnham, 1998).

Of more significant concern for some commentators and researchers has been the prominence of food brands for products classed as poor in terms of their nutritional value. Such brands were represented among the most liked brands named by UK tweens and teens in the Brand Republic survey reported above (Harris, Pomeranz, Lobstein & Brownell, 2009; Powell, Szczypka & Chaloupka, 2010; Sutherland, MacKenzie, Purvis & Dalton, 2010). In addition, the appeal to children of alcohol brand advertising and their early awareness of brand names has been cited as a cause for concern in relation to underage drinking.

It is understandable that children might become aware of food brands that they consume in their family household. There are other product categories targeted at adult consumers for which widespread child awareness has also been measured and linked to early onset of product take-up. There is research evidence spanning several decades which shows that children can identify widely advertised alcoholic beverage brands. Pre-teenage children as young as ten years have been found able to recognise alcohol brands taken from television advertising campaigns (Aitken, Eadie, Leathar et al., 1988; Wyllie, Casswell & Stewart, 1989; Wyllie, Zhang & Casswell, 1998).

There have been popular advertising campaigns, often with memorably humorous or rebellious scenes, that have drawn in the attention of teens and pre-teens (Cragg, 2004). Alcohol advertising campaigns have been nominated by children far below the legal drinking age, as being among their favourite commercials (Davidson, 2013; Nash, Pine & Messer, 2009). Advertising characters such as the Budweiser frogs of the famous 1990s campaign could trigger recall of the brand name even among kids as young as 9. So popular was this campaign that kids' recall of Budweiser was more widespread even that that of Kellogg's 'Tony the Tiger' or 'The Mighty Morphin Power Rangers' – both brands targeted at young consumers (Leiber, 1998).

Some agencies make their living from proffering this kind of message: we are all encouraged to believe that unless we are branded, we are somehow less fully formed as individuals and as valid members of society. With the dramatic rise of the internet and within this network of 'social' network sites (or 'social media'), marketers have developed a wide range of new methods for reaching young consumers with brand promotions (Clarke & Svanaes, 2012; Nairn & Hang, 2012).

One New York marketing strategist and branding consultant, 3A Media, have even extended the idea of branding from products to people themselves. In this respect they take the branding concept beyond the more usual idea that consumers project a self-identity through the product brands they are seen to use, and this 'identity' is often shaped in part by the presence of specific celebrity endorsers who lend their names to product brands. The qualities of the celebrity, especially if they are talented, rich, and successful, are believed to rub off on the brands they endorse and then in turn on the consumers who purchase those brands. 3A Media have extended this concept further by offering advice services to parents about how to choose fashions or events for their kids that will project a particular image and internalise a mindset that will enhance their kids' chances of realising whatever dreams they have.

According to 3A 'it is never too young to start branding'. The branding context being promoted here is a coaching and make-over advice service for parents who want their kids to get into entertainment or fashion. In its home page promotion blurb, the company asks, 'how would parents position their children in the highly competitive world of modelling? Would it be like children's pageants we see on *Toddlers & Tiaras*? Or would it be more in the line of stage moms pushing their kids relentlessly to secure the next paying gig?' (3A Media, 2013)

Parents are being overtly invited to buy into a range of commercial advice and coaching services through which they treat their children as branded commodities that are entered into various competitive markets as merchandise to be judged and sold. In 3A's words, 'whatever the road may be, we do think for parents wanting their children to enter the competitive world, it is important to brand their children from the start. *Establish* a consistent identity. Have an *engaging* story about your child, and *excite* the casting agent and the client why they want your child in their next ad campaign (3A Media, 2013; original emphasis throughout).

Early brand experiences

The branding of children more usually operates through brands that are targeted at them. This should not come as any surprise. Children are consumers just as much as their parents and other adults are. In fact, they are consumers even before they are aware of it. From the moment they are born there are commodities that are made for them. Babies have to be fed, clothed, cleaned, and entertained. As they grow older, they have to learn about things that will enable them to function as independent, civilised, and productive members of society. In all these various aspects of their lives, therefore, suppliers have created products and services designed for different child age groups. Just as commodity and service supply markets have got bigger and more diversified for adult consumers, the same process has occurred in relation to kids. There is nothing intrinsically asocial or evil about this. It might be conceived as an outcome of the constantly changing activities of an evolving species.

For manufacturers and service suppliers the importance of early branding exposure stems from the belief that by capturing the attention and interest of consumers when they are very young, brand loyalty can be cultivated that may last a lifetime. Whether this kind of lifelong commitment is possible for any except a few exceptional (and essential) brands is debatable. Certainly the earliest attempts to demonstrate consumer brand loyalty from childhood into adulthood produced mixed results.

Lester Guest followed through a sample of young American consumers who were aged between 7 and 18 at the start of his study in 1941 over 20 years. They were initially tested on their ability to recognise products from 80 brand names representing 16 product categories. The children were accredited with having brand awareness if they could correctly assign four of the five brands per product category. Twelve years later when he retraced members of this sample, he found that brand preferences stated when they were younger were mentioned again by 32–39% of the participants. After 20 years, brand preferences from 1941 were restated by 26% of those participants who were located again. There was some evidence that participants from higher socio-economic status households displayed greater brand awareness across this study (Guest, 1942, 1955, 1964).

We should probably not be surprised that brand preferences change over time from childhood into adulthood. Since the middle of the twentieth century, markets have expanded in many product categories, with population growth, growth in sources of supply, and increased numbers of competitive brands all creating opportunities – and in some cases threats to their existence – for manufacturers and suppliers. Brand choices have changed and in most product and service categories they have diversified, giving consumers more choices.

Belief in the potential power of early socialisation stems from ideas about the role played by parents and peer groups in conditioning early consumer behaviours and brand preferences. These sources of social learning have been hypothesised to cultivate deeply conditioned brand orientations that once established will remain with the young consumer for a long time. Socio-economic class is also an important factor here because greater affluence can lead to expanded life space for individual consumers. For the young consumer, going through the early stages of consumer socialisation therefore, this can result in exposure to more product and brand opportunities. In the case of the poorer consumer, in contrast, their limited financial position means that they are restricted to fewer product choices and the cheapest brands. Young people from better-off households can therefore become aware of a wider range of goods over time (Hess, 1970; Ward, 1974; Moschis, Moore & Stanley, 1984). Despite their relative economic disadvantages, however, even children from poorer backgrounds have been found to exhibit brand consciousness, to aspire to own premium branded items such as Nike sports shoes, and to hold in higher regard other children that do wear highly regarded brands (Elliott & Leonard, 2004).

Over time, economic growth in major developed countries, and increasingly in many developing nations, has produced a wider spread of consumer affluence across expanded 'middle classes'. More consumers enjoy expanded life spaces and this change has brought a broader range of products and services within their financial reach. This phenomenon has also triggered greater involvement of younger members of these large numbers of more affluent family households in consumerism. Marketers have responded by engaging in more vigorous and more creative promotional activities to bring brands to the attention of young consumers.

As with all life experiences, however, there is usually an optimal level at which it can be deemed 'in proportion' or 'healthy'. Whenever any single activity emerges and continues to grow in terms of its influence over the way people think, feel, and behave, there is a risk that it can throw people's lives out of balanced alignment and change their core values and behavioural norms in ways that could be damaging to themselves or others. If this observation is true of the level of branding we find in the world today, there are searching questions we must begin to ask.

In a world of ever present branding, has expanded choice come at a price that is worth paying? While it is unavoidable that some products and services will be aimed at children – because they are legitimate targets and comprise a consumer marketplace that has developed out of essential items they need in their lives, and it is important that young people should become savvy as consumers – should brands be allowed to play a significant part in shaping the early personal identities of kids?

In responding to these questions, another question emerges about where responsibility lies for the protection of kids' best interests. Does it reside with parents, with manufacturers, with branding agencies, with governments or elsewhere? There is certainly a degree of responsibility that can be laid at the door of brand creators and the techniques they use to engage with consumers. They have developed a marketplace in which competition between brands is acute and where brands are constantly being refreshed to stay ahead of the rest.

One technique of cultivating brand awareness among kids (and their parents) has been the introduction of inter-generational brand extensions. These are kids' brands that have spun off from earlier established adult brands. This is a subtle marketing strategy that plays on the idea that parents are the source of earliest social learning for their kids. These brands tend also to operate within more affluent consumer markets, in which parents can afford and are willing to pay adult-level prices for premium branded children's goods. This phenomenon has been witnessed in the world of fashion where leading designers for adult clothing markets such as Diane von Furstenberg – who has dressed icons such as Michelle Obama and Gwyneth Paltrow – has developed kids' clothing lines such as Gapkids and BabyGap for Gap. Other brand extensions have included cosmetics (Baby Dior) and even luxury furniture (Pottery Barn Kids) (Brennan, 2012).

Are kids susceptible to branding?

One of the critical issues with kids and branding is that children can be particularly susceptible to marketing techniques, and open to their influence because socially and psychologically they are not yet fully formed. In their early years, children's ability to understand and decipher the real purpose of branding and its associated advertising or other promotional activities is still developing and there is a concern that this can render them more likely to believe what advertisers tell them (Gunter, Oates & Blades, 2005). As well as this type of influence, there are the more subtle side-effects of branding and its symbolic cultural and social meanings that create reference sources in terms of social and personal identity. Thus, if a particular clothing brand is fashionable and all the kids are wearing it, parents will find their own child pestering them for the same item because they don't want to be left out or to appear different from the norm.

This kind of social influence of branding can cause tension in family households especially if the trendy brand in question happens to be twice as expensive as most other brands in the same product range. These social pressures can become most acute once kids get into their teens and the need to project the right kind of personal image and belong to the coolest social cliques are more important to their lives than anything else. It is this pool of insecurity that brands tap into with promises of instant social status (Leonhardt & Kerwin, 1997).

Observations that children are becoming brand conscious earlier have also been coloured by the sense that this is a social problem. Marketers that target children are criticised for doing so. Yet, we could also argue that since we live in a consumer society of our own making and that few of us would choose to return to a pre-branded era of limited product and service choice, early brand consciousness does not need invariably to be seen as a bad thing. Instead, if it forms part of early consumer socialisation which enhances the consumer literacy of children in terms of their abilities to identify quality and value in commodities and services, this could actually be seen as a positive outcome. The downside of this socialisation process would be if spinning off from it also was a self-consciousness that is overly sensitised to a need to be seen as trendy and fashionable and where self-identity is centrally defined in terms of commercial brand associations.

An unhealthy obsession with brands can be created where premium brands drive young consumers' commodity preferences with essential items such as food and clothing. These are items parents cannot avoid buying and so for marketers these are captive markets. The idea behind school uniforms was to remove brand differentials from the everyday clothing of kids in the place where they spend many of their waking hours. It also serves to remove class distinctions – between the 'haves' and the 'have nots' – and creates a more level playing field and atmosphere of equality in which learning is the main objective. Even then, kids will try to personalise their uniforms through pushing at specific boundaries. Girls might observe standard colours and designs, but try to modify skirt lengths (usually making them shorter). Boys might leave shirts hanging out of trousers for as long as possible.

These anecdotes reveal manifestations of personal branding but we need to know more about what branding means to kids. We have already looked at the origins of branding to define what it is and where it came from. As our analysis of branding has shown, however, its meaning has evolved as developed and developing societies around the world have become more consumerist in their orientation. Making the observation that even young children today are brand conscious is one thing, but defining what this actually means is something else. The difficulty here stems in part from the fact that brand consciousness itself is not a constant but changes in its nature and manifestations as children become physically and psychologically more mature over time.

As we will also see later in this chapter, we need to examine closely the nature of the measurement of brand awareness. Researchers have tended to rely on measures of memory a lot for indicators of brand awareness, but there is more than one type of memory and the tests of recall and recognition that dominate this research evidence are sensitive only to one type. Failure to register children's brand awareness could therefore be explained by inappropriate research methodologies, while registration of awareness using these measures may provide a one-dimensional view of children's general understanding of brands.

Understanding early consumer development

We cannot begin to understand how brand awareness and comprehension come about without also understanding what is known about the way children become consumers. To understand how children learn about consumerism, we need to consult models of child development. Although these models were not established specifically to explain children's socialisation as consumers, they describe processes or stages of development that provide an essential underpinning to how children learn and are able to comprehend what is going on around them in their environment. There has been an ongoing debate among child psychologists about the efficacy of 'stage' versus 'process' models of cognitive development, with the debate extending over into theorising about other areas of social and emotional development.

A great deal of early child development psychology was influenced by the thinking of Jean Piaget. He made a detailed study of children's development from birth to adolescence and identified a number of specific stages of cognitive development which he believed formed the basis of development for all children (Piaget, 1970, 1972; Smith, Cowie & Blades, 2003). His work was based on a small number of case studies, however, and despite his initial influence on child development theory, over time his model has been challenged and today largely superseded by newer conceptual models (Ginsburg & Opper, 1988; Smith et al., 2003).

Rather than presuming, as Piaget did, that there are fixed stages of development that occur during specific age ranges, later models conceived of children's cognitive development as a continuous process, with different sets of cognitive abilities emerging gradually and at varying times. Despite this debate among psychologists, a great deal of marketing research and theorising about how children learn to become consumers has been shaped by Piaget's model. As a starting point, it is worth outlining it here before looking at other more recent thinking about children's development. Piaget proposed that there are four key stages of cognitive development that shape the way children think about the world around them. He called these the sensori–motor stage (from birth to 2 years), preoperational stage (2 to 7 years), concrete operational stage (7 to 11 years), and formal operational stage (11 to adulthood).

In the sensori–motor stage, children learn how to interpret basic sensations from the world around them, including simple object recognition, and how to perform and control their physical movements. For example, a child at play will at first need someone else's help if they drop or throw a toy out of their physical reach. Over time, as the child's physical coordination develops and they learn that they can control specific movements, they will reach for it for themselves. During this stage of their development, their language and underlying cognitive abilities are very limited and this means that understanding of brands and related marketing messages tends to be beyond their capabilities.

In the preoperational stage, children begin to acquire language skills through which they can verbally label objects and communicate internal thoughts and feelings to others. At this stage, however, they retain a highly egocentric view of the world despite entering into a broader range of social interactions and relationships with other people. Children can begin to engage in simple logical reasoning about the world but the judgements of which they are capable are still crude. In a classic experiment, for instance, a child is presented with two glasses, one of which is tall and the other short. The short glass is also fatter and both hold exactly the same amount of fluid. The short glass is filled with water and the child watches while its contents are poured into the tall glass. The child is then asked whether the tall glass contained more water than the short glass. In focusing only on the height dimension, the child fails to record and use information that the amount of water is exactly the same and during the preoperational stage will state that there is more water in the tall glass.

The limited abilities of children to take into account more than one variable at a time when making judgements about objects has been identified as an explanation of their limited understanding of advertising. The differentiation between advertisements and programmes on television, for example, can depend upon being able to identify a number of distinguishing features in each case. On a simple level, programmes tend to be longer than advertisements. In addition, advertisements have other distinctive production features in their visual and verbal narratives that make them recognisable to adult viewers. This form of multi-faceted evaluation of the ingredients of advertisements and programmes requires information processing skills that remain beyond children of pre-school age (Kunkel, 1988; Young, 1990).

Children in the pre–operational stage of development are also very egocentric in the way they view the world. This is a characteristic we will return to later because it is an important factor underpinning how young consumers can relate to specific brands and be influenced in their preferences by other people – especially their peers. To test whether children are capable of adopting another person's viewpoint, child psychologists have devised tests using dolls. The children in these experiments are encouraged to imagine they are the doll or to guess at what the doll's experience might have been in a specific setting in which something happened to it. Piaget constructed a study of this kind in which he sat a doll on a table facing a landscape scene on the other side. He then asked children of pre-school and school-age to describe what the doll could see. Those kids who were still at the pre-operational stage of development had great difficulty performing this task because they could only think about it from their own point of view and not from the perspective of anyone else (Piaget & Inhelder, 1956).

In the concrete operational stage, children learn to retain and reproduce ideas about objects and processes without always needing those things to be physically present and visible. They can also process puzzles, taking into account more than one variable at a time. By the concrete operational stage, in undertaking the water in the two glasses task, for example, children start to recognise that they should not allow the height of the vessel to govern their perceptions. They learn to conserve the information that the mass of the liquid being poured remains unchanged regardless of the height of the glass.

Although children's logical reasoning abilities were believed to evolve during this stage, they were found still to be confined largely to manipulation of physical objects. Children's abilities to extrapolate general sets of rules in more abstract and internalised ways remained limited. This might mean that children could still experience difficulty with their interpretation of some promotional messages about brands because of their ephemeral nature (Gunter,

Oates & Blades, 2005), but they might also begin to make their own judgements about products linked to brands if they can physically handle and experience the products.

By the formal operational stage which, according to Piaget, children generally reach from the age of 11 years, they learn to think analytically and in far more abstract ways. Children can engage in abstract puzzles which require them to use rules to reach solutions in the absence of being able to see or touch or handle physical objects, the properties of which are being judged. In my book *Advertising to Children on TV*, written with my colleagues Caroline Oates and Mark Blades, we cited a classic puzzle of this type. In this case, children are told the following: 'All cats with pink eyes have six legs. Fred is a cat with pink eyes. How many legs does Fred have?' (Gunter et al., 2005, p. 66).

Following the abstract rule here, the answer of course is 'six'. For children at the concrete operational stage, however, this puzzle can often cause a problem to them because they are required to put aside what they know about cats from their real life experience, to adopt an abstract rule-based scenario on its own merits, and to reach the solution that the rule of logical reasoning in this case requires. By the time kids have reached the formal operational stage this kind of puzzle is generally more straightforward for them.

On entering this stage, children also become aware of the need to weigh up the implications of actions not only for themselves but for others. Children begin to lose the continuing egocentricity they display during the concrete operational stage, during which their repeated social encounters with other children teach them that other people often have different world views and perspectives from the ones they hold. From this experience, they gradually learn to accommodate the needs of others in their own behaviour. This accommodation often occurs on a person by person basis and is dependent upon a child's previous experiences with specific children.

By the formal operational stage, teenagers have become attuned to group-level norms and expectations in terms of personal appearance and behaviour, and internalise these constructs in their plans for themselves. They can visualise outcomes in their own minds before actually entering social settings to find out what the outcomes will be. In relation to brands, therefore, children that have reached this more abstract level of reasoning can consider not only the value of brands in terms of personal likes and dislikes but also demonstrate an awareness of how other consumers, in particular their peers, might also react to a brand. If peer group approval in such contexts is important to them, they might allow group tastes to overrule personal tastes in their own brand selections.

As we can see, Piaget's work indicated that children are restricted in their range and flexibility of thinking at each of these stages, but especially during the first three stages. There can be individual degrees of variation in the speed with which children progress through these stages, with some children advancing from one stage to the next at an earlier age than others. Thus, even though Piaget believed that children must complete their passage through one stage before progressing on to the next, speed of progression can be influenced by the nature of environmental experiences that can stimulate new modes of thinking.

Later psychological theories of cognitive development moved away from Piaget's model but still retained as core concepts the idea that children progressed through different phases of development and that their cognitive abilities changed as they matured. Piaget's model tried to explain the different ways in which children processed information, embracing ideas about how they learned from their experiences, acquired new knowledge, and organised and stored this knowledge in their memories. He claimed that children's inabilities to perform specific tasks at specific ages could be explained by the level of cognitive maturity they had reached at specific stages of development.

Other writers have challenged this explanation and argued that in some of the tests used by Piaget, children's failure to perform tasks resulted from a lack of clarity in the instructions they were given (see John, 1999; Moses & Baldwin, 2005). As we will examine later on, more recent research has indicated that even pre-school children can engage in some forms of relatively abstract reasoning in relation to brands and this is linked to specific skills they demonstrate in relevant tests of their cognitive abilities. With Piaget's original tests, pre-operational children could have failed because there was a strong reliance on verbal skills they did not possess. However, if verbally based tests are switched to ones in which judgements are made via non-verbal responses, underlying cognitive skills can become more apparent. In other words, even 3- and 4-year-olds can demonstrate reasoning abilities, but they cannot always put their judgements into words (Siegel, 1997; Smith et al., 2003).

Cognitive theories and understanding consumer development

Piaget's stage theory of children's cognitive development seems to provide an elegant model to use in formulating ideas about how children evolve as young consumers, but its theoretical implications have not really ever been fully and systematically tested in relation to children's reactions to brands and branding activities. Many early research studies of children's consumer socialisation have cited Piaget's model as a backdrop to their research, and assumptions have then been made, largely on the basis of the age of the children recruited, that they must have reached a specified level of cognitive development (Ward, 1974; Wartella, 1982; Young, 1990).

For many years, such assumptions were not directly tested through relevant support tests of cognitive abilities (John, 1999). It was therefore presumed that if 8-year-olds in a sample differed from 4-year-olds this must be a reflection of their respective Piagetian stage of development. In fact, what needs to happen is for researchers to establish through direct cognitive tests the status of each child's cognitive reasoning abilities and then to relate their scores on these tests to their performance on brand-related tasks.

In the consumer field, the influence of the stage-model of development was manifest in particular in early studies of children's understanding of advertising (Wartella & Ettema, 1974; Ward, Wackman & Wartella, 1975, 1977; Wartella, 1980; Gaines & Esserman, 1981). As we saw earlier, the notion of 'brand' evolved alongside the growth of the advertising industry to embrace more abstract ideas about what a product variant could bring to the lives of consumers. No longer was a 'brand' simply a mark of origin or ownership. It had a meaning of its own that was greater than the functional definition of the product.

Advertising promotions contributed greatly to this notion of brand image. Advertising has also represented a principal focus of attention of researchers who sought to enhance what we know about the consumer learning that we must all go through as children to become informed and selective consumers. Research with children over the second half of the twentieth century initially developed a model that conformed with the idea that kids go through several stages of cognitive and social development and that within each of these stages, their ability to make sense of advertising – or even to recognise that it is something distinctive – is restricted by the cognitive skills available to them at the time (see Young, 1990; Gunter, Oates & Blades, 2005).

The first step in understanding that advertising is not the same as, say, a television programme takes on a very crude perceptual form with the child noticing that advertisements tend to be shorter than programmes or that they are separated physically from other content in a website (Zuckerman, Ziegler & Stevenson, 1978; Levin, Petros & Petrella, 1982). Second, children start to develop a basic understanding that advertisements have a specific purpose that is distinct from that of other media content in which it is embedded. Initially, this recognition enables a child to know that an advertisement is telling you something about a product you can buy and use (Donohue, Henke & Donohue, 1980). This ability is prevalent among youngsters by the ages of 6 or 7, but appears in only small minorities of children younger than this (Macklin, 1987). Children's earliest experiences in this context will tend to focus on products targeted at their age group, such as toys and games. Eventually, it spreads to cover other commodities. In a further stage of development, children come to realise that not only do advertisements provide information about products but that they also try to persuade you to buy the specific product or 'brand' that is being promoted (Christenson, 1982; Brucks, Armstrong & Goldberg, 1988). Children realise that advertisements try to get you to like the product and then to want it (Kunkel, Wilcox, Cantor et al., 2004).

In a further and more advanced level of understanding, children become aware of the economic implications of advertising. These include the fact that advertisers do what they do to make money and that they also pay media operators for space to advertise. Thus, advertisers and those who work with them have a number of agendas and many of these agendas are motivated by self-interest (Gunter & Furnham, 1998). Coupled with this type of knowledge is an array of beliefs about advertising that, for instance, the information it provides cannot always be taken at face value. On passing through these various stages of development, young consumers acquire what has been called 'advertising literacy' (Livingstone & Helsper, 2006).

As we will see later, the notion of literacy used here is grounded in a cognitive defence orientation which argues that children can be taught how to critique advertising and other forms of brand marketing, and thus become less susceptible to their promotional effects. This internalised inoculation against the influences of marketing derives from the acquisition of knowledge about persuasion processes, how they work, and how to recognise when they are present (Friestad & Wright, 1994). A newer model has emerged which challenges the position adopted by this cognitive defence perspective and recognises that sometimes – especially when consumers become emotionally involved with advertisements – young consumers fail to implement their learned defences against persuasion (Buijzen, van Reijmersdal & Owen, 2010; Rozendaal, Lapierre, van Reijmersdal & Buijzen, 2013).

Returning to general developmental patterns in childhood, movement in scholarly thinking towards the idea that children's cognitive (and consumer) development may occur in a gradual way rather than stepping up in a saccadic fashion from one stage to the next occurred at the end of the twentieth century when one researcher in this field presented a process-driven model of children's development as consumers. In 1999, Deborah Roedder John outlined three categories of information processing relating to the study of children's socialisation as consumers. These were called strategic processors, cued processors, and limited processors (John, 1999). Her initial thinking about an information processing approach to assessment of children's abilities as young consumers had begun twenty years earlier (Roedder, 1981). In many ways, although they have different names from the Piagetian stages, they embrace the idea that over time children's thought processes become more complex, and that children are able to understand the world around them in increasingly sophisticated ways.

Information processing theories have underpinned studies that have investigated how children learn to pay attention to the world around them and then select which of their experiences they will process and store information about for later use. These theories also address how children organise this internalised information – or knowledge – and are then able to retrieve and use it later on. It is important to recognise that children's abilities to process complex information are limited during their early years, but then gradually evolve over time to approach adult levels as they reach their teens (Schneider & Pressley, 1997). Research in this field has therefore tried to understand and explain how human beings develop and operate as information processors. Do we – as children – develop particular strategies for processing information? What are these strategies? Are the same or different strategies used for different experiences? What are the limits to our information processing abilities? Do these limits also vary with the types of experiences we encounter and how often we encounter them?

The adoption of an information processing approach to understanding children's consumer development does not mean that stage theories are rendered redundant. It is still feasible to distinguish 'stages' through which cognitive development progresses, but modern cognitive thinking takes the view that this is a phenomenon that happens gradually rather than in dramatic jumps from a lower to a higher level (Siegler, 1998).

John believed that strategic thinking is – or eventually becomes – an aspect of young consumers' cognitive arsenal, but it tends not to emerge until age 12 or sometimes a little later, and shares certain qualities with Piaget's formal operational stage. By this stage of their development, children have usually developed a number of different ways of thinking about products and marketing activities. They can process information from advertising campaigns and articulate different reasons for liking and disliking brands that reflect not just a brand's physical and functional qualities but also the symbolic meanings that frequently become attached to brands and define their appeal to mature consumers (John, 1999).

According to the Persuasion Knowledge Model, as they mature as consumers children acquire the ability to identify marketing tactics and discern marketers' motives (Friestad & Wright, 1994). This learning can mediate the attitudes and beliefs they form about brands and the advertising campaigns that accompany them (Wright, Friestad & Boush, 2005). Children initially learn that advertisements provide information about brands. Later they also come to realise that advertisements are designed to make you want to buy things (Wright et al., 2005).

In articulating their early ideas about the world, children can display many of the qualities of strategic thinking. A child's abilities to think about products or services and brands, however, are more difficult to carry out in a totally abstract fashion without the relevant items being present. Children need to be prompted to a greater extent to think about brands not just in terms of their physical and functional attributes, which they can often readily describe in the presence of a product (Brucks et al., 1988). During the age-range of 7 to 11 years, children need to be cued before they apply their knowledge to make critical judgements about brands and advertisements. Once they get into their teens they can manage this more readily by themselves (An & Stern 2011).

'Strategic thinkers' can spontaneously enter an advanced mode of thinking about products and brands, whereas 'cued thinkers' need to be helped. Cued thinking about a brand requires the product or aspects of it to be physically present and resembles in many ways the concrete operational stage of Piaget. Here Piaget made reference to the ability of children to assess objects in a multi-dimensional fashion. This outcome is best achieved when they can see the object in question, rather than having to imagine it. This level of thinking tends to show itself from around the age of 7.

Cues can be presented in the form of clearly demarcated advertising 'breaks' that separate advertisements from surrounding media content. Such breaks prompt children to realise they are being confronted with advertising and that advertisements are persuasive messages designed to influence their purchase decisions. These breaks are not always sufficient as triggers of children's consumer literacy skills. In interactive marketing environments such as advergames, for example, they demonstrated mixed success in influencing pre-teenage children's persuasion knowledge (An & Stern, 2011).

Before the age of 7, children are conceived to be limited information processors. This means that their abilities to make specific evaluations of products in terms of what they can do and why they are important are not fully formed (Schneider & Pressley, 1997). Very young children, as we will see later, can recognise certain products and their brand names, but only manage to do this successfully when required to make simple judgements, for example, that hamburgers are available at McDonald's. If asked to say why McDonald's is good, they will struggle to give a coherent explanation.

Social development and emergent consumerism

As well as cognitive development, as it relates to children's abilities to process and make sense of information they obtain from the world around them, their social development is also important in the context of their relationships with brands. The reason for this is that the premium value that attaches to a brand can be determined not only by its physical qualities but also how other people in a child's social environment respond to the brand. This 'other person' reaction only begins to exert an influence on the child's own brand evaluations and choices when they have reached a stage of maturity at which they can take the other person's perspective on things.

This means that perspective-taking is an important factor in children's consumer socialisation. According to leading psychology theorists, children are initially egocentric in their outlook on the world (Selman, 1980). This is especially true of pre-school children and can persist for a while during early school years. Hence, from ages 3 to 6, when children begin to socialise with a broader spectrum of people, their reactions to social situations are shaped by self-centredness and the only point of view that is important to them is their own. In their social interactions with other children, pre-schoolers' tactics for persuasion when trying to get others to play specific games with them would be based on the offer of specific incentives that the child knew they might be responsive to if their positions were reversed. Alternatively, children can use various forms of emotional blackmail such as getting upset or angry. This tactic might also be used with parents when pestering them to make specific purchases on the child's behalf (Clark & Delia, 1976; Weiss & Sachs, 1991).

As children mature further, between the ages of 6 and 8, their social lives begin to change. At this stage of their development, when they spend more time out of home in school and playing with friends, they come to understand that their perspective is not the only one that exists. Others around them have their own perspectives on things and children come to realise that they cannot always expect to get their own way. Sometimes it is important to give way to others' wishes in order to maintain friendly relations. This does not mean they necessarily understand the other person's perspective, but they do at least acknowledge that it exists. This means that in their own persuasion tactics with others, children entering their 'tween' years might adopt various deceptions knowing that these might work more effectively than cruder approaches such as simple reward exchanges between them ('If you do this for me, I'll do that for you') or emotional persuasion ('I don't like you anymore!'). Manipulative deception can begin to surface by the age of 5, but it becomes more widespread and advanced in form two or three years later (Erftlier & Dyson, 1986; Peskin, 1992)

As they grow older through the ninth and tenth years of their lives, children develop abilities to become more inwardly reflective and to empathise with other perspectives than their own. They not only recognise their existence but also start to understand what these different perspectives may mean in terms of behavioural outcomes. As they approach their teens, these ideas become internalised to a point where children will weigh up other potential perspectives as well as their own before acting in different situations. In their teen years, as peer groups attain greater significance, children's perspective taking does not only consider what another individual's perspective might be but also when their behaviour is in keeping with the perspective they know a key social reference might adopt (Gunter et al., 2005).

In a consumer context, separate stages have been outlined by some marketing scholars that have been influenced by the cognitive and social development models outlined by psychologists. In addition to her three cognitive processes, Deborah Roedder John outlined three social development processes which she called perceptual, analytical and reflective. These processes evolved over time and were underpinned by changes in children associated with both their cognitive and social maturation (John, 1999).

Social changes occur in the lives of children as they grow older and gain more and more independence from their parents and the family home. This is not a one-dimensional process of friends and peer groups gradually taking over from parents as main reference points in terms of how to behave or which self-identity to wear. How kids can relate to their friends and acquaintances at school or in their out-of-home social lives also depends on their level of cognitive development which underpins such essential skills as 'other' perspective taking. John's (1999) social development processes were an attempt to describe gradually emergent children's abilities to understand complex verbal and nonverbal information. It was further theorised that such abilities would also enable kids to adopt different social perspectives in relation to marketing messages and brands.

The explicit association of limited, cued and strategic process development with ages of onset has led this model to be referred to widely by marketing researchers who have used it as a 'stage' theory. The problem with this simple conceptualisation is that it presumes − as is often done with Piaget's theory − that until they reach a specific age, children are incapable of thinking beyond a certain level of sophistication. Yet, there is ample evidence that this is a grossly over-simplistic generalisation about children's cognitive development. There are occasions, for example, when children can display a level of cognitive reasoning beyond what a stage theory predicts for them but only in relation to certain puzzles or reasoning tasks with which they are well practiced (Schneider & Pressley, 1997).

In applying this understanding to a child's consumer experiences, it is possible that a child, classified as being in the concrete operational stage by Piaget and Inhelder (1956) or a 'cued process' thinker by John (1999), that plays with two computer games on a regular basis and learns many different strategies for progressing through to the end may be able to make more complex judgements about the relative merits and complexities of each game than an adult. When asked to engage in other reasoning tasks with which they are less well practised such a child may fail altogether. The outcome here can be explained more by the nature of the child's learning experiences than by the 'stage' of cognitive development they have reached. Similar principles can be applied to any stage model, whether it attempts to describe and explain cognitive development or social development.

Returning for the moment to John's social development model, the perceptual stage characterises children between the ages of 3 and 7. During this stage children can begin to recognise and name products and brands. They can place such objects into categories based on their physical dimensions and the functions they can perform. However, children are perceptually bounded at this stage and are able to recognise products by their outward appearance, but are rarely able to make deeper judgements about them in terms of how other people use them or in terms of symbolic values they have acquired through advertising or the ways they have been adopted as social status signifiers by social groups (John, 1999).

Upon entering the analytical 'stage', between the ages of 7 and 11, children start to acquire a range of cognitive and social skills that enable them to make much richer judgements about products and brands. Not only do they know what functions are performed by specific products, they are also able to make more detailed comparisons between brands within a product range on the basis of how they differ from each other on multiple dimensions (Randrup & Lac, 2000). Hence, they might make comparisons based on outward appearance but also the basis of a brand's relative performance in terms of its functionality. Thus, is one brand of cereal tastier than another? Does one type of computer game have more complex narratives or production techniques than another? Children draw on their own experiences which they then compare with marketing claims about the brand (Bartholomew & O'Donohue, 2003). Their growing awareness of the perspectives of others means they also draw upon the critiques of other young consumers in reaching their evaluations of specific brands (Mangleburg & Bristol, 1999).

By the reflective 'stage', these multi-dimensional judgements about products and brands evolve still further and children start to take into account social meanings that attach to brands. Their perspective taking makes reference to perceived normative assessments by social groups to which they belong or aspire to. In effect, young consumers become fashion-conscious in a way that requires more complex judgements about products, product variants and specific brands. Quality of performance, cost and marketing messages might all be weighed up and positioned alongside collective opinions of specific peer groups that are important to the individual teenage consumer (Gunter, McAleer & Clifford, 1992).

In a further analysis of this developmental process, the position of branding in the wider context of whether children display a materialism orientation has been examined in relation to the psychology of young consumers and in particular the role played by possessions in their definitions of their self-identity. Materialism is known to form part of a wider suite of psychological and social factors that define the individual, including the types of parents they have, family affluence, parental attitudes to possessions, the quality of communications between children and their parents, the materialistic orientations of peer groups, and their media habits and patterns of exposure to marketing promotions (Goldberg & Gorn, 1978; Churchill & Moschis, 1979; Moore and Moschis, 1981; Hite & Eck, 1987; Achenreiner, 1997; Goldberg, Gorn, Peracchio & Barnossy, 2003).

One interesting developmental pattern that has been found is that the value children attach to material possessions is linked to their self-esteem (Kasser, 2002). One further observation is that materialism evolves across childhood (Achenreiner, 1997). There is further evidence, however, that this is not a smooth, unrelenting progression towards increased preoccupation with possessions (Goldberg et al. 2003). The link between materialism and self-esteem is important because self-esteem is sensitive to the physical changes that occur as children grow up. Self-regard varies between children, of course, but in general, children in their 'tweens' (8 to 11 years) feel quite good about themselves or are simply not concerned about self-image. During their early teen years, and as children begin to develop adult characteristics as they enter puberty, all this changes. At this point, their self-image becomes a major preoccupation. Once they have got through this stage by their mid- to late teens, their self identity settles down again in most cases and they begin to feel better about themselves – at least compared to a few years earlier (Kasser, Ryan, Couchman & Sheldon, 2004).

The significance of material possessions in this context stems from their link with the pursuit of happiness and also in relation to the role played by brands in imparting specific types of social identity to their consumers (Csikszentmihalyi & Rochberg-Halton, 1981; Solomon, 1983; Belk, 1985; Richins & Dawson, 1992). At first, children seek to acquire specific goods usually through their parents. Despite being able to identify goods by brand names even from pre-school years, brands mean little to them beyond being labels by which products can be called (John, 1999). As they grow older, brands acquire new meaning for children in that they convey symbolic meanings about social status, lifestyle and the types of people who use them. Their relevance and importance to individual consumers then derives from the degree to which those meanings are transferred to them as individuals in the way they believe they will be seen by others. There must also be a different sense of self in this context whereby the child displays an awakening of their own self-concept not just as a distinct identity from other children around them, but also in an evaluative sense in which they make comparisons with others and form a view of their own identity that is positively or negatively toned. These symbolic meanings of brands have little relevance to children before this awakening occurs, but afterwards they can become critically important to the way a child feels about him- or herself.

Materialists tend to define themselves and the quality of their lives largely in terms of their possessions (Richins & Dawson, 1992). Purchasing goods can make them feel better about their lives and about themselves (Fournier & Richins, 1991). We have often heard people talk anecdotally about 'retail therapy' whereby they treat themselves to purchases when depressed in order to lift their mood. Such anecdotes have received scientific backing with research evidence showing that people's materialistic orientations can be manipulated by interventions designed temporarily to lower their self-esteem or enhance feelings of social insecurity (Braun & Wicklund, 1989; Kasser, 2002; Solberg, Diener & Robinson, 2004).

With children, changes in self-esteem are cyclical and related to the levels of cognitive, social, and physical development. A sophisticated understanding of brand symbolism emerges during their 'tween' years and this enables them to relate to commodities at a level that means they begin to have relevance to self-identity definition. Consumption takes on a different meaning during this developmental phase of life as do brand images (Achenreiner & John, 2003). As we have also seen already, at this stage, children become more aware of how brands are perceived by their peers (Selman, 1980).

In their early teen years, therefore, children experience a dip in their self-esteem as rapid physical changes create uncertainties about their self-image. This lowered self-esteem, combined with sensitivity to peer group pressures, leads them to become more brand conscious and to seek to acquire possessions that enhance their self-image and boost how they feel about themselves. Once they have passed through this developmental stage, usually by the ages of 16–18 years, their self-concept stabilises and their hunger for material possession abates to some extent (Belk, 1988).

Research has confirmed that kids aged 12–13 years define themselves more in terms of their material possessions compared with those aged 8–9 and those aged 16–18. Furthermore, within each age group, interventions designed to heighten self-esteem can result in reduced materialism urges (Chaplin & John, 2007).

Reconciling stages and processes: cognitive skills and branding

Models of child development that take a 'stage' perspective have been enthusiastically adopted by marketers in conceptualising the consumer socialisation of children (Gunter et al., 2005). One reason for this could be that these models have provided useful frameworks for the construction of research. Piaget's model has been especially popular in this context. Developmental psychologists, however, have moved beyond Piaget's original thinking, which has been regarded as presenting a structural model that is too rigid in its representation of children's gradually emergent cognitive and social skills. Even some marketing scholars have called for a more flexible and sophisticated model that takes into account individual differences in cognitive abilities that can occur among children at the same stage of cognitive development (John, 1999). This observation has received some empirical support from psychological experiments carried out with children, and initial evidence has emerged that individual variances in development can mediate the way children in the same age group think about brands.

The study of consumer socialisation and the emergent advertising and branding literacy that goes with it, have continued to be influenced by psychological models of cognitive development. Despite debates about stages versus processes, throughout the 1980s, 1990s, and 2000s, researchers working on this subject have adopted an age-based framework in which the capabilities of children are age-defined. In reflecting on this point, it is perhaps not hard to understand why this should be so. Ultimately, we need to impose some kind of conceptual structure on our understanding of consumer socialisation. While it may comprise a gradually evolving maturation process, there is evidence that even allowing for individual differences, most children within a specific age range tend to display a characteristic level of cognitive development.

There is evidence from a number of published sources that children up to the age of 5 have difficulty with taking on board any perspective of the world other than their own. They also have problems with reaching cognitive judgements in which they aggregate across more than one dimension of experience at the same time. In other words, taking into account both the height and width of vessels rather than just one of these features when deciding which of two holds the most liquid. Thus, when looking at advertisements they distinguish them from surrounding material at a simple perceptual level only (Blatt, Spencer & Ward, 1972; Butter, Popovich, Stackhouse & Garner, 1981; Buijzen, Van Reijmersdal & Owen, 2010). Some children of pre-school age however may also be able to provide insights into the informational function of advertisements (Macklin, 1987). Because of their inability to acknowledge and understand other perspectives on the world than their own immediate view, they are unable to recognise the intentions of advertisers and the possibility that advertisers might be attempting to deceive them (Baron-Cohen, Leslie & Frith, 1985; Kunkel et al., 2004).

By the time they get to the ages of 6 through to 9 years, children's cognitive abilities will have moved on. It is true that these abilities will not be at the same level for every child of the same age, nor will each child demonstrate the same rate of improvement in their intellectual abilities across this age bracket. Nonetheless, at some point during these years, most children will show some knowledge that advertising does not just have a particular appearance in different media, but it generally has a specific purpose as well. Functional judgements therefore emerge that enable many children to say that advertising gives them product-related information, and some children also to know that advertisements try to get you to like and to want to buy products (Bever, Smith, Bengen & Johnson, 1975; Macklin, 1985, 1987; Wilson & Weiss, 1992; Kunkel et al., 2004). For some children towards the upper end of this age bracket, who are among those making the greatest cognitive advances during this period, insights into the persuasive intent of advertising have been detected (Lawlor & Prothero, 2003; Mallalieu, Palan & Laczniak, 2005).

By the time children get to the ages of 10–12 years, their cognitive abilities mature still further. Once again, not all children within this age range will demonstrate the same levels of ability, and some will show faster growth in their abilities than others. This period of their development, however, has been identified as one during which the persuasive intent of advertising becomes clearer and also that this activity is being perpetrated by others who have a specific agenda of their own. We noted that during pre-school years up to age 5, children see the world in a self-centred way. During the next age group, from 6–9 years, their more frequent interactions with other kids teach them that other people may have a different view of the world. Even though you might not readily identify with these alternative perspectives or want to abide by them, sometimes you have to in order to get along with other people.

By the pre-teen years of 10–12, children's abilities to take into account the perspectives of other people matures further such that they can incorporate it into their advance thinking about events that lie ahead (Baron-Cohen et al., 1985). In other words, they can begin to think about the implications of their own actions for other people. This 'other' perspective taking can be important in the consumer context because it can cause children to think through the implications of purchasing a specific brand they have seen advertised. The advertiser might make one set of claims about the brand, while the child's social experiences have taught him or her that their peers or their friends might have a different opinion about it. Children can then weigh up their final decision, taking into account not only their personal desires but also the reactions of others. The key point here is that this level of thinking about brands and their associated advertising campaigns requires a higher level of cognitive development. This ability is emergent during the pre-teen years (Moses & Baldwin, 2005; Wright, Friestad & Boush, 2005; Rozendaal, Buijzen & Valkenburg, 2010; van Reijmersdal, Rozendaal & Biujzen, 2012).

One Dutch study found that the extent to which children's attention is drawn to specific brands that are advertised on television can have some effects on the brands they seek as gifts at Christmas, but this relationship is not a consistent one across different television channels to which children might be exposed. The prevalence of brand gift requests also became progressively less across age groups, being greatest among children aged 7 and 8 years and least amongst those aged 11–12 years, with those aged 9 and 10 years in between. There was a possibility however that on the television channels where advertised brands were monitored, there were many more brands targeted at the youngest than at the oldest age group in this case. Nevertheless, the researchers also floated the explanation that the older children, being at a more advanced stage of cognitive development, were also more cynical about advertising and less inclined therefore to have their gift ideas controlled by commercial messages (Buijzen & Valkenburg, 2000).

Another interesting study by Esther Rozendaal and her colleagues at the Amsterdam School of Communications Research has found that the age of 10 seems to mark an important development threshold, after which children display more adult-like assessments of advertisers' intentions (Rozendaal et al., 2011). This research began with the observation that advertisers have used various tactics to persuade consumers to buy their brands, but among the most widely used are: to repeat the advertisement a lot; to include within the advertisement a demonstration of the product; to give an impression that the product is already popular with the target audience's peer group (e.g. showing kids playing with a advertised game); using a well-known celebrity to endorse the product; to use humour; and to offer incentives to purchase such as free gifts.

The research was conducted with professional advertisers, an adult sample, and a sample of children aged 8–12. None of these samples could be regarded as representative of their original populations, but the research allowed for direct comparisons to be made between children and grown ups and to compare their respective perceptions about advertisers' tactics with the opinions of experts. The children and adults were asked what advertisers intended when they used any of the six tactics discussed earlier. The professional advertisers had confirmed the importance of these tactics. The researchers also asked about specific types of effects they might wish to achieve with these tactics – all of which concerned impacts upon child consumers. These effects included helping children to learn about the advertised product, to recall the advertisements, to believe the advertisement, to make the advertisement more likable, and to male children ask their parents to buy the product (see Rozendaal et al., 2011, p. 337).

The children were divided into two categories by age: 8–10 and 10–12. Each of these sub-groups of children was compared in their understanding of advertising tactics with the adults. The mean scores for understanding about these tactics, overall, were highest for adults. Even so, the older children, aged 10–12, performed almost as well as the grown ups on four out of the six marketing tactics: use of repetition, showing the brand's popularity with the child's peer group, the use of humour and the use of special offers. The youngest children aged 8–10 performed significantly worse than both the adults and older children in their understanding of all the tactics, except for humour. Interestingly, the oldest children performed significantly better than the adults in their understanding of the use of celebrity endorsers. The researchers concluded that between the ages of 8 and 12, children exhibit a progressive growth in their understanding of advertising, and that after the age of 10, an understanding of the persuasive intent of advertising becomes more apparent. Children's advertising and branding literacy extends to an awareness of various marketing techniques and tactics that are used in promoting brands (Rozendaal et al., 2011).

During these 'tween' years leading up to adolescence, evidence has emerged that exposure to advertising on television not only triggers a desire for the advertised products but also increased materialism. The cultivation of materialistic views of the world can emerge over time between the ages of 8 and 11 and seems potentially to be influenced by exposure to advertising and by the enhanced product desire that stems from this exposure (Opree, Buijzen, van Reijmersdal & Valkenburg, 2013).

Once young consumers have reached their teenage years, their cognitive development will have reached a level of maturity approaching that of adults. This means that many will begin to make complex judgements about brands and their advertising campaigns based on the information contained in advertisements, personal experiences with brands, knowledge of others' experiences with brands, and an understanding of the different agendas of advertisers (Gunter & Furnham 1998; Valkenburg & Cantor, 2001). Even within this age bracket, however, not all young consumers are the same in terms of their cognitive and social maturity and therefore in terms of their abilities to reach specific kinds of judgements about brands and advertisements. This last point has been found to apply particularly to young consumers' understanding of the tactics used by advertisers to persuade consumers to buy their brands (Boush, Friestad & Rose, 1994).

Consumer literacy, brand advertising and children's vulnerability

As we have seen from much of the evidence reviewed already, a prevailing view has been that children are vulnerable consumers. Their initial inabilities and subsequent limited abilities to know what advertising is, its purposes and the agenda of advertisers and marketing professionals who design marketing campaigns, render them susceptible to brand marketing influences. As they grow older and develop more advanced intellectual skills, children's abilities to interpret advertising messages and to make up their own minds about brands also improve. This growth of knowledge about advertising and brand marketing has been termed 'advertising literacy' (Livingstone & Helsper, 2006).

It has been further postulated that as advertising literacy develops, then children become less vulnerable as they develop 'cognitive defences' against the persuasive influences of advertisements (Friestad & Wright, 1994). As they mature, young consumers acquire an internalised knowledge about persuasion and the techniques that accompany it in the context of brand advertising and other promotions. The Persuasion Knowledge Model was outlined by Friestad and Wright to explain this specific component of the consumer socialisation process and how it eventually operates to help consumers draw their own conclusions about brand promotions.

This knowledge has been identified as representing the cornerstone of informed, critical consumerism (Verhellen, Oates, De Pelsmacker & Dens, 2014). At the core of the Persuasion Knowledge Model is the concept that children learn eventually to recognise that they are a target and that the advertiser is a source of attempted persuasion. Accompanying this initial understanding is the eventual identification also of techniques used by advertisers to persuade consumers to buy their brands (Mallalieu, Palan & Laczniak, 2005; Wright, Friestad & Boush, 2005). Once advertising and other brand promotions are more closely integrated with surrounding entertainment content, however, children may be placed in more vulnerable positions because their persuasion knowledge is not sufficiently developed to detect the more subtle persuasion cues (Panic, Cauberghe & De Pelsmacker, 2013; An, Jin & Park, 2014).

This has directed the focus of attention of those who would seek to find ways of protecting children from the influences of advertisers and brand marketers towards finding ways of promoting youngsters' awareness and understanding of advertising and its techniques (Gunter et al., 2005). There is an implicit assumption in all this reasoning that if children can be made more advertising literate, they will be better equipped to cope with advertisements in different forms and also less likely to believe everything they see and hear in commercial messages about advertised brands. What is less clear, and has been called into question by relevant empirical tests, is whether advertising literacy actually protects children and ensures they are not taken in by advertising messages (Mallinckrodt & Mizerski, 2007; Rozendaal, Buijzen & Valkenburg, 2009).

Rozendaal, Lapierre, van Reijmersdal and Buijzen (2011) have proposed an extension to current ideas about advertising literacy and children's cognitive defences in relation to brand marketing. They acknowledge that children's internalised defences against advertising are limited by the status of their overall cognitive development (Moses & Baldwin, 2005), but also posit that the appearance of these abilities and defences does not guarantee they will always be used. Furthermore, whether cognitive defences are used might depend upon whether they are appropriately triggered by specific advertising or brand marketing exposure experiences. This response in turn can be influenced by the make-up of the advertising or marketing messages and in particular by whether they are attributes that trigger emotional involvement that can distract attention to cognitive defence eliciting features.

Rozendaal and her colleagues introduced two new concepts: 'advertising literacy performance', which represents the deployment of cognitive defences after they have developed, and 'attitudinal advertising literacy', which relates to specific attributes of advertising that can trigger emotional responses or engagement with it. The latter response is especially likely to occur with advertising that fails to involve children cognitively and this may often happen because the type of product or service being promoted is low in terms of involvement (i.e. it does not represent the kind of item consumers need to think carefully about before making a brand commitment).

This new conceptual development is important because it directs our attention also towards attributes of brands and advertisements that can make a difference in terms of the specific processing mode that achieves ascendancy during any brand or advertisement exposure experience. Although there is evidence that the cultivation of cognitive defences against persuasion can result in a reduction in children's acceptance of promotional messages (Hobbs & Frost, 2003; Chernin, 2007), such interventions are not always successful (Chernin, 2007). We therefore need to know what else might be going on to ascertain when consumer literacy (i.e. greater awareness and understanding of brands and advertising) can be effective.

At a cognitive level, it is important that children can 'stop and think' about advertising messages (Rozendaal et al., 2011). Only when they do this can they begin to deploy any internalised defences they have learned against unconditional persuasion. Next, they must be able to deploy executive functioning processes so as to critically deconstruct persuasive messages before deciding whether to comply with them or reject them. There are three subprocesses that come into play here: inhibitory control, attentional flexibility, and working memory. At the outset, children must learn to control initial urges and not to act upon them without forethought. Next, children must weigh up benefits and risks, both in the short- and long-term, which are associated with certain choices of action. Thus, an advertised brand might seem attractive at first, but initial impressions could be deceptive, and rushing into purchase could result in disappointment if the full range of benefits (or risks) associated with the brand or its value for money are not carefully weighed in the balance.

Finally, all these varied assessments take place in working memory which is an early processing stage for new information. The capacity of this structure is limited and complex judgments may quickly exhaust it. Working memory capacity is not fully developed during childhood. This means that complex, multi-faceted judgments can often be beyond the processing capacity of very young consumers and this means that not all relevant factors are taken into account before responding to a persuasive message.

At an emotional level, children must develop a number of abilities and skills that they can use to modify their affective responses to stimuli, either to enhance the enjoyment of an experience or to avoid disproportionate and inappropriate responding (Calkins & Hill, 2007). When very young, children rely on their carers to comfort them when they have unpleasant experiences and to intervene to regulate their emotional responses in different social settings. As they grow older, they learn to internalise strategies designed to enable self-regulation of their emotions (Gross, 2007).

Inappropriate and most especially excessively severe emotional reactions to social experiences can impair both cognitive performance and behavioural control (Carlson & Wang, 2007). This observation has resonance with children's advertising experiences because commercial messages frequently use production techniques designed to trigger emotional responses in consumers. Any failure to cope with this arousal during exposure to complex advertising messages could result in inappropriate emotional responses and also a failure to invoke cognitive defences to deconstruct persuasive content. Advertisements that engage children emotionally are less likely to be processed in an elaborate fashion. This means that the central arguments presented by advertising about a specific brand are less likely to be processed and assessed. Nevertheless, the emotional experience generated by an advertisement could produce a lasting memory which would be sufficient to enhance its persuasive impact (Buijzen, Van Reijmersdal & Owen, 2010; Rozendaal et al., 2011).

Quality of research

There have been discordant observations about whether young children can or cannot really understand brands. The attraction of marketing professionals to consumer categories, differentiated by trendy name-tags, has probably not helped develop a broader and better informed understanding of the nature of children's emergence as mature consumers. Research evidence has been put forward that brands are important not only to young people in their teens, but also to those in their 'tweens', aged between around 7 and 11. There have even been claims that younger children who have not yet started school display an understanding of brands. Whether this is true or not and what it means to say that a 3-year-old or 4-year-old has brand awareness is still an open question. Such children might be able to recognise brands as objects when placed in front of them when they are 3 or 4, but can they engage with brands in more abstract ways as older children can, for example, by identifying that certain types of people might be expected to adopt particular brands?

Questions have been raised as well about the quality of some of the research in this area. Some conclusions have been reached about the cognitive and social abilities of pre-school children on the basis of research carried out with school children. There is also a concern that some research has explored an overly narrow range of products in studying very young children's brand responses. In these cases, the products examined may have had little relevance to pre-schoolers and therefore their answers concerning the particular brands may simply have reflected a lack of interest on their part (McAlister & Cornwell, 2010). This observation echoes what was said earlier about how children can display advanced levels of thinking about things they are familiar with and that are important to them, but then fail to replicate this same level of performance when confronted with things that do not interest them.

Anne McAlister of the University of Wisconsin-Madison and Bettina Cornwell of the University of Michigan completed a ground-breaking study that explored whether pre-school children do show some understanding of symbolic meanings of brands (McAlister & Cornwell, 2010). What this meant was that as well as being able to recognise Kellogg's Corn Flakes, could they also be able to offer their impressions about this brand, not just in terms of whether they like it or not, but also by describing something more abstract such as the kinds of people who might consume it. Bearing in mind the established ego-centricity of children at this age, would they be able to adopt a perspective on brands other than their own?

McAlister and Cornwell conducted two separate studies, the first of which fed into the second. In spite of the researchers being based in the United States, the research was carried out in Australia. Initially the researchers recruited a sample of 38 children from around Brisbane who were aged 3 and 4. The children were shown 50 brands from 16 product categories. Brand names and their logos were presented on white cards. The children, who were tested one at a time, were shown each card and asked 'Have you seen this before?' If they could not immediately recognise the brand, they were probed still further by being asked if they knew what types of things they make. Fast food brands were the best identified (correct in 93% of cases) while brand recognition rates for products such as cereals, toiletries, and hardware were at or close to zero. Recognition rates were far higher for brands targeted at children aged under 12 than for other products.

The second study was interested in whether children in this age bracket could understand brand symbolism. Before this study, common wisdom was that pre-school children were incapable of engaging with brands in an abstract fashion. McAlister and Cornwell felt, however, that this was an issue that deserved further investigation because there was a blanket assumption that all children under 5 were the same in terms of the cognitive and social maturity (McAlister & Cornwell, 2010).

Psychological evidence, outside the marketing context, had emerged to question this presumption. Other writers working in the marketing sphere had theorised that children's consumer development before school did not proceed in the same way and at the same pace for all youngsters (Moses & Baldwin, 2005). Here it has been recommended that constructs such as 'theory of mind' and 'executive functioning' in young consumers could provide measures of individual differences and explain why some pre-schoolers perform better than others in explaining what brands mean to them.

Theory of mind is concerned with articulating the nature and progression of children's social development (Smith et al., 2003). Initially, young children adopt a self-centred view of the world. This is manifest not only in terms of wanting their own way, but also in believing that their perspective is the only one that counts or exists. The ability to empathise with others and to recognise that other people may hold different beliefs, motives, and objectives, and see the world differently from us emerges at a later stage and represents an internal theorising on our part about the mental states of others. We formulate our own theories about the state of mind of another person and this enables us to anticipate how they might react to specific situations. This can be useful in the context of forward planning on behalf of other people. It might also influence decisions we might take in specific situations where we consider the perspectives of others as well as our own.

The approach adopted to demonstrate 'theory of mind' – or the ability of the child to take someone else's perspective – has used a doll technique first mentioned a while back. The methodology adopted by child psychologists has become known as the 'Sally-Anne' task. In this particular instance, there are two dolls, called 'Sally' and 'Anne'. Sally is accompanied by a basket and Anne by a box. In a classic study, children taking part in this exercise witness Sally place a marble in her basket before being removed from the scene. In her absence, Anne, with the researcher's assistance, takes the marble out of Sally's basket and puts it in her box. The other doll (Sally) is returned to the scene and the child is asked where he or she thinks Sally will look for her marble.

An adult observer's answer here is likely to be that Sally would look in her basket. Putting ourselves in Sally's position we would reason that the last time she saw the marble, it had been placed in her basket. On her return therefore this is where she would be likely to look first. For a young child, below the age of 4, however, the answer is not so straightforward. They had witnessed the marble being moved from the basket into the box, and in their egocentric mode of viewing the world would answer based on their own experience rather than taking an 'other' perspective – in this case that of one of the dolls (Baron-Cohen et al., 1985).

Executive functioning is another concept associated with how we plan our future behaviour. Very often, our future plans are shaped by rules that determine objectives and how they can be achieved. There may be occasions when we need to be mentally flexible enough to change course, but still keep our eye on the final objective. McAlister and Cornwell provide an interesting illustration of this point by describing a card sorting task involving yellow circles and red squares.

Children can be asked to sort these cards initially by shape and this is something even under-5s may be able to do. Then, before completing this task, they are told to switch to sorting cards by colour. While children 6 and over may be able to cope with this, many younger children are unable to comply and continue to sort by the original dimension.

Executing functioning refers to the cognitive processes that enable a child to put aside one rule and adopt a new one and still complete the task that was requested. This ability has been found to emerge between the ages of 3 and 5, but any two 3-year-olds or 4-year-olds might differ significantly in their relative ability in this respect (Frye, Zelazo & Palfai, 1995; McAlister & Peterson, 2006).

The executive functioning ability is relevant in a marketing context because if children can distinguish between sorting rules following different physical dimensions of simple figures such as differently coloured squares and circles, such skills might also be applicable to differentiating between brands and their logos that are also characterised by distinctive colours and shapes. It is also possible that brands might be differentiated by pre-schoolers on the basis of their functions. This possibility was supported by the finding that children under 4 could distinguish accurately between objects that are used indoors or outdoors (Zelazo & Reznick, 1991).

'Theory of mind' abilities have relevance to understanding brand symbolism in that it encompasses the idea that children can take on board the perspectives of other people, and this ability can be applied to recognition of the social significance of brands. Hence, a brand may have been endorsed by other people in the child's environment and its popularity is noted. Personal preferences could therefore be shaped by the child choosing brands known to be popular with others because of the belief that this might enhance their own popularity. Children must first be able to make assumptions about other people's thoughts relating to brands before judging brands in this way.

In a further study, McAlister and Cornwell (2010) recruited 42 Australian children aged 3–5 years. Colour pictures of 14 different brands were printed on white cards. There were six pictures per brand. Three depicted the product, two depicted venues where the product is sold, and one showed either a character associated with the brand (e.g. McDonald's Hamburglar) or a spin-off item of merchandise (e.g. Bratz pyjamas). The children were then instructed to construct collages of brand items associated with a specific brand. This exercise was carried out two brands at a time, with a third collage being constructed out of other items deemed not to belong to either of the two brands. This was done for seven categories of products: drinks, fast food, boys' toys, girls' toys, entertainment-related items, cars, and clothing fashions. The last category was dropped because the children generally performed poorly with it compared to the others.

Understanding of brand symbolism was indicated by those children achieving a score of four or more correct assignments of brand-related items to each brand. The maximum possible score per brand was six. Further questions were then asked about each brand for which a collage had been constructed. These questions asked the children to comment on the quality of the brand and also to indicate whether using the brand would make a person popular with other people. Psychological tests were given to each child to determine their score on a theory of mind scale and an executive functioning scale.

The age of the child, their language ability, and their cognitive ability (IQ) did not predict their ability to select brand relevant items such as visual brand images, logos, and other related features, but both theory of mind and executive functioning scores did predict brand representation ability. Those children who showed more developed executive functioning and theory of mind insights were better at identifying the different features that represented a specific brand. Both of these cognitive skills, along with their language skills, also predicted children's capabilities to identify brand symbolism.

Summing up, McAlister and Cornwell provided empirical evidence that children of pre-school age can correctly identify product brands, especially if those brands are targeted at their age group. They also displayed an ability to identify different ways in which brands are represented in marketing activities associated with them. Finally, there was evidence that some of them could also make more abstract judgements about the quality and social prestige of a brand. These skills were significantly more pronounced among children who also displayed more advanced cognitive skills associated with making judgements about items along more than one dimension at a time and being able to consider the wider social consequences of being associated with a specific brand.

Measures of brand awareness and comprehension

As well as debates about the best ways to measure children's level of cognitive development and how this interplays with their understanding of branding, there have been wider discussions of how even mature comprehension of brands is assessed. In determining whether brand marketing has an impact on consumers, researchers have identified a number of levels at which 'impact' can be defined and measured. Although the ultimate interest lies in the ability of marketing techniques to promote and produce greater consumption of brands, brand marketing does not work simply by triggering consumers to buy the promoted brand. Marketing techniques are designed to draw in consumers' attention to a brand so that they notice it and remember it. Next, these techniques are designed to create positive impressions about brands in the form of favourable attitudes. Attitudes also represent 'memories' of a type in that consumers store feelings about brands, which in turn stem from attributes or features (that often have personal value attached to them) that are learned associates of brands.

In measuring brand familiarity and attribute knowledge, therefore, researchers tend to relate this back to specific marketing experiences that consumers can remember. Typically, in surveys of consumers, respondents are questioned about the brands they can remember seeing in a recent controlled or uncontrolled brand exposure experience. This exposure experience might be linked to a recent advertising campaign that was run in the major media or it might even be a controlled exposure manipulated by researchers in an experiment they run with recruited participants. The tests that are used in these settings ask respondents to recall the names of brands they have seen or heard about, or to select or recognise correctly brands they have seen from a longer list of brands that includes ones they have not been shown.

This type of memory has been called 'explicit memory' by marketing researchers (Shapiro & Krishnan, 2001). Cognitive psychologists have also referred to it as episodic memory (Tulving, 1972). Episodic memory was conceived as one aspect of long-term memory storage, with the other major memory component being called semantic memory. Episodic memory stores information that is temporally dated. It is, in effect, a memory of personal experiences.

In addition, there is a second memory concept that marketing researchers have called 'implicit memory' (Duke & Carlson, 1994). Cognitive psychologists had earlier coined the term 'semantic memory' (Tulving, 1972; Tulving, Schachter & Stark, 1982), although other cognitive researchers also made reference to the term implicit memory (Schachter, 1987; Richardson-Klavehn & Bjork, 1988). Semantic memory contains our language lexicon or dictionary, rules about the use of language, and factual information or our knowledge of the world (Houston, 1981). A number of different models of semantic memory have been conceived that have envisaged it to take the structure of a network of links between different memory 'nodes' that contain factual knowledge of different kinds or as a repository of knowledge units about specific topics organised in a hierarchical configuration. If a specific topic or object is experienced, its meaning is not defined simply by the nature of the experience but also by the attributes or features that have already been stored about it in semantic memory with which it is matched up (Collins & Quillian, 1969; Meyer, 1970; Smith, Shoben & Rips, 1974).

This book will not provide a detailed review of this memory literature here, but makes reference to it because of its relevance to our understanding of the value of specific types of research methods in measuring brand awareness and brand image. When explicit memory is tested, researchers invite consumers to demonstrate whether they have been exposed to a particular brand on an earlier occasion, using brand recall or brand recognition tests. Consumers may show failings in these kinds of tasks that are then often interpreted as demonstrations of weak brand registration in their memories. Yet, other tests that call upon implicit memory have been shown to demonstrate the existence of brand knowledge in terms of factual details about brands or feelings about brands even when episode related brand exposure recall is poor (Shapiro & Krishnan,

2001). Such implicit memory can be primed or triggered by brand exposure experiences, but such memories are not explicitly linked back to those exposures by consumers.

Some marketing researchers believe that implicit memory could provide a better indication of brand ideas held by consumers than explicit memory. Moreover implicit memory for brands probably comes into play when consumers are shopping in retail environments and catch site of brands that then stimulate their pre-existing knowledge (both cognitive knowledge and feeling knowledge) about the brand which in turn helps them to decide whether to purchase it (Park & Hastak, 1994).

The significance of this research in the context of the theme of this book is that when children have been tested for their brand awareness, explicit memory tests have tended to dominate research methodologies just as they have in research with adult consumers. Children have been invited to indicate which brands or brand promotions they can recall or which ones they can recognise from an extended set that might include made-up brand names (in a survey setting) or brands they did not see in a controlled exposure test (in an experimental setting). As with research conducted with adult consumers, explicit memory failures have often been interpreted as indicators of a lack of brand awareness. The reality could be quite different.

Even young consumers might, over time and following repeated brand exposure they have not consciously catalogued, develop a series of ideas or feelings about brands that are not linked to specific exposure experiences. Thus, we need to know not only whether children can demonstrate an awareness and understanding of brands through their ability to complete explicit memory tests (i.e. recall or recognise brands after specific exposure experiences), but also whether they have more lasting and developed memories about brand meanings that need a different type of test to unveil. The importance of implicit memory to our understanding of young consumers' learning about brands and their meanings becomes even more important in relation to more disguised forms of brand marketing where consumers may not always know that they are being confronted with brand promotions. This trend has become prevalent in relation to marketing techniques used to reach children on the internet. This is something we will return to in later chapters.

3

Emergence of brand consciousness

There is compelling evidence that children have brand consciousness from an early age. As we will see, this fact has been confirmed by both academic and marketing industry research. While industry researchers have been interested in finding out which brands are best known and best liked among young consumers, and how brand awareness levels and preferences vary across different child age groups, academic researchers have been occupied more with finding explanations for why brand consciousness exists, the different forms it can take, and the key factors that underpin the way it evolves as children grow and mature physically and psychologically (see Hite & Hite, 1995; Dammler & Middelmann-Motz, 2002; Valkenburg & Buijzen, 2005; Costa, 2010; Bussey, 2011).

For marketers, up-to-date data about kids' brand likes and dislikes can form essential input to marketing campaigns and can represent metrics for tracking the effectiveness of different types of brand promotions (Kapferer, 1992). Such data enable brands to benchmark themselves against their competitors and to track back and make comparisons of the apparent effectiveness of different brands' campaign strategies. At the level of individual child consumers, brand promotions can prime them to choose advertised brands over other brands shortly after exposure (Chernin, 2008; Boyland, Harrold, Kirkham et al., 2011). Such is the power of branding, that it can influence product experience. For instance, in taste tests with two identical food products, the one presented packaged with a well-known brand name has been found to taste better (Woolfolk, Casetellan & Brooks, 1983; Robinson, Borzekowski, Matheson & Kraemer, 2007). This brand effect can be further strengthened with children as young as 5 or 6 when it is associated with a well-known celebrity (Lapierre, Vaala & Linebarger, 2011).

In the UK, brand consultancy Brand Republic teamed up with market research agency Harris Interactive in 2011 to produce the Kids Brand Index. They conducted a survey of 4000 children aged 7–11 years (the so-called 'tween' market) and 12–15 years to get their opinions about 166 different brands. The brands covered a number of product types including clothing, drinks, foods, electronic gadgets, mobile phones, shops, sweets and chocolate, toys and games, television channels, television shows, video games, and websites. Respondents were tested for brand awareness and how much they liked specific brands, as well as what their parents and other kids thought about different brands. Brand league tables were then created from these different metrics (Bussey, 2011).

Marketing scholars have known for many years that we often define ourselves through our possessions (Belk, 1988). What this means is that the way we see ourselves and, more especially, want to be seen by others can be projected through the items we choose to consume (Sirgy, 1982; Solomon, 1983). When we talk about the things we like to own and possess the most – 'our favourite things' – we are opening up ourselves to others and saying to them, 'this is the kind of person I am' (Wallendorf & Arnould, 1988). Brands play on this process by offering to consumers a 'brand image' or an 'identity' that they might like to try on.

The appeal of a brand, therefore, can derive from the degree to which the consumer perceives a good fit between the kind of publicised identity offered by the brand and the kind of person they want to be – or be seen as being. This identity can take on a social flavour in that the identity offered by a brand resonates with the identity associated with an attractive reference group for the consumer. Brands may be advertised in ways that associate them with particular lifestyles that the consumer desires, or to social categories of 'other person' that the consumer holds in high regard. The popularity of specific brands with peer reference groups can be a particularly powerful factor in shaping the brand preferences of young people. Even association of food brands with tempting taste description or health messages can sway children's choices and taste experiences (Barry & Gunst, 1982; Lapierre et al., 2011).

The key question for those interested in how these dynamics develop is when in a child's life does their involvement with brands first appear? Linked to this question are other interesting puzzles, including whether brand involvement appears all at once or whether it develops through a series of stages? Can a child at the age of 3 exhibit brand awareness? Does this represent the same kind of thinking about brands as that exhibited by a 6-year-old, a 10-year-old or a 15-year-old? Research into these questions has revealed that brand awareness can appear at a very early age, but that the meanings of brands can change as children grow older, alongside their understanding of what brands are and their abilities to give more sophisticated reasons for liking or disliking specific brands.

Children can begin to recognise products they have become familiar with at home and when they go shopping with their parents by the age of 3. They are particularly likely to be attuned to products that are targeted at them, such as games, toys, and clothing (Haynes et al., 1993; Derscheid, Kwon & Fang, 1996). They will soon after begin to recognise familiar brand names, logos, and even characters that are associated with specific products. As their language skills develop between 3 and 5 years, they will recognise brands not only by the visual appearance of their packages but also through being able to read brand names.

After starting school, as their cognitive abilities continue to improve, children will acquire a broader knowledge about different categories of product and their functions and purposes (McNeal, 1992; Otnes, Kim & Kim, 1994). As they mature through the ages of 6 to 11, their ability to recall brand names also grows. Children who are given a product category with which they are familiar as a prompt are able to name progressively larger numbers of brands within that category as they approach their teen years (Rossiter, 1976; Ward et al., 1977). At Christmas, when their minds turn increasingly to gifts, this emergent ability is manifest in the number of specific brand mentions children make in their letters to Santa Claus (Otnes et al., 1994).

Once they get into their middle school or 'tween' years, between the ages of 7 and 11, children develop a broader structural knowledge of products. This means they are able to take specific products and identify which category they belong to. This understanding begins with distinctions between broad categories such as clothes, games, toys, and other products targeted at them, and more general products in fast-moving and luxury goods ranges, such as different types of foods and drinks, household products, and so on. They use external perceptual cues initially but then later make deeper connections between items based on their functionality (Markham, 1980; Markham & Callahan, 1983).

At first, product categorisations are dominated by the physical attributes of products that can be perceived by children. Later, unseen and more symbolic features are taken into account and used to determine which products belong together and which do not (John & Sujan, 1990). Upon reaching their teens, children can deploy a more sophisticated level of insight into products, drawing upon brand meanings, to classify product variants not only in terms of their functions but also the status they confer on users. Even very young children have been found to display brand preferences but these are probably driven be seeing their friends using specific brands and simply wanting what someone else has got in a self-centred way (Hite & Hite, 1995). Later, however, a young consumer may only want what someone else has got if the brand is endorsed more normatively by influential reference groups (Belk, Bahn & Mayer, 1982). In this type of case, it is not only the brand that is assessed, but also the person using it. As they mature, young consumers begin to judge each other on the basis of the brands each adopts (Belk, Mayer & Driscoll, 1984).

Gwen Achenreiner of the University of Wisconsin and Deborah Roedder John of the University of Minnesota are two marketing scholars who have succinctly articulated a number of levels of thinking that children must display and that can be used to determine their understanding of the concept of a brand.

> First, children need to recognize brand names as a way to identify a specific product within a product category. Second, children must recognize a brand name as a unique and separate element of the product, distinct from the packaging or the product itself. That is, children must be able to decompose a given product into separate and distinct dimensions, viewing brand name as one of those separate elements. Third, once children are able to recognize a brand as a separable product element, they must be able to think about the brand name at an abstract level, connecting the brand name to non-observable features or associations such as quality, prestige, or trendiness. (Achenreiner & John, 2003, p. 206)

These authors then go on to explain that children can display an awareness of brand names as early as age 3 or 4. In being able to do this, young kids might even pester their parents to buy them these brands, asking for them by name. Closer analysis shows, however, that brand names can be compounded with product category names and a when a child asks his or her parents to buy them a specific confectionery brand, the request may actually be for any version of the product rather than for a particular branded variant of that product (John, 1997).

The picture that has emerged from research into children's brand awareness and understanding is that their initial engagement with brands can begin even during their first two years of life. Even 2-year-olds can exhibit what appear to be brand-related product preferences (Hite & Hite, 1995). Brand preferences become more widespread by the age of 5 and continue to increase through the pre-teen or tween years into adolescence (Fischer, Schwartz, Richard et al., 1991; Derscheid et al., 1996; Macklin, 1996).

There is a danger here in jumping to conclusions about the brand involvement of children. Critics might claim that evidence showing even 2-year-olds know about brands is a worrying sign that brands have too much influence over our lives and that they are contaminating the early development of innocents. What we really need to take on board here is that 'brand awareness' as measured with a 2-year-old does not represent the same phenomenon as the brand-related conversations we might be able to have with a 10-year-old or a 14-year-old.

Some of the best results in terms of showing some semblance of brand awareness among very young children have derived from studies that used simple recognition tasks. One example was a study carried out by researchers at the University of North Carolina who recruited children aged 3–6 to match brand logos to branded products (Fischer et al., 1991). This test was conducted with a total of 22 brands including 10 brands targeted at children, while the rest were products aimed at the adult market. Five brands were for cigarettes. The task was very simple. Each child was tested on his or her own in a quiet room to one side of their classroom in school. They were told they would play a game matching cards (containing logos) with products. A picture of each product was available together with the cards and they simply chose the logo that they believed went with a specific product. No indication was given to them of whether they were correct or not.

The findings showed that their brand-logo matching abilities varied from brand to brand and were generally a lot better with the children's brands than the adult brands. There were some cigarette and adult brands, such as the Old Joe camel cartoon character for Camel cigarettes and logos for Chevrolet and Ford cars, that were better recognised than logos for children's brands such as bowls of cereals with Cheerios and Kellogg's and surprisingly Mickey Mouse with Walt Disney. In addition, performance improved progressively across all categories of brands with age. Three-year-olds performed worst, followed by 4-year-olds, then 5-year-olds, while 6-year-olds achieved the highest correct recognition scores.

The ability to know that a brand, as identified by its distinctive brand name, is something different from a product category name represents a level of conceptual awareness that surfaces a few years later. There is no precise age threshold when this capability suddenly appears. Much depends on the complexity of the specific brand itself and whether it is defined by one overriding attribute or by a combination of ingredients and features. The ability to relate to a brand name as something that is different from the broader product range of which it is a member has been observed to occur as early as age 6 (Kemler, 1983; Smith, 1989).

As Achenreiner and John (2003) went on to explain, a more abstract level of brand differentiation and understanding emerges next and represents a more adult-like connection with brands, whereby their meanings derive from features that can be conceived but not always sensed. Initially, children must acquire and demonstrate an ability to classify objects into types according to their physical attributes and functions. Then, they might begin to differentiate between sub-categories and then finally individual exemplars of the category. It is at this last level that brand differentiation occurs.

Sufficient intellectual development to enable some of these judgements to be made can emerge even during pre-school years, but the ability of children to make these distinctions consistently and by themselves tends to take longer and might not surface fully until they reach 7 or 8. Even then, these judgements tend to depend on making physical distinctions between brands rather than more abstract ones related, for example, to what they might say about you as a person. Abstract-level distinctions have been observed among some 8-year-olds. They become more common by the age of 10 (see John & Sujan, 1990; John, 1999).

Achenreiner and John tested the abilities of children aged 8, 12 and 16 to make brand-related judgements to find out whether awareness of brand meanings would influence their preferences, their perceptions of other people who might wear a brand, and the appeal of brand extensions to other types of product. They showed pairs of adverts for jeans and for athletics shoes to groups of children. The premium brand for jeans was Levi and for athletics shoes was Nike. In both cases, an unknown brand – K-Mart – was used as the point of comparison.

There was a significant brand label effect on the product preferences of 12-year-olds and 16-year-olds which did not appear among 8-year-olds. Thus, when shown adverts for jeans in which exactly the same product image was used throughout but where in one image a famous brand name was used and in the other an unknown brand name was used, the brand name alone was sufficient among older children to make the product appear as more attractive, of higher quality and prestige, and an item they would like to own. Eight-year-olds did not show any preference based on brand name. Similar findings occurred when the children were asked to rate the brands on the basis of the type of person who might own them. In this case, they were invited to rate brand users in terms of their attractiveness, popularity, and wealth. Finally, the children were given a list of five possible extensions of each brand to other product fields (e.g. Nike shampoo) and asked whether they would like this product. Again positive brand extension perceptions were detected for well-known brands but not for the unknown brand among the two oldest age groups, while this effect did not emerge among the 8-year-olds.

Richard Elliott of Warwick Business School reported a study conducted with his student, Clare Leonard, that interviewed 30 English children aged 8–12 years about their perceptions of brands of training shoes. All the children who took part were from poor homes and their families had received help from Social Services Departments. Despite not having much money, these children were drawn to well-known brands and most claimed to own a pair. Nike was singled out more than any other brand as the most popular brand (Elliott & Leonard, 2004).

The highest regarded brands were often the most expensive ones. Nonetheless, they were worth the price because symbolically ownership signalled social status and this was important for these children because it meant they were more likely to be accepted by their peer groups. Being seen with unfashionable and cheap brands of trainers could trigger ridicule from their peers and even worse make them targets of teasing or bullying.

As one girl remarked:

well if we don't wear like what our other friends wear, like cool stuff and that, we get picked on like and we won't quite fit in there and that cos we just get, like picked on and stuff. And I don't think that's fair really, because it's not fair on other people if their mums and dads can't afford stuff like other people, it's not their fault so I don't know why people have a go at them. (Elliott & Leonard, 2004, p. 356)

Other research has shown that pre-school children aged between 3 and 5 can recognise brands targeted at their age group. Not only can these children recognise brand names and symbols, they can also pass judgements about them. According to Anna McAlister and Bettina Cornwell who work at the University of Wisconsin Madison and University of Michigan, kids learn to use brands in the same way as adults as identifiers to narrow down product variant choices. Given a number of product categories and brands to look at, these young children demonstrated some competence at placing brands with the correct category (McAlister & Cornwell, 2010).

The importance of brand identity for all consumers, regardless of their age, is that it provides shortcuts to brand comparison making in increasingly crowded marketplaces in which consumers can readily become overwhelmed by all the brands and promotional information laid before them. From an early age, kids are exposed to the big brands in different settings and along with other life experiences need to sort through brands and make judgements about them that they can internalise and file away for ready reference whenever needed (Dell'Antonia, 2010).

Research commissioned by *Marketing Week* from consultancies Fly Research and Discovery Research combined focus groups and survey research with children aged 6–11. The best known brands were ones from the soft drinks sector, such as Coca-Cola, Pepsi, Tropicana, Ribena, Sprite, Fanta, Robinsons, and Capri Sun. Other widely recognised brands were Nike and Adidas from the sports sector and Disney and Apple from the media and technology sectors. Focus group interviews with kids revealed that they can relate to the physical attributes of brands, but can also make comparisons between brands, and exhibit their own brand preferences that do not always coincide with those of their parents. Hence one 8-year-old remarked that although his father allowed him to play with his iPhone, given the choice, he would prefer a Blackberry (Costa, 2010).

Despite the evidence from earlier research that indicated more sophisticated brand comparisons among children aged 12 and over than those aged just 8, the *Marketing Week* researchers reported that the 'coolness' of brands was remarked upon even by 6-year-olds. In fact, what emerged was that cool brands changed with age and that the under-9s tended to name different brands as their favourites from those rated most highly by the older children. Another interesting finding was that premium brands were rated as better than super-market's own brands in the same product categories.

Reasons for liking some brands more than others included conformity with peer pressure, recommendations by family members, and the use of well-liked celebrity endorsers. There was also a gender divide at play. Girls and boys differed in their most liked brands overall but these differences were often linked to the different priorities of each sex. Girls tended to be more brand conscious than were boys when it came to purchasing clothes or footwear, while this gender difference was reversed with games or consoles (Costa, 2010).

Stuart Roper and Binita Shah of Manchester Business School conducted qualitative research with pre-adolescent children aged 7–11 years, and with their teachers, that investigated brand awareness and the perceived importance of brands in children's lives. The teachers were interviewed in groups and the children were given questionnaires that invited them to write about brand issues in their own words. It became apparent that kids in this age bracket knew and could write about brands.

The significance of brands stemmed from how they were linked to member-ship of specific social groups. Owning and using the right brands could make a difference to their popularity with classmates and the extent to which they were one of the 'in-group' or socially excluded. There could be further knock-on effects on the self-esteem of children who were teased or picked on for not having the brands perceived as most fashionable. What is also interesting about these findings, however, is that they occurred among children from a devel-oped country (UK) and also from a developing country (Kenya).

Open-ended group discussions with children and a survey of their parents in England confirmed that brand recognition surfaces at an early age, and that brand awareness expands as children grow up. Once again, brands were impor-tant to kids for self-esteem and social status reasons. Acceptance by their peers was often dependent upon using the right brands (Ross & Harradine, 2004).

A further investigation conducted by researchers at Manchester Business School used the picture collage approach with children aged between 7 and 10 years to examine their perceptions of clothing fashion brands (Hogg, Bruce & Hill, 1999). A sample of over 200 children was divided into small groups where they produced collages as a team exercise. The collages could draw upon images and words from magazines they had been given to build up an identity for a clothing brand. They were also invited to comment on the process and the choices they made for their collages. The products that the study focused on were sweatshirts and T-shirts. These had emerged from pilot work as items that were important to children in this age bracket.

There was evidence that these pre-teens were able to establish a distinctive identity for specific brands and that references were often made to specific sports and prominent sports stars in doing so. For some of the children, specific brands were also associated with named retail outlets. This was especially true for girls. Brand descriptions were not always positive, and some collages were used to critique as well as define specific brands.

Unravelling the emergence of branding in children

One reason why there is conflicted evidence about the age at which children start to demonstrate brand awareness is that researchers have used different methods for measuring it. Researchers have used recognition and recall techniques to measure children's ability to identify brands. In the case of recall tests, children have been asked to name from memory the correct brand after being presented with brand logos, characters associated with brands, or advertisements for brands (minus the brand name). In recognition tests, these kinds of stimulus items are presented along with brand names, and children are required to match the correct name to the correct visual prompt (Goldberg, 1990; Fischer et al., 1991; Derscheid et al., 1996). Some researchers have argued that although these two techniques are measuring different psychological processes, both are important in the consumer context (Macklin, 1996).

When we find ourselves in a retail setting, confronted with a shelf of branded goods, we have all the brand-relevant information we need to recognise brands and make comparisons. However, we still need to make a judgement based on what we know about brands or as a function of assessing the information set out before us. If we are required to make a brand decision in a situation where the product range is not physically present, however, then we must rely on our ability to recall brand-related information stored in our memories.

Recognition can yield better results than recall in terms of accuracy of performance in brand identity. As a measure of brand understanding therefore it might provide a generous assessment of very young children's abilities because with recognition you can guess the answer and sometimes get it right. Moreover, in recognition tests you are given all the material you need to make a judgement; you do not need to retrieve it unseen as is necessary with recall. The distinction outlined earlier between explicit and implicit memory is also relevant here. Tests of brand recognition or recall tend to be time bound and invite research participants to remember specific instances of brand exposure. However, consumers develop more diffuse knowledge repositories about brands that build over time and in which specific items of factual brand learning or brand meanings cannot be readily linked back to specific moments when brand exposure experiences occurred. Such implicit memories can nonetheless be drawn upon at appropriate times, such as when in retail settings, to make judgements about brands which then guide purchase decisions (see Shapiro & Krishnan, 2001).

Age can also benefit recall performance because as we grow older, we gain more experience and with that, greater knowledge of the world. As we become more familiar with the world we are better able to remember things about it, because whenever faced with something new, our pre-existing knowledge can provide a ready-made framework within which we can process fresh information. In addition, the more practised we are at recalling information across a range of circumstances in which this cognitive process is called upon, the better we get at it. We may also develop our own internal strategies for organising and storing our memories and subsequently retrieving information from them when it is required. All these skills develop over time and thus give older children an advantage over younger children in brand identity tasks dependent upon their abilities to recall information from memory (John, 1999; Siegler, 1998).

Chaplin and John carried out a series of three studies in which the young participants were asked to provide descriptions of themselves in response to the question: 'Who Am I?' After this, they were given a separate task in which they evaluated brands. In the first study, carried out with children aged 8–9 and 12–13, five different product categories were used: cereal, beverages, confectionery, clothing, and restaurants. Twenty brands associated with each product category were displayed on five poster boards (one per category) (Chaplin & John, 2005).

The participants were invited to decide which brands were the 'easiest or most helpful' in answering the 'Who Am I?' question. They were invited to generate their own reasons for explaining why they felt that particular brands were useful in defining who they were as individuals. Clothing emerged as the product category most popularly selected for this exercise. Cereal and confectionery were regarded as less helpful in describing their self-identities. The older children named more brands and gave more complex reasons for choosing them than did the younger children. There was a concern here, however, that the younger children were at a disadvantage in this task because their language skills had not reached such advanced stage of development as those of the older ones. Hence, it was not clear whether their understanding of brands was more simplistic or whether their ability to articulate this understanding was limited.

To get around this problem, Chaplin and John constructed two more studies in which the participants were given opportunities to express their identities, which were not solely dependent upon their relative language abilities. Instead of responding only to verbal labels of brands or other non-branded self-descriptions, they were also given pictures of these descriptive items, again stuck on a poster board. They were then instructed to select from these pictures and build a collage of images that they felt represented the kind of person they were. Further explanations were then sought from the children about why they had chosen specific images and organised them in the way they did. In one of these studies, three groups of participants were recruited, aged 8–9, 12–13, and 16–18.

Even the youngest were familiar with most of the brands used, but brand awareness became progressively better with age. The older the participants were, the more brand names they referenced in building a picture of their self-identity. Among the older participants, larger proportions of self-descriptions were based on branded than on non-branded items. Thus not only do teenagers, as compared with pre-teens, access more brands when describing themselves, suggesting that they have greater overall brand awareness, but they also perceive their own identities as being more extensively defined in terms of commercial brands.

In their final study, Chaplin and John asked children aged 8–9 and 12–13 to build 'Who Am I' collages using brand names and non-branded self-descriptors and then to use the same materials to produce a similar collage for a specific brand of their own choice. Earlier results in terms of numbers of brand selections made by the younger and older age-groups were confirmed. In addition, there were more overlaps in the non-branded descriptors used in the self-concept and brand choice collages of the older children than in those produced by the younger children. Throughout this and the earlier study that utilised pictures, the older children were able to talk about brands in more abstract ways that often made reference to their specific qualities and the types of people who they would normally associate with these brands (Chaplin & John, 2005).

Research by Patti Valkenburg and Moniek Buijzen of the University of Amsterdam examined the brand awareness of children aged between 2 and 8, and investigated factors that might influence this awareness, such as their parents, peers, and potential advertising exposure on television. After an initial survey they recruited nearly 200 parent–child pairs to take part in a brand identification exercise. The children were taken into a room with one of the researchers and were shown pictures – one at a time – of 12 brand logos. To begin with they were asked to give the name of the brand associated with the logo. This represented a test of brand recall. Next, they were shown three further cards, each of which contained one brand name. One of these brand names was the brand linked to the logo on display. The child had to select the correct brand. This represented a test of brand recognition.

Parents were separately interviewed to obtain information about: their child's television viewing habits; the family's socio-economic status, determined by education and income; parental awareness of the brands on which the children were tested; and finally, indicators of the extent to which, in parents' perceptions, their child was influenced in their brand preferences by the brands used by their friends.

Valkenburg and Buijzen found that brand recognition and recall improved significantly with age. The children were divided into four age groups: 2–3, 4–5, 6–7 and 8-year olds. Brand recognition improved by a significant margin between each of these age groups up to 6–7. Eight-year-olds performed marginally, but not significantly, better than those aged 6–7. Brand recall remained fairly flat across those aged 2 to 5, and then improved by a significant margin at 6–7, and then again at age 8. Looking at background factors, brand recognition was related to amount of television viewing, family education level, and parental reports that their children's brand preferences were dependent upon brands used by their friends. Brand recall performance, however, was related significantly only with parental brand awareness.

In explaining these findings the researchers argued that television frequently displays brands visually, and that this experience can enhance children's abilities to recognise brand names and logos and to match them up. The more difficult task of recalling brand names is not enhanced by television. Family education influences were linked to regularity of visual exposure to brands because in households that are better off, more time (and money) could be spent on consumer activities and children have wider brand exposure experiences as a consequence. The influence of peers could also function through more frequent exposure to brands that their friends use. Recall performance was apparently enhanced by parental brand awareness and this might be explained by more frequent mentions of specific brands by parents rendering these brands more memorable and available in memory for recall (Valkenburg & Buijzen, 2005).

There is evidence that critical psychological developments occur between mid-childhood (aged 8 to 10) and teenage years in the level of sophistication with which children make judgements about themselves as individuals and about brands. As they grow older, children display greater brand awareness, but this is manifest not simply in terms of the numbers of brands they are familiar with, but also in the ways they think about and evaluate brands (Valkenburg & Buijzen, 2005).

The power of branding

In our analysis of branding we have seen that a brand represents a sign of product or service distinctiveness. In their earliest applications, brands confirmed ownership or origin of production. Over time, as consumer markets became more crowded and competitive, brands signalled much more than this. Their meanings for consumers derived from their reputations for delivery of quality, or at least for being consistent in giving consumers what they expected. Brand images also derived from often symbolic meanings they conveyed about lifestyle, social status, and personal identity. These more abstract meanings generally depended on the things consumers were told about brands in promotional campaigns that sang their praises. These meanings could often be confirmed (or not) through conversations consumers had with other consumers about specific brands.

Ultimately, the power of successful branding for the brand owners and producers, and for those who delivered brands to consumers, derived from its ability to command consumer loyalty, produce a healthy market share, and sometimes to create an impression of value, meaning the product variant could be sold at a premium price. As well as the power of brands to drive consumer markets for specific products, there have been other questions asked about the wider influences of a world full of brands on children's values. Can the early introduction of brands to children's lives place too much emphasis on consumerism too soon and condition a generation of excessively materialistic individuals?

Branding and product-related effects

We have focused so far in this chapter on trying to understand how young consumers engage with brands and develop an understanding of what brands are. What we know about young consumers' awareness and involvement with brands has derived from studies that asked them directly what they thought about brands and what kinds of attributes they associated with them. There is another way of finding out about the power of branding among children that also provides an indirect, but nevertheless compelling indicator of brand awareness. There is mounting evidence that children's experiences of products are different when they believe a product is a well-known brand. In one example, food and drink was rated as tasting better when children thought it was provided by a well-known food outlet.

In research reported in the Archives of Pediatric and Adolescent Medicine, Thomas Robinson and his colleagues asked children aged 3–5 years to say which of two food items placed before them tasted better (Robinson, Borzekowski, Matheson & Kraemer, 2007). Five types of food were tested in this way: a hamburger, chicken nuggets, a bag of French fries, a carton of milk or apple juice, and a carrot. In each instance, one item of the pair was branded as being from McDonald's. The first four food items were all available at McDonald's outlets, while the carrot was not.

The key finding to emerge from this study was that in general the taste of these food and drink items was rated as being better for the McDonald's branded item than for the other item. The differences were pronounced in most cases. Throughout, much larger percentages of the children preferred the taste of the food/drink item in the McDonald's packaging than in the unmarked packaging: hamburgers (48% versus 37%), chicken nuggets (59% versus 18%), French fries (77% versus 13%), milk or apple juice (61% versus

21%) and baby carrots (54% versus 23%). This finding was true for both those children who recognised the McDonald's branded item on their own and for those who had to be told that one item in each pair was from McDonald's.

The researchers went to great lengths to ensure that there were no experimental design effects that could have contaminated their results. The left versus right positioning of the branded item and non-branded item was balanced throughout. The children could choose which item they tasted first. The research assistant who asked the children to taste the items and say which one they liked best could not see the child or where the food/drink items were positioned. The nature and quality of the packaging of the branded and non-branded items was exactly the same, except for the presence of the McDonald's brand name on the packaging of one item in each pair. Hence, what this study appears to show is that even amongst pre-school children, many have become familiar with the McDonald's brand and that this awareness leads most of them to prefer the taste of food items which they believe have been produced by that outlet.

In addition to the influences of branding on children's choices between products aimed at them, there has been a lot of interest in how branding can cultivate an early interest in products not intended for them. We have already seen that there has been evidence produced in a number of countries that children display a keen awareness of the brand names of alcoholic beverages. This awareness can occur among children several years before they reach their teens (Aitken et al., 1988). There is clear evidence also that alcohol advertising, especially that appearing on television, attracted a lot of attention from kids (Nash, Pine & Lutz, 2000). Some researchers have argued that 'liked' commercials might also be more influential (Covell, 1992; Kelly & Edwards, 1998).

The early recognition of alcohol brands by children in their pre-teenage years, before they have begun to consume alcoholic beverages themselves, has been accepted by some researchers as evidence that alcoholic brands are being lined up as aspects of self-identity from an early age. Furthermore, this early brand awareness may form part of a suite of factors that encourage children to consume alcoholic drinks under-age (Aitken et al., 1988; Aitken, 1989; Wyllie, Zhang & Casswell, 1998).

Others have argued that brand interest and liking, and persuasion and behavioural outcomes are not the same and are not invariably linked (Waiters, Treno & Grube, 2001; Nash, 2002). The attraction of children's attention to advertisements for alcoholic drinks does seem to depend on specific attributes, such as the presence of animated characters. The use of humour, cartoon characters, and celebrities has been linked to children's greater attention to alcohol advertising and also to their liking of advertisements and brands (Lieberman & Orlandi, 1987; Nash, Pine & Lutz, 2000; Cragg, 2004; Chen, Grube, Bersamin et al., 2005; Collins, Ellickson, McCaffrey & Hambarsoomians, 2005)

Young children are attuned to cartoon characters. In one test in which animated figures from beer commercials were presented as prompts, even kids as young as 9 showed a greater ability to recall the brand than when other prompts were used (Collins et al., 2005). It is unclear, therefore, whether alcohol brands were recalled because they meant something to children in the audience in terms of being a product category they would wish to consume or whether their significance stemmed from the association of specific product variants with interesting cartoon characters.

Other evidence has emerged that among teenagers, at an age when many might just be starting to consume alcohol or to take an interest in doing so, brand names on their own might be rated as dull, but once they were linked to other factors that were appealing to young people, such as the presence of young adults having a good time, or scenes from popular sports, brand promotions were received much more positively (Slater, Rouner, Domenech-Rodriguez et al., 1997).

More qualitative approaches to the study of alcohol branding and children have also revealed that there are significant socio-cultural context factors that underpin the ideas young people develop about alcohol consumption. These factors can result in highly distinctive orientations towards alcohol among different socio-cultural communities. In one major study that spanned seven countries (Brazil, China, Italy, Nigeria, Russia, South Africa, and Scotland), and questioned young adults aged 18 to 25 years about their early drinking experiences, most reported that they first tasted alcohol between the ages of 10 and 14 and that this initiation occurred with parents or among peers. Brands and brand marketing were rarely mentioned among this international sample, but attitudes towards alcohol consumption were often shaped by local norms surrounding the use of alcoholic beverages in different social settings (Martinic & Measham, 2008).

Further research studies from Northern Ireland and Scotland have confirmed the overriding importance of local social conditions in determining whether young people drink or not. Introduction to drinking occurred usually through a parent and was subsequently determined by peer group norms. To be a non-drinker meant having to depart from local cultural norms and having also to explain your 'unusual' behaviour to your peers. Getting drunk was also part of the social scene, and not being willing to participate and 'let go' was seen as failing to conform. Branding was not mentioned in relation to the onset or subsequent nature of drinking behaviour. The types of beverages young people chose to drink was influenced by pricing factors, especially among those less well-off, but among most young drinkers the type of tipple you preferred was defined by the social group or network to which you belonged (Seaman & Ikegwuonu, 2010; Percy, Wilson, McCartan & McCrystal, 2011).

There is evidence with product categories such as alcohol and tobacco that brand recognition, and more especially the meanings given to specific brands by teenage consumers, are determined by social cliques to which they belong, or aspire to join, rather than by any attempts at promotion or persuasion by brand marketers. In extended interviews, teenagers have admitted taking up drinking or smoking to impress friends and peer groups and often to gain entry to a highly regarded social group (Lucas & Lloyd, 1999; Stewart-Knox, Sittlington, Rugkasa et al., 2005; Percy et al., 2011).

We can conclude that although brand awareness can surface early in life, the impact of brands and branding on children as consumers cannot be assumed to derive only from the efforts of marketing professionals. Knowing about a brand and liking a brand can be consequences of brand marketing experiences, but they can also derive from quite distinct social experiences and non-marketing influences. So far, however, we have examined children's experiences of brands that come from overt brand promotional activities. Children's developing awareness of brands has been linked back to their emergent cognitive abilities, but usually in relation to clear and transparent branding phenomena. As the rapid spread of digital technologies has empowered consumers to become more engaged in brand creation and promotions and to avoid brand advertising if they wish, marketers have turned to more subtle and often disguised techniques to promote brands. What are the implications of this shift in marketing approaches for young consumers' understanding of brands and related activities?

Media changes and disguised branding

The ability of children as consumers to know when they are being targeted by brand marketers is linked in large part to their level of cognitive and social development, but it is also mediated by the explicitness of the marketing techniques that are used to influence brand-related beliefs, attitudes, and behaviour. Children are initially hampered by their crude understanding of the world around them, and cannot explain brand advertising and its purposes until they have reached an appropriate point in their psychological development. What can help them get to this point is when brands are honest about what they are, and marketing activities likewise operate in a transparent fashion.

Changes to the nature of the media landscape during the final decade of the twentieth century meant that new methods emerged for consumers to be reached by the conventional mass media, and new methods were also available to consumers to control the reception of media content. There were numerous consequences of these developments, including the empowerment of consumers to avoid traditional forms of advertising in major media such as radio and television. The enhancement of personal recording technologies encouraged more viewers to watch playback rather than live broadcasts and in doing so to use the technology to fast-forward through advertising breaks (Balasubramanian, 1994; Piccalo, 2004). Marketers needed to find new ways of reaching consumers, which they could not avoid so readily. This need led to creative solutions that embedded brands within programmes and films and – as we will see later – within interactive online games. This approach, known as 'product placement', has become more widely adopted (Consoli, 2004).

Product placement has become almost ever present in many mainstream television programmes and motion pictures. In spite of the recent attention it has received because of high profile campaigns and changes in governments' regulations in respect of it, product placement is not a new marketing device (Gould, Gupta & Grabner-Kraurer 2000). It can be traced back as far as the late nineteenth century in relation to the Lumiere films of that time (Newell, Salmon & Chang, 2006). What has happened in recent times is that brands have become more closely integrated with entertainment content to a point where the two become almost indistinguishable (Hudson & Hudson, 2006).

Product placement has been attractive also to marketers seeking to promote their brands on the internet. Early forms of online advertising adopted similar principles to that in older media of creating a space for a brand that was separated from surrounding content. Banner advertisements and pop-ups were the most popularly used formats in the early days of the internet. As with advertising in conventional media, advertisements would appear at points determined by the media operator and would frequently be regarded by consumers as a distraction or nuisance intrusion during their entertainment or information-seeking.

With product placement, the brand is not separated from the surrounding entertainment or information content but is integrated within it. A brand might be depicted sitting on a cupboard or table top, or being used by a character on-screen. Its visual presence is captured by the camera to a point where not only the product but also the brand name can be perceived by viewers. It is featured as a seamless aspect of the ongoing narrative of the programme.

The disguised nature of this form of brand advertising has attracted much criticism from commentators, who have argued that it disadvantages people as consumers because they need to know they are being targeted in this way to raise their internalised critical faculties in deciding whether or not to accept and act upon the commercial message. This concern has been especially acute when it comes to children because their critical faculties, and indeed their basic understanding of persuasive processes, have not yet reached maturity. Furthermore, this technique has been used widely with products known to appeal specifically to young consumers, which some commentators claim leads youngsters to pester their parents more often to buy them items or, in the case of some products such as food, to encourage unhealthy eating habits with other short-term and longer-term health consequences (Sigman, 2010).

Some writers on the subject have tried to redress the critical balance by pointing out that product placement is not an anonymous marketing ploy, but a technique that has been used for some years and one that has been widely written about in the marketing trades press (La Ferle & Edwards, 2006; Wiles & Danielova, 2009; Sutherland et al., 2010). Specific high profile cases of product placement have also entered the wider public domain through coverage received in the popular press. This coverage raises questions about whether consumers are as unaware of this marketing method as its critics claim (Bhatnagar, Aksoy & Malkoc, 2004). Of course with children, such questions are more serious because children are less likely to pay attention to wider public debates about product placement, and they possess relatively ill-formed comprehension of marketing and persuasion techniques.

Product placement appeals to marketers because it is a method of circumventing consumer avoidance and also because when used discretely it does not trigger consumer irritation. Marketers need to take care in using this technique, however, because experienced consumers can sense when a brand has been 'placed' if cameras dwell on it too long or it is repeatedly handled by on-screen actors. Such placements could then attract the scepticism of more obvious forms of advertising (e.g. Calfee & Ringold, 1988; Friestad & Wright, 1994), and this reaction to explicit sales attempts occurs also among some young consumers (Boush et al., 1994). When consumers are sceptical of advertising, they examine and question their claims more closely and are less likely to be persuaded (Aksoy & Bloom, 1999).

With experience, consumers both become more aware of product placements and accept that they have become part of the established marketing mix. In addition, product placements can invoke a level of more detailed interpretation of brands that nonetheless does not necessarily lead to persuasion. This outcome has been demonstrated by research into consumers' changing reactions to movie product placements as a function of repeated exposure to them (DeLorme & Reid, 1999).

Mediating factors linked to product placement impact

In the end, the effectiveness of product placement as a marketing technique is linked to a number of mediating variables known to influence the impact of more regular forms of advertising. Whether consumers are persuaded by a specific marketing campaign is associated with their level of involvement with a product or service, which in turn determines how they process information about it. Products that are important to consumers demand more of their attention and can be promoted more effectively by techniques to provide distinctive information about the brand. Consumers tend then to seek out informed arguments that persuade them about the specific merits of the brand being promoted.

With products or services with which consumers are less involved, detailed factual arguments are less important and such brands may be promoted more effectively by the use of more peripheral forms of promotion linked to production techniques designed primarily to make the brand and its surrounding advertising look attractive. So, for such brands, advertising can rely on attractive settings and music, endorsements by popular celebrities, and special effects designed simply to attract attention (Petty & Cacioppo, 1979; Petty, Cacioppo & Schumann, 1983).

Other factors include ensuring that a placed brand is given visual prominence and that it makes a good fit in terms of the nature of the surroundings in the movie or programme in which it is embedded. Thus, a brand of fast car might make a good fit in a James Bond film in which the main character is seen driving the brand. In contrast, if the secret agent is depicted repeatedly picking up a branded soft drink, this could be seen as less in keeping with his public image and therefore a more gratuitous form of marketing. Nevertheless, it is feasible that with child consumers, seeing James Bond consuming a branded soft drink could lend a certain image of 'cool' to the brand and with what might be seen as a relatively low involvement product this exposure alone could render it more attractive to them.

The nature of product placement integration with surrounding media material has been differentiated into a number of types. Winkler and Buckner (2006) distinguished between associative, illustrative, and demonstrative placements. In the case of an associative placement, a brand is placed in a programme and shown in the background only. With an illustrative placement, a brand is more prominently positioned and might be used by an on-screen character. With demonstrative placement, the brand occupies a position that is integral to the narrative of media content in which it is placed. In a game setting, for example, it might be manipulated as part of the game. In theory, the more integral to the surrounding narrative a brand becomes, the more its prominence will grow and the more of the viewer's attention it is likely to command. From an information processing perspective, the meanings conveyed by the brand will be progressively more likely to reach the long-term memory of the consumer as its placement shifts from associative to illustrative to demonstrative.

Evidence for product placement impact

It is worth taking a look at research evidence that has been published about product placement effects. We can theorise about the effects of this type of marketing as much as we like, but in the end we need to see hard evidence of its impact. To begin, with, at a relatively superficial level, this form of brand promotion has been found to enhance consumers' awareness of brands (Babin & Carder, 1996; Gupta & Lord, 1998; Nelson, 2002; Russell, Norman & Heckler, 2004). Product placement can also promote more favourable attitudes towards a brand (d'Astous & Seguin, 1999; Russell, 2002). There has also been some indication that product placement effects on consumers' attitudes and beliefs can also translate into behavioural impact (Morton & Friedman, 2002).

There is further evidence that product placement influences on consumers can depend upon more than simply being visible on camera. The way in which the brand is integrated with the narrative of a television programme or movie can serve as an important mediator of product placement effects. Product placements can take different forms in movies and television programmes. Products can be shown visually and receive audio mentions. Even when shown in camera shot, there may be some variance in the duration of the shot and how centrally the brand is placed in the scene. Such production techniques can make a difference to how well viewers subsequently remember the brand. One study of post-viewing brand recall found that a subtle (i.e. non-central) brand display produced worse recall than when the brand was more centrally or prominently displayed in the scene. The addition of an audio mention produced better brand recall from a non-prominent visual placement but made little difference to recall levels for a brand that had been prominently positioned (Gupta & Lord, 1998).

The degree to which a brand is linked into the plot can make a difference to the attention it receives from viewers, and may even affect subsequent brand-related attitudes (d'Astous & Seguin, 1999). This outcome can depend upon how on-screen characters behave towards the brand. Bonds that can form between on-screen characters and brands through repeat exposure can play a part in this process (Karrh, 1998). One study found that if viewers perceived that a character in a situation comedy show displayed a positive attitude towards a product this could encourage viewers to adopt a similar disposition. This outcome could be magnified when the viewer had formed an attachment to the character as well (Russell & Stern, 2006).

The disposition of viewers towards a television programme can play an important role in determining the impact of product placements. The effectiveness of product placement can be diluted when consumers know they are being targeted with a marketing campaign (Friestad & Wright, 1994). With experience, consumers develop the form of scepticism about the persuasive message (Bhatnagar et al., 2004). When consumers are exposed to brands in product placement scenes, because these occur in the context of movies or television shows where their primary experience is one of 'being entertained' they are not triggered to interpret the placement experience as one linked to marketing (Wright, 2002). Their consumer defences may therefore be down and their susceptibility to marketing influences is greater.

The recognition of the true purpose of product placement can surface with repetition of a brand within a programme or movie or even in a magazine, and inappropriate or ill-fitting use of a brand can produce irritation in audiences (Ha, 1996). In addition, the visibility of a brand within a television programme can be enhanced by greater liking of the programme on the part of viewers, which can in turn lead them to pay closer attention to it. Making a brand even more visible through placement enhancing production techniques could therefore have negative rather than positive consequences for the way it is received by viewers. Research has shown that brands placed within well-liked programmes are likely to prove more visible to viewers compared to their placement in programmes that are less well-liked. Furthermore, this increased brand visibility can produce more negative attitudes about the brand. Subtle brand presentation in less well-liked programmes can still register a presence, but without triggering persuasion knowledge, and in consequence can produce more positive brand attitudes (Cowley & Barron, 2008).

Children and product placement

Concerns about children and product placement effects have been fuelled by evidence that this technique has been widely used by products targeted at young consumers, most especially food and drinks products. Although this might not seem to be a cause for concern at first glance, further evidence shows that the kinds of products that use this method of reaching young consumers are most often those classified as poor in nutritional value (Kunkel, McKinley & Wright, 2009; Powell, Szczypka & Chaloupka, 2007, 2010).

Research has shown product placement to be widespread in mainstream media – especially in peak-time television programmes and movies (Dalton, Tickle, Sargent et al., 2002; Bell, Berger, Cassady & Townsend, 2005; Sutherland et al., 2010). Studies have concentrated a great deal on specific product categories such as alcohol, food, and tobacco. A lot of attention here has been devoted to the potential impact of product placements on children. The main perspective was that the brands that were most often featured within movie narratives represented products that posed health risks for young people.

The most often debated issue linked to food brand placements in the media has been the contribution they make to the unhealthy eating habits of children and the rise in rates among youngsters of being overweight or obese. One American study reported that out of the 200 most watched movies between 1996 to 2005, nearly seven out of ten (69%) contained at least one product placement for a food, beverage, or food retail chain brand (Sutherland et al., 2010). These placements were most likely to occur in action-adventure, comedy, and horror films. The most prevalent brands of all were for confectionery and salty snack foods, sugar sweetened drinks, and fast food retail outlets. In general, therefore, the most prevalent brands in movies were ones that represented foods and drinks of poor nutritional value.

Despite the concerns here for kids' exposure to unhealthy brands, movies directed at the youngest viewers tended to be least likely to contain these kinds of product placements. Nevertheless, movies that can be watched by older kids or by kids when accompanied by an adult still frequently carried product placements for sugary foods and beverages and fast food chains. This type of research exposes the prevalence of product placements for specific types of products, but it does not measure the potential impact of these placements.

Research on product placements in peak-time television programmes has confirmed that this form of brand marketing has become widespread on mainstream television in countries such as the United States, but that child exposure to this type of marketing may not be as extensive as we might think. In an analysis that used television industry research data, the appearances of food, beverage, and food outlet brands in programmes were combined with audience viewing data (Speers, Harris & Schwartz, 2011). Brands for these three product categories were found to have appeared 35,000 times in peak-time programmes in 2008. It was estimated from the viewing figures for these programmes that the average child aged between 2 and 11 years saw 281 of these brand appearances compared with 444 for adolescents (aged 12–17 years) and adults (aged 18–49 years). Most of the exposures for children were accounted for by soft drinks brands (218 out of 281), and these in turn were mainly for Coca-Cola. For most food and drinks brands, the average child experienced between one and five exposures to product placements during the year. The researchers made much of the exposure to Coca-Cola placements, which when placed alongside an active advertising campaign, meant that kids saw the brand a lot on television. However, what is perhaps equally significant is that with most product placement brands, average levels of product placement exposure over a 12-month period were low.

These findings concerning the prevalence of product placement on television and in consequence the extensive exposure opportunities for children have been used to back calls for tighter regulation of this type of advertising. Despite more market domains relaxing their rules about product placement in broadcast outputs, many regulators have acknowledged the concerns about the way this technique has been extensively used by food and soft drinks brands and inserted restrictive codes that attempt to prohibit the presence, for example of foods deemed to be high in salt, sugar, and fat content (for the UK, see Ofcom, 2011). Noting the presence of product placement is only part of the story. When exposed to this subtle form of brand promotion, how do children respond? So far, the evidence on this question is limited.

In an experimental study, groups of children aged 6–7 years and 11–12 years viewed one of two sequences from the movie *Home Alone*. One sequence depicted a can of Pepsi Cola being spilled during a meal, while the other sequence depicted a meal scene minus the branded product. In follow-up interviews, all the children were invited to help themselves to a choice of Pepsi or Coca-Cola at the start of each session. Those children who had watched the scene with the product placement were more likely to choose that brand afterwards. The ages of the children made little difference here (Auty & Lewis, 2004).

To date, there is limited evidence of how product placements might influence children. Despite understandable concerns that this form of marketing may place young consumers at a particularly acute disadvantage because their consumer literacy is still under development, an analysis of the degree and nature of their vulnerability when confronted with product placement is still needed. We know that opportunities for product placement exposure are extensive. We also know that brands that adopt this marketing technique include ones that are well known to and widely used by children. Whether the quality of the brand exposure experience in the case of product placements in television programmes and movies is sufficient to register cognitively and emotionally with children in ways that might translate into greater brand preference and use remains an open question. As we will see later on in this book, a new form of product placement in the shape of 'advergames', which engages children more interactively could represent a type of marketing that has a more powerful and lasting impact on young consumers.

4

Children and digital branding

The popularity of online digital media as a marketing platform has surpassed the advance of research designed to inform our understanding of how this medium works and how effective it can be at delivering results in the marketplace. Industry research has generated surface level market statistics that profile internet traffic linked to brands, but what do consumers really make of this type of marketing and how responsive are they to it? In the context of the theme being examined here, what are the implications of brand marketing in this environment for young consumers? The answer to this question is not just of interest to brand manufacturers, their suppliers, and their branding agencies, but also to governments and regulators seeking to maintain control over marketing of any kind that is targeted at children.

The attraction of digital media to marketers working with brands targeted at children is driven in the first place by the widespread adoption of these communications platforms by young people. The EU Kids Online research programme surveyed over 25,000 children and their parents across 25 European Union countries in the spring and summer of 2010. This research reported that 93% of 9 to 16 year olds said they went online every week, with 60% going online virtually every day. Internet use is less prevalent among the pre-teens than teens, but even among the youngest children surveyed here, one in three were regular internet users (Livingstone, Haddon, Gorzig & Olafsson, 2011).

Around the world, evidence has amassed that the under-18s have been the most enthusiastic adopters of digital media of any age group (ITU, 2008; Lenhart et al., 2010; Green, Brady, Olafsson et al., 2013). Internet adoption was found to be more prevalent among children from relatively affluent households with more disposable income (Hasebrink, Gorzig, Haddon et al., 2011). As they grow older, children are not only more likely to go online but also to spend more time there each day (Livingstone et al., 2011). Penetration levels for internet use and the amounts of time spent online vary from one country to the next, but large-scale international surveys have confirmed that children around the world are spending more of their disposable time online, that their parents often don't know they are doing this or what they are looking at, and that a great deal of socialising now takes place there (Symantec, 2009).

Within the broader internet environment, online social network sites have become the cornerstone of many children's social lives. This is where they go to keep up with the latest news from their friends and to publish content about themselves. By 2009, nearly three out of four American teenagers (73%) who used the internet said they were registered to social networking sites, compared to less than one in two adults (47%), although online adults aged 18 to 29 years (72%) were almost as likely as teens to use social networking sites. Children in the 14 to 17 age group (82%) were especially likely to use social media (Lenhart et al., 2010).

Children are active consumers who have purchase power through their parents as well as in their own right (McNeal & Yeh, 1993; Kuhn & Eischen, 1997; Marshall, 1997; Buckingham, 2009). Understandably, therefore, as the attraction of brand marketers to the internet and, in particular, to online social network sites grows, children will be seen as targets because of their indirect and direct spending power. Brand marketing has had to adapt to this new promotional environment because consumers engage with it differently from traditional mass media. This has also meant that conventional advertising methods – although still present in the online world – are not as effective in many online environments, and indeed are not as welcome either as far as consumers are concerned.

For brand marketers, online promotion of brands offers a distinctive advantage not provided by other advertising media in terms of being able closely to monitor the extent to which children are exposed to promotional messages. Real-time online behaviour can be mapped via tracking data obtained through the placement on consumers' computers of electronic files, commonly known as 'cookies'. When consumers visit brand websites directly or by clicking on a banner or a pop-up advertisement, they may be invited to provide personal details including contact addresses (i.e. linked to their email) and this enables online marketers to establish a database about the nature of their customers as well as tracking their online behaviour as it relates both to brand exposure and online purchase (Hallerman, 2008).

There are other marketing techniques that have opened up through the internet, which entail the recruitment of consumers to act as endorsers of brands to their friends and other people they know. The use of consumers as brand representatives is an activity that pre-dates the digital era, but the internet has facilitated its wider use including amongst children (Montgomery & Chester, 2009). This is a subject we will return to later.

The power of interactivity

One of the reasons why the digital world has excited brand marketers is that it provides a platform on which consumers can be engaged with brands in a more dynamic way than through traditional mass media. The internet invites users to search it and to interact with the content they find on the World Wide Web. Once content has been located on specific websites, there may be further facilities made available to visitors to undertake two-way communications rather than the more traditional one-way link afforded by the older media.

Since children have been found to take to the digital world enthusiastically, it is understandable that digital platforms have been regarded as having particular potential for reaching young consumers. As well as brands that are designed for the children's market, there are many other brands for products consumed by all age groups that nevertheless seek to capture the attention and loyalty of consumers while they are young. Many traditional forms of brand advertising have struggled to reach young consumers, either because they display a lack of interest in older media or because they are unable effectively to process brand information through these media (Dreze & Hussher, 2003).

As we have already seen, with interactivity, marketers hope that consumers will become more involved with brands, especially if they are encouraged to take part in online activities in which brands take centre stage (Montgomery & Chester, 2009). In other words, the online world does not simply represent yet another platform for brand exposure, but provides an environment in which consumers can contribute views directly about brands, can offer new branding ideas, and even play games in which brands are manipulated on screen (Adams, 2006). Furthermore, in some interactive digital environments, as we will see, consumers may even be recruited to represent brands to other consumers.

The digital world has provided marketers with a new toolkit through which to represent their brands to consumers, but how do different interactive tools stack up in terms of how they work and how effective they might be expected to be? The main online media tools adopted by brand marketers are: sites on which brands have a physical presence, such as company websites; web communities that provide channels through which people can engage in conversations with each other on topics of common interest; web stores that provide virtual shopping environments from which people can select brands for offline delivery; banner advertisements; pop-up advertisements; newsletters; and promotional emails (also known as spam when unsolicited).

Banner advertisements and pop-up advertisements represent online versions of traditional media advertising whereby the advertisement content is separated from other content and consumers have little or no control over exposure to these promotions because they appear spontaneously. Newsletters and solicited email promotions provide consumers with some degree of control in that it is usual that people must sign up to a company or brand first and give permission for these messages to be sent. Consumers may not know when these messages are going to arrive. With unsolicited email messages or spam, consumers have little control, and these tend to arrive as a result of the sender obtaining the receiver's email address without permission from another source (Liu & Shrum, 2002).

With websites, shops, and online communities, consumers choose to seek out these platforms and also to enter into memberships that permit access and give approval for promotional messages to be sent to them. With brand manufacturers' and retailers' sites, people tend proactively to seek them out to get brand information or to make purchases.

One key aspect of interactivity is the communication feedback loop from consumers to brand marketing sites. While traditional media send out promotional messages in the offline world, in the online world, interactive marketing vehicles also engage with consumers to solicit communication from them. Even with banner and pop-up advertisements, consumers can click on the ads to open up a channel to further brand-related information or even to purchase opportunities. When consumers click-through or register their presence on websites, an electronic record of these visits or subsequent requests or transactions is maintained, providing advertisers with a database about consumer traffic.

The potential potency of interactivity was believed from early on in the digital era to derive from its capacity to get consumers more 'involved' with brands and their promotional campaigns. When consumers became more involved, which here meant in a cognitive sense, they would pay more attention to web-based information and also be more likely to process it more deeply, particularly if they also produced their own communications to the brand site or actively engaged with the brand on a website through some form of game playing. In the offline world, there was a belief that advertising effectiveness could be enhanced through more consumer involvement, which would in turn cause consumers to engage in more elaborative processing of brand-related information (Batra & Ray, 1985).

In this state of mind, consumers were expected to acquire and retain brand-related knowledge more effectively (Ariely, 2000). Interactivity can also give consumers a sense that they have more personal control over the brand promotion process and have more than a passive role as unquestioning recipients of marketers' claims about brands. Thus, interactivity can enhance the 'self-efficacy' of consumers which can again motivate them to weigh up brands and brand claims in a more diverse fashion and also to store all this information much better (Zimmerman, 2000). Consumers can feel more in control during interactive online engagement with brands, making them want to learn more about brands, which in turn should render brands more memorable and likely to be 'top-of-mind' when consumers are shopping for purchases (Liu & Shrum, 2002).

Children and web advertising

The use of websites to promote brands has been a source of concern where they are used to target children. It is important for consumers, whatever their age, to know when they are confronted with a message that has been designed to influence their attitudes, beliefs, or behaviour. Creating a boundary between a promotional message and surrounding content is one action that marketers can take to enhance consumers' recognition of information that is aimed at persuasive influence. Making such distinctions explicit is particularly important with children, whose consumer socialisation is not complete and who may therefore have a poor understanding of the purposes of advertising (Brady et al., 2008).

The growth of the internet as a source of information about products and services and as a platform for purchase transactions has occurred at such a pace that our understanding of how young consumers can cope in this environment has been left behind. Most previous research on children's understanding of advertising, for example, focused on televised advertising (Livingstone, 2005). The experience of brand marketing on television is quite different from the range of promotional experiences a child consumer might encounter on the internet.

Despite research findings that have suggested children begin to recognise advertisements as having distinctive identities, for example on television when set against programmes, being able to make simple distinctions based on crude physical comparisons (e.g. programmes are longer than advertisements) does not mean young children understand and can articulate the more complex promotional and persuasive purposes of advertising (Oates, Blades & Gunter, 2002; Oates, Blades, Gunter & Don, 2003; Andronikidis & Lambrianidou, 2010).

In an internet setting in which the nature of advertising messages and brand promotions differs from that present in other media, the structural cues initially deployed by children to distinguish branding or advertising messages can be quite different (Ali, Blades, Oates & Blumberg, 2009). When children aged 6, 8, 10, and 12 years from Indonesia and the UK were shown printed copies of web pages created by the researchers, 6-year-olds could identify only about a quarter of advertisements embedded in them, compared with 8-year-olds who recognised around half and 10- and 12-year-olds who recognised about three quarters. The oldest children were most likely to recognise an advertisement when it contained price information linked to a brand (Ali et al., 2009). Yet despite evidence showing that online advertising may not be instantly recognisable, exposure to brands in an online setting can shift consumers' attitudes and make them more favourably disposed towards specific brands (Yoo, 2008).

We might ask how this can happen. The inability to separately differentiate a brand advertisement dos not mean that the brand itself is not noticed or that information about it is not encoded into the consumer's memory after exposure to it. Although the brand exposure may not be remembered as a distinct episode or event, separate from other media content to which the consumer was exposed at the same time, the brand itself could still makes its way into the consumer's memory. It is possible that the consumer is already familiar with the brand, in which case further online exposure to it would serve as a reminder about it and might also provide new information about it that is then added to what the consumer already knows.

In the online world, we are frequently invited to engage with content in an interactive mode. This means that we do more than simply consume content that is presented to us on websites. We might be encouraged to seek out further information about a brand; to offer opinions about it; to engage in competitions that offer rewards linked to the brand; or to take advantage of premium offers for immediate online purchase requests. These different kinds of interactivity are designed to bring us psychologically close to the brand by engaging with it one-to-one (Steuer, 1992; Hoffman & Novak, 1996). These techniques can result in a more vivid brand experience that is in turn more memorable or might, in the moment, encourage us to think more highly of it (Coyle & Thorson, 2001; Voorveld, Neijens & Smit, 2009, 2010). These observations are especially relevant to understanding the impact of the most advanced forms of interactive online brand marketing, such as advergames, which we will examine in greater detail in Chapter 6.

Corporate websites and branding

The internet has opened up other opportunities for brand owners to reach and influence consumers. As well as explicit advertising, more subtle forms of promotions have been deployed to enhance brand awareness, positive brand attitudes, and intentions to purchase. These activities have been used widely to reach young consumers, given their enthusiastic adoption of the internet and related tools. There have been concerns about marketers' movements in this direction because of the disguised nature of this type of brand advertising.

As we saw in the last chapter, even with older media, marketers have turned increasingly to more subtle forms of brand promotion – in particular product placement. This development has been motivated by the impact on consumers' television behaviour of new content recording technologies that enable them both to circumvent scheduling restrictions on when they consume specific programmes and enables them to fast-forward through advertisements.

Corporate websites are ostensibly produced to enable companies to provide people with information about their organisations, products, or services, and to enable consumers to provide feedback about brands. As companies have become more internet literate, many have introduced other elements to their websites, such as competitions and games, areas in which consumers can talk to each other about the company and its products or services, and premium offers. In effect they are sources of information and entertainment and sources of brand promotion.

There are concerns about the use of websites as disguised advertising platforms, especially where children are the target market. These concerns stem from a belief that children are already vulnerable as consumers because they often lack the level of understanding of brands and of brand advertising that adults have. This may mean that they are more at risk of influence in a context in which insufficient cues have been given to them to trigger any internalised defences against persuasion they have learned. A further concern has stemmed from the observation that the advertisers that most frequently use this approach with child consumers are those representing products that pose specific health risks to children. These include sites that represent food products high in sugar, salt, and fat content. Advertising for these products is believed to contribute towards higher rates of childhood weight problems and obesity (Ogden, Carroll & Flegal, 2008).

A major study conducted by the Kaiser Family Foundation in the United States examined the corporate websites of the most advertised food brands on television. The sites that were included for close scrutiny were ones classed as presenting content for children aged under 12. The researchers eventually identified 77 websites that promoted 107 brands, and generated 4,000 pages of content for analysis. Data obtained from the Nielsen agency reported that these sites were visited by over 12 million kids aged between 2 and 11 years during a three month period in the middle of 2005. The Kaiser Family Foundation research also found that an overwhelming majority of food brands that advertised on US television also used the internet to target children. In fact over three-quarters of these brands produced websites that were targeted specifically at pre-teenage and teenage children (Kaiser Family Foundation, 2006).

The sites studied by the Kaiser Family Foundation researchers were found to use a range of digital marketing techniques that included advergames (see also Chapter 6), brand mentions and advertisements, viral marketing, competitions and promotions, club memberships and incentivised surveys, premium purchase offers, customisation spaces and social media links, nutrition information and brand-linked educational pages (also called 'advercation').

Research conducted by Andrew Cheyne, Lori Dorfman, and Eliana Bukofzer of the Berkeley Media Studies Group, University of California, and Jennifer Harris of the Yale Rudd Center for Obesity and Food Policy reported that websites operated by companies marketing breakfast cereal brands at children often used a range of interactive techniques to enhance children's involvement with the sites when they visited. This involvement in websites was called 'telepresence' (Cheyne et al., 2013). The researchers measured the use of a range of features on each brand promoting website that included: links to games, quizzes, and videos; the presence of the brand (e.g. images of product packs); the way the product was presented; and product-related claims. Each site was further classified using a system of 'telepresence' measurements developed earlier (see Keng & Lin, 2006) to determine whether it was high, medium, or low in its potential to capture young people's attention. This analysis was carried out with 26 branded websites.

This study found that the great majority (82%) of these sites had games, with many having more than one. Very often, advergames were present which invited children to play interactive online games in which the brand was integrated into the game narrative. Virtually all the advergames involved playing with food, and in many cases treating the brand as more than just a food item. Brands might be integrated, for example, with vehicles that on-screen characters, manipulated by kids, would use to travel around the game environment. Many of the sites contained video material and much of this material comprised explicit branded promotions. Some of these websites adopted cross-promotion techniques whereby the cereal brands were combined with established cartoon characters (e.g. The Flintstones).

Under half the sites (47%) were classed as using 'low immersion' techniques that drew in kids' attention with games and videos, but used fairly low levels of interactivity. Over four in ten sites (41%) were categorised as 'medium immersion' and used larger numbers of techniques designed to grab a child visitor's attention, such as interactive games and serialised video episodes with continuing storylines. The remaining minority of sites were classed as 'high immersion' and used more advanced interactive games such as advergames or virtual worlds through which children could engage with branded products and make purchases. The researchers concluded that cereal manufacturers have used websites as effective marketing platforms to draw in young consumers to more frequent, lengthier, and psychologically more engaging (or immersive) visits that add up to intensive brand experiences. Outwardly, these sites can appear as sources of entertainment or amusement for kids, but all the time there is an underlying brand marketing imperative that is not always obvious to users. The potential of such sites to influence the food preferences of children is a source of concern when they are used extensively to promote products classed as too sugary to represent a healthy nutritional choice (Cheyne, et al., 2013).

Within websites, a variety of platforms have been adapted to carry brand advertising. In Chapter 6, we will turn our attention to the phenomenon of 'advergames'. These are electronic games that are designed to promote specific brands, the brands being integrated as active components within the games. This form of brand integration is a digital equivalent of certain forms of product placement in analogue media. In addition to brand integration, however, games have been used to carry stand-alone advertisements for brands.

Product placement in computer or video games pre-dates the internet, and the first examples emerged in the 1980s in relation to arcade games that carried banner advertisements for tobacco brands (Glass, 2007). Most of the research concerning the impact of brand advertising in video games has measured consumers' memory for brands and their attitudes towards brands after playing. The placement of brands in video games can enhance brand awareness in terms of consumers' memory of a brand, but research has indicated that only a minority of brands tend to be effectively recalled even immediately after playing a game and that this memory is often short-lived (Nelson, 2002).

Brand memory can be mediated by the different ways in which the brand is presented in a video game. As we will see in the discussion of advergames in Chapter 6, the impact on consumers of this type of marketing can depend upon the degree to which game players interact with the brand. There is also an interaction between the type of memory in which a brand is stored and the degree to which the brand is integrated into the game. In Chapter 3, we saw that a distinction has been made by marketing researchers between 'explicit memory' and 'implicit memory'. Explicit memory comprises memory for specific brand experiences whereby consumers are asked if they can recall any awareness of the brand during a particular media exposure.

Cognitive psychologists have referred to this type of memory as 'episodic', in that it is concerned with our ability to remember specific experiences or episodes in our lives. Implicit memory concerns a more generalised knowledge we might hold about a brand that we cannot link back to any specific exposure experiences. Cognitive psychologists have also labelled this 'semantic memory' because it consists of a repository of meanings that may be interconnected in a permanent or long-term memory store, but where there are not necessarily any explicit linkages back to points in time when, or to a place where, a particular piece of factual knowledge was learned (Meyer, 1970; Tulving, 1972; Eysenck, 1977, 1984).

We have already seen that in relation to research into product placement effects, three different types of placement were identified that were called associative, illustrative, and demonstrative. With associative product placement, the brand is simply inserted at some point in a game as part of the background. In the case of illustrative placement a brand may be positioned more centrally within a specific scene in the game, so that it is potentially more noticeable than a brand placed in the background. The player's attention may therefore be more likely to settle on the brand, but he or she does not manipulate it in any way. Finally, with demonstrative placement, the brand is not only centrally positioned but may be engaged with by the player in an interactive fashion (Winkler & Buckner, 2006).

A research group in Taiwan recruited consumers to play with desktop computer games in which brands were situated either as background items (associative placement), foregrounded items (illustrative placement), or as part of the game that was played (demonstrative placement). Table tennis and puzzle games were used. In a test of explicit memory, recall and recognition of brands was best when demonstrative placement was used and was worst when associative placement was used. In relation to a test of implicit memory in which participants indicated their brand preferences in terms of intention to buy a brand from a list that included brands placed in the games and other brands, the effects of types of product placement were reversed. Associative placement generated the strongest intention to purchase and demonstrative placement produced the weakest. A more 'in your face' style of product presence in a game environment promoted raw awareness of brands, but its lack of subtlety could mean that the brand was perceived as less appealing, with fewer positively toned associative attributes in implicit memory to render it more attractive to consumers (Ho, Lin & Yang, 2011).

Children, brands, and interactive online settings

This kind of evidence derives from an analysis of a single type of advertising. Advertising messages can, however, take on a number of formats on the internet. In addition to pop-up brand messages, brand logos and messages in sidebars, advertising slogans and brand mentions embedded within websites, other more subtle and yet at the same time dynamic and engaging techniques have been developed. With these techniques, it may not always be apparent to young consumers that the activities in which they are encouraged to take part on specific websites are really designed to persuade them to like and purchase branded products or services.

Brands have recognised the need to utilise the new communications and entertainment formats that have emerged within online social networks. One approach has been to embed brand exposure and related promotional messages within social networks and virtual environments. While some brands have positioned themselves within established online social networks, another approach has been for brands to produce their own stand-alone social media sites that adopt many of the practices found in the most widely used mainstream sites such as Bebo, Facebook, MySpace, and Twitter. Having examined what we know about consumers' and more especially children's responses to basic forms of advertising on the internet, we will now look at some of the newer forms of digital brand advertising and promotional formats that have taken centre stage.

These new developments in marketing and advertising have taken advantage of social media settings and the electronic environments created within virtual world and computer or video games. The next two chapters will examine these new developments in brand promotions targeted at children and review what has been learned so far about their impact on young consumers. Chapter 5 will focus on the use by brands of social media or social networking sites as promotional platforms. Brands have adopted two broad approaches in this context. The first of these is to become embedded in established online social networks by creating their own profile presence alongside other users and to engage with other users not only as consumers but also as brand endorsers or brand 'champions' whereby they support the brand by promoting it to other consumers like themselves.

Chapter 6 will examine the way brands have entered the world of video games to engage with consumers. Brand owners have negotiated directly with existing video games manufacturers to obtain product placement within mainstream games. In addition, they have produced their own interactive games that consumers can access via the brands' corporate websites.

5

Branding potential of online social media

When it comes to eating Nestle's Polo Mints, do you suck them or crunch them? On a website created by the company, visitors are invited to click on whether they see themselves as one type or the other (www.polomint.co.uk). They are then directed to join fellow 'Suckers' or 'Crunchers' on a social media site. These two types of fans of the brand could then exchange brand experiences with each other.

The Wrigley's Extra website (www.wrigleys.com/uk/brands/extra.aspx) provides access to a social media community in which visitors can talk more generally about food and eating. The site does not focus visitors' attention solely on the brand itself but encourages broader discussion of food and where they like to go to eat out. The Wrigley's site created more enthusiastic participation and arguably greater consumer involvement because of the nature of its content, while the Polo Mints site ran out of steam because little effort was made by the company to create discussion topics around the brand or indeed about anything at all (Stokes, 2011).

Cadbury launched a 'Spots and Stripes' advertising campaign in 2010 and linked this to a social media site (www.spotsvstripes.com) through Facebook, Twitter, and YouTube. The aim of this campaign was to create two teams (Spots and Stripes) to compete in various online competitions in the run-up to the 2012 London Olympics. During this campaign, the company launched a new product, the Challenge Bar, which was made of milk and white chocolate and had three sections, one spotty, one stripy, and one in the middle which the Spot and the Stripe had to play for. The inside of the wrapper of this product had different games printed on it which members of the Spots and Stripes teams could play in the offline world for the third 'chunk' and could then go online and claim points for their chosen team. In this campaign, social media platforms were dynamically linked to a major offline marketing campaign for a new brand and created a sense of purpose among the online social communities that the company established (Stratman, 2010). Throughout all this game playing and the accompanying social media exchanges, the brand was never far away.

The internet has provided a major platform on which companies can present and promote their products and services in a multitude of modalities and formats on the World Wide Web. As it has evolved and become more interactive – allowing users not only to search for content but also to produce and upload it – the Web has become more 'social'. This has meant that as well as linking people to information and entertainment oriented websites, the internet conveys sites that have created online communities allowing people alternative ways of keeping in touch with their offline social networks and of extending these networks.

The emergence of these 'social media' has changed the way product manufacturers and service suppliers can create new brands, bring them to market, and promote and refresh existing brands (Kaplan & Haenlein, 2010, 2011). Social media comprise a wide range of online forums that people can join, follow, contribute to, and obtain information from. They include interactive websites that are frequently updated, known as weblogs or 'blogs', chat rooms and discussion boards, product and service ratings websites, and social networking sites.

Blogs can vary in terms of their thematic content, whether they are text based or also include audio or video content, and in terms of the maximum lengths of messages they will accommodate. In recent times, micro-blogging sites that enable users to post very brief messages in live streams and to engage in almost immediate interactions with others have become very popular. The best known of these is Twitter. When examining the impact of social media in the consumer context, however, most attention has been directed towards social networking sites. Several of these sites have each attracted hundreds of millions of users. The most widely used and recognised of these sites is Facebook.

These online tools have been widely deployed by corporations that target brands at young consumers. This is not surprising given that millions of children around the world belong to at least one online social media site. As well as inserting themselves into established online social communities, some corporations have developed their own websites, increasingly with high levels of social interactivity, that are designed to pull in children by offering various incentives such as competitions, games, opportunities to link with other kids, and premium offers on products and services.

The promotional purposes of these sites tend to be disguised or mixed in with a multitude of other, apparently 'non-marketing' activities. One technique that has grown in popularity is the use of young consumers as brand 'champions' or 'ambassadors', who are incentivised to promote brands among their friends online. These new marketing trends raise important questions about children's brand engagement that go beyond those we have already been asking in relation to more traditional forms of brand promotion to young consumers.

Understandably, the popularity of social media sites with children, and their increased use by marketers for brand promotion campaigns, have together fuelled public disquiet about these marketing practices and the way they might influence children. Concerns have arisen both in regard to the potential exposure of children to brand promotions on social network sites that are intended for adults, and about promotions targeted specifically at children.

As we will see later in this chapter, there are many social network sites and virtual worlds designed explicitly for young people and in many of those made for children, commercial brands have a prominent presence. In addition, commercial brands produced for adult consumer markets that have been restricted by various government or voluntary codes and regulations concerning their advertising activities have turned to social media as alternative promotional venues. In these settings, however, child members of social network sites can gain access to branded sites that contain advertising for brands that they might not be able to see so readily in other regulated media such as television, radio, newspapers, and magazines.

The use of Facebook by alcohol brands provides one case example of where a category of commercial brands that cannot be marketed or sold directly to children, because they are legally banned from consumption of alcohol beverage products, has utilised a social network with many child members who can gain access to brand promotions and wider consumer chat about alcoholic brands. Although explicit advertising on the internet was restricted in the same way as it was on other media, online discourses involving ordinary users of the Facebook site were not covered by the advertising codes of practice because technically they were not classed as 'advertising'. Advertising regulators have had to be fleet of foot to re-classify advertisers' Facebook sites as advertising (Carah & Brodmerkel, 2012).

Marketing and mainstream social networks

There are many brands that have established a presence on social media sites such as Facebook, Twitter, and YouTube. Despite the adult branding of these sites, many of the brands that use them for promotional purposes are popular with children, including many fast food restaurants and sugared drinks. One analysis showed that 11 of the top 12 fast food chains in the United States in terms of sales in 2009 had at least one Facebook account. Within another year, the missing chain joined Facebook. More than 30 leading brand sugared drinks also had Facebook accounts (Richardson & Harris, 2011).

Branded Facebook pages displayed many of the same format characteristics as those of any other user of the site. There were picture profiles of brands;

information about brands; opportunities for customers to provide feedback about old and new brands; input into brand developments; and competitions and promotions offering opportunities to win prizes linked to the brands. Customers were often invited to post comments and could upload pictures of themselves posing with the brands. Customers could also place orders through the brand's Facebook site in many cases (Richardson & Harris, 2011).

Harris and colleagues examined the new online marketing strategies of products targeted at children, including breakfast cereals, fast food, and sugary drinks. Manufacturers of these products used social networking sites to promote their premium brands to kids. In addition to developing their own sites, they also made use of established, mainstream social media sites such as Facebook.

The corporate appeal of online branding

Online social networks and micro-blogs are themselves among the most powerful brands on the internet and have accumulated vast numbers of users. They also generate huge volumes of chatter every day (Javitch, 2008). Very often, this chatter concerns brands that people have used. Research conducted by Nielsen in 2011 found that over half of active social media users followed a brand and displayed significantly greater than average expenditure in specific product fields such as clothing, shoes, and accessories (Walker, 2013).

Research by online branding consultancy, Syncapse, with over 2,000 online US consumers and Facebook users, tracked the fan bases of 20 leading brands including Coca-Cola, Disney, Levi's, Nike, Oreo, Skittles, Victoria's Secret, and Walmart. Respondents indicated whether they were 'fans' of a brand by stating whether on Facebook they 'liked' it. These respondents were then invited to indicate why they had become fans of a brand. The most popular reasons given were that they wanted to support a brand they liked (49% of those saying they had 'liked' a brand on Facebook), to get a coupon or discount (42%), and to receive regular updates from these brands (41%) (Kalehoff, 2013).

Within these environments, where many millions of people spend hours of their time each week, there are opportunities for brands to establish new and powerful relationships with their customers. These tools can be used to build brand awareness, find new customers, and to track the performance of brands in the marketplace (Weston, 2008). Companies can create their own profiles on social network sites and provide various incentives for consumers to visit and engage with brands (Araujo & Neijens, 2012). This process can be used to cultivate relationships between brands and consumers that traditional forms of advertising cannot produce (Palmer & Koenig-Lewis, 2009). These methods for reaching consumers are used with children as well as adults. This approach has been used to capture consumers while they are young and has included not only brands traditionally targeted at children but also adult brand extensions in product fields such as clothes and accessories.

The volume of daily use of social media sites further underlines the vast potential they have as a branding environment. Daily users of Facebook around the world can reach 172 million, while Twitter can attract 40 million and LinkedIn can reach 22 million. Ernst and Young reported here that a survey they conducted in 2011 with UK online poling agency, YouGov, found that 67% of social media users claimed that social media sites influenced their purchases. Consumers have already been empowered by digital technologies in respect of their purchases. Applications such as RedLaser can be downloaded onto their mobile phones and by using their phone to scan the barcodes of products they see in retail settings, they can check on the price of the same item in other stores to see how the one they are looking at compares.

The business potential of social media is underpinned by the more general expansion of the internet. One report predicted that by 2016, half the world's population will be using the internet. The internet economy in the G–20 countries will by then be worth around $4.2 trillion. Within these countries, social media users amount to 80% of all those people who are online.

The importance of social media in the branding arena also stems from the social functions of these platforms. An overwhelming majority of social media users utilise these sites to maintain connections with family and friends. These contacts can also provide sources of information about products and services and even sources of recommendation. As well as being a platform for a growing number of transactions, consumers also use the internet for window shopping and then interact with their online social networks for further recommendations before making offline purchases (Hoffman & Fodor, 2010).

Commercial organisations have not failed to recognise the business potential of the cyber-world and some have begun to build new business models within online social media settings (Sutter, 2009). The growing recognition on the part of marketers that, in today's media rich world, integrated marketing campaigns often represent the best route to promotional success and market share growth from their products, means that social media have increasingly been incorporated into the marketing mix. Leading consultancies such as McKinsey have advised corporate chief executives that social media can no longer be perceived as a side show in their business planning. They represent platforms on which brand assets can be created, enhanced, and refreshed (Divol, Edelman & Sarrazin, 2012).

The attractive feature of social media in promotional and persuasive contexts is that they combine interpersonal and mass communication. The size of their user populations can mean that brand names, logos, and related promotional activities can be presented to millions of people as swiftly as through the more traditional broadcast or print media or outdoor advertising routes. Another important aspect of social media sites is that they can be used to promote brands in a much more subtle fashion than traditional advertising. Although some brands have used social media sites as extensions of their normal marketing practices through the use of placed advertisements, many social media users have displayed low tolerance for this kind of brand marketing intrusion in their social arenas. Tolerance of advertising on social media sites can be enhanced if users believe that it is a price they must pay for continued free access to other services they receive from an online social network (see Millward Brown, 2011).

Large corporations can use social media to get in closer touch with their customers. Growing numbers are now doing this (Barnes & Mattson, 2008; Araujo & Neijens, 2012). The more traditional marketing activities that were conducted through mainstream mass media could allow big corporations to reach out to their customer bases, but they always retained a great distance between themselves and consumers. With online social media, companies can talk to their customers and present to large audiences the messages they want to get across. At the same time, customers can talk back to companies letting them know what they think and feel about specific brands or brand campaigns. Customers can also talk to each other and formulate their own views about brands, while companies can, from the sidelines, witness this chatter and learn a lot about the people they try to sell to that their own market research might not reveal to them (Evans, 2011).

In the social media world then, consumers have been empowered to proffer their opinions on brands and to get these opinions seen or heard potentially by many thousands of other consumers. Collectively, social media users can spread opinions and recommendations about brands to others very quickly. As a 'social' environment, these networks provide a lot of informal chatter about brands that could influence their market performance. It is important for corporations to understand the dynamics of this branding environment so that they can develop effective promotional activities that are social media based (Bergstrom, 2000).

Social media have become important also because consumers increasingly seek brand-related information from corporation sites, and recommendations from other consumers about specific products and services. Consumers use social network sites to carry out their own research into brands. This type of consumer research goes beyond the use of search engines to find brand websites that contain brand-related information. It takes on a more 'social' flavour as consumers seek personal evaluations of other consumers such as themselves. The brand-related chatter that takes place on online social forums has become increasingly important to consumers, both adult and children alike (Smith, 2013).

Companies can use social media proactively to trigger online conversations about their brands. This chatter can be triggered by brand manufacturers and suppliers, or their advertising agencies. Online brand-related chatter not only raises the profile of a brand, it also represents a source of feedback about brands and, as such, provides commercial organisations with a constant stream of market research. The rapid spread of conversations about brands has been termed 'viral marketing'. As we will see later, this online chatter needs to observe certain rules, one of which concerns the transparency of its purpose. Brand owners who engage with social communities pretending to be something they are not can suffer from a consumer backlash if their disguised marketing activities are exposed (Hoffman & Fodor, 2010).

One further advantage of using online social networks for marketing purposes for brand owners is that these sites can provide on-tap market research in the form of quantitative data from site traffic and qualitative data manifest as expressed sentiments in online chatter that indicate levels of interest in their brands. Although corporate chiefs have been concerned about the impact of social media activities on the bottom line and seek metrics that show a clear financial return on investment, other 'social' metrics have grown in significance, such as whether online chatter about brands raises brand awareness, generates positive sentiments about brands, and gets consumers generally more interested in them (Hoffman & Fodor, 2010).

Visitor traffic to brands' websites, numbers of views for online videos, and registered followers on social media sites have emerged as valuable performance indicators in relation to online branding campaigns (Hoffman & Fodor, 2010). On Facebook, where users can indicate how much they 'like' specific brands and on Twitter where brands can receive mentions, marketers have ready-made market research tools with which they can monitor what consumers think and feel about brands. This information might also cover consumers' opinions about competitor brands, enabling brand owners to gain insights into where their brands stand in the marketplace alongside others (Funk, 2011).

This feedback could be more valuable than expensive offline market research in that the opinions that may be voiced about brands stem from naturally occurring conversations rather than contrived research interviews. This type of platform can therefore be used to enable a company to promote its brands worldwide and to receive feedback about them from different markets relatively inexpensively (Hanna, Rohm & Crittenden, 2011). It has also been reported that consumers' opinions about brands could be shaped by brand owners' interventions in online chatter so as to increase consumers' intentions to purchase and use the brand (Weinberg & Pehlivan, 2011).

It is important that brand owners and their agencies do not presume that online social media spaces are theirs to control. Just as consumers can grow tired of unrelenting advertising in traditional media locations, marketers can overplay their hands on social network sites. It is important to get the balance right between establishing an online presence sufficient to yield value in terms of raised brand awareness (and market share), and not irritating consumers who use these sites for many other purposes (Palmer & Koenig-Lewis, 2009). The attraction to social media sites of corporate brand owners has therefore been reinforced by the integrated, one-stop shop package they offer for brand promotion, consumer engagement, and brand performance assessment (HWZ/ BV4 Brand Report, 2012, 2013).

Positive word-of-mouth recommendations have been known to have a great deal of currency in the offline world (Keller, 2005; Doyle, 2007). In the pre-internet era these interactions were confined to face-to-face conversations between consumers. Even though these conversations might occur between a few hundred customers out of tens of thousands or even involve a few thousand customers out of millions, their impact was generally minimal because they were never joined up into a single community of brand-related discourse. Social media were observed to facilitate the spread of word-of-mouth or consumer-to-consumer communications about all kinds of issues from their earliest days (Rheingold, 1993; Goldenburg, Libai & Muller, 2001).

Where social media have become real game changers for brands and their underlying corporations is that they enable all these disparate conversations to become quickly shared by hundreds of thousands or even millions, making people aware of how many other customers there are like them who perhaps have been dissatisfied with a brand's performance. An opinion about a brand published online by one consumer can reach another consumer who may then express their opinion about that brand. These two opinions may then circulate among other users and within a relatively short period of time widespread brand chatter can surface that involves hundreds or even thousands of consumers and which potentially could be read by many tens of hundreds of thousands more (Constantinides & Fountain, 2008). Online brand chat can, of course, be turned to a brand's advantage if it is positive (Mayzlin, 2006).

Given that growing numbers of people now turn to social media for product and service information, the power of these forums to influence brand performance has also increased (Vollmer & Precourt, 2008; Safko & Brake, 2009; Skaar, 2009). Although online social media platforms provide potentially influential tools for corporate brand owners, they also require more power sharing with each consumer, who is no longer isolated in his or her relationship with a brand. Consumers can quickly link with other consumers, and are not restricted in this activity to talking only to people they know locally. This scaling up of consumer influence over brands through online social media has created fresh challenges for large companies and forced many to alter the way they communicate with their customers (Mangold & Faulds, 2009).

This relatively new environment for promoting brands can also be very challenging. The same rules of engagement do not always apply in the online world and offline world. Becoming embedded within the social media sites of their customers can open up potentially profitable new channels for strengthening consumer loyalty. Equally, if brands misplay their hands in this environment, bad news can spread very quickly and a brand's reputation can be damaged within hours (Bernoff & Li, 2008). What can focus the minds of large corporations is chatter that is critical of their brands and of their company's own service level performance. Criticism of brands can spread rapidly in social media environments. Companies are learning that if their brands fail to satisfy their customers, negative word-of-mouth publicity can escalate to dangerous levels within a matter of days or even hours (Gillin, 2007).

Criticism of brands can occur not only when they fail to deliver what consumers expect. Any changes that are made to a brand can also incur the ire of consumers, who might feel a sense of ownership over it following years of loyal patronage. When clothing retailer Gap decided to make its logo more modern and contemporary and introduced its new look on Facebook in October 2010, there was a severe backlash from consumers, who felt that the brand had abandoned the image with which they identified. Much of the negative chatter about the new version of the brand occurred online. After a subsequent attempt at soliciting consumers' input to a further revision of the brand logo failed, Gap reinstated its original logo (Walker, 2013).

One further finding of market research in this field that has indirect implications for the security of child consumers is that adult consumer tolerance for brand promotions in their online social networks is limited in the case of more transparent forms of advertising. Despite being recognisable, they are also regarded by many social networkers as intrusive, and traffic monitoring confirms that they generate low click-through rates – that is, online users clicking on advertising that pops up on their social network screen to obtain further brand information (Millward Brown, 2011). One method of disguising a marketing campaign that has been facilitated by online social networks has been to recruit consumers on those sites to act as brand champions, writing and generating online chatter about them, and spreading positive opinion about specific brands (Hoffman & Fodor, 2010; Gupta, Armstrong & Clayton, 2011).

The brand ambassador technique has been criticised when it is used with children, and when a company tries to get away with marketing of this kind in a less than transparent fashion, it can come badly unstuck. Soft drinks distributor Dr Pepper/7UP launched a campaign for a new flavoured milk brand called Raging Cow in 2003 in which it enlisted six teenagers and young adults to spread favourable reviews and comment about this new drink via blog posts. The company failed to disclose that these young bloggers were linked to it and incentivised to promote the new brand. Other bloggers grew suspicious of the campaign and exposed it. Following negative publicity across the blogosphere the brand disappeared (see Hoffman & Fodor, 2010).

We will return to the implications of social media branding applications for kids a little later. Next, it will be useful to pause and take a look at what has been discovered to date about branding promotion methods and impact on consumers.

Do social media benefit brands?

The use of online social networks for marketing purposes has grown as the prevalence of social media has expanded. More and more businesses have acknowledged that the level of brand-related chatter than can occur on these sites quite spontaneously and without any prompting from specific brand owners means that it cannot be ignored as a potentially highly influential environment for brand development and image maintenance. Social media can be used to enhance brand awareness, develop a brand's identity, promote positive brand opinion, find new customers, and cultivate stronger brand loyalty among existing customers.

The potential significance of online media chatter about brands has been underlined by direct assessments of its prevalence and sentiment. Bernard Jansen and his colleagues at the College of Information Sciences and Technology, Pennsylvania State University, analysed more than 150,000 postings on Twitter over a 13-week period in 2008. Around one in five of these 'tweets' (19%) were found to contain a mention of a brand and of these, a further one in five contained some form of evaluative sentiment about the brand that was mentioned. Half of these evaluative brand mentions were positive in tone and one-third of these tweets were critical (Jansen et al., 2009). This feedback can be gathered relatively inexpensively and provides companies with insights into current brand sentiments among a section of the public. What is not known is whether the 'tweeters' are representative of consumers in general or even of a brand's usual customer base.

Social media and brand awareness

Brand owners can engage directly with customers in social network sites and they can observe and listen to whatever is said about their brands. Social network sites can also provide platforms on which more traditional forms of advertising message can be conveyed, but this is probably not their most beneficial use as part of a company's marketing strategy. These sites are not an alternative to traditional media platforms, but according to some experts should be regarded as a new dimension in brand marketing that is likely to be most effective when brands use these environments and play to the strengths they have to offer (Brandt, 2008).

A New Orleans catering company called Naked Pizza engaged in a Twitter campaign about its pizzas and drew in thousands of followers within a few months. The company found that sales of its pizzas increased dramatically during the campaign and that most of its new customers made reference to the Twitter campaign when giving their reasons for buying from Naked Pizza (Baldwin, 2009).

Social media and brand identity

Social media can play an active role in enabling consumers to engage with brands, and in shaping brand identities. Product and service suppliers can use social media to engage directly with their customers. Conversations about brands can be triggered between suppliers and their customers and between customers and other customers. Companies can invite customers to contribute new product ideas, thoughts about existing brands and their promotional campaigns, join debates about brands, share experiences with brands, and also to get involved in wider competitions and campaigns that go beyond the brand. Companies' own employees can use social media as a channel through which to speak to their management and employers as well as to each other about brands. Other interested parties – including a company's suppliers, regulators, and other stakeholders – can also engage in public discussions about brands.

Social media campaigns have successfully been used to engage consumers with brands. Brand involvement has been manifest in terms of the volume of online activity linked to a brand as well as in terms of eventual sales. In the United States, Southwest Airlines included a revamped blog with podcasts, online videos, and other social media activities in a campaign designed to support a re-branding exercise. The blog was used both to enable the company to make announcements about its services and to invite comments from its customers. Visits to the site increased significantly during the campaign and visitors stayed longer and contributed more opinions about the quality of its aircraft and service (Berg, 2009).

Social media can fulfil a number of deep-seated needs for users, particularly at a social needs level. Thus, social media are sites where people can feel connected to others, and which provide environments that make people feel they have joined a community where they belong. Social media sites also provide sources of entertainment and information. Information is not just about users' personal lives. It can also be about products and services. Even then, it has a social dimension because these media offer environments in which users can converse with each other and generate evaluations of brands through open discussions and from these might arise recommendations.

One interesting case study of the way social network sites can be used by brands not simply to cultivate their own brand identity but also to bring consumers' personal identities closer to the brand is an online competition run by Skittles, the candy made by Mars. This brand is one of the most popular brands on Facebook. By May 2013, it had acquired over 25 million fans on the site (Tobin, 2013). Around half of its fan base is located in the United States (Nieburg, 2013). In 2013, the brand ran a 'Greatest Fan in the World' campaign in which users were invited to post the best pictures of themselves showing how much they loved the brand.

Social media and brand opinion

The importance of other personal recommendations in relation to decisions about product or service purchases is important because other people may be regarded as more credible sources than brand owners. One survey, conducted by eMarketer, found that when asked about the sources of product information to which consumers would attach confidence, top of the pile was 'a friend's recommendation (mentioned by 76%). In second place, was the respondent's previous experience with the company (68%). Less widely endorsed were recommendations that appeared in the mass media (22%), in an advertisement (15%), or on the company's website (8%) (Doyle, 2007).

Word-of-mouth recommendations are therefore extremely important to brands. In the social media world, there are many opportunities for brands to cultivate positive 'word-of-mouth' chatter about them. In this case, such chatter might be called 'electronic' word-of-mouth recommendations. This online chatter can be positive or negative in tone, and negative comments have proved to be especially potent in their impact upon a brand's reputation. The well-known American communications technology blogger, Jeff Jarvis, engaged in a critical campaign about computer distributor Dell, in which he complained about the quality of its after-sales service. His experience had been shared by many others, who also joined in an online rampage about Dell, causing its customer satisfaction rating to plummet (Williams, 2009). Despite this negative case study, other research has found that more generally, digital social media can provide very useful platforms for brand marketers to reach consumers and generate positive mindsets towards brands.

As we have already seen, disguised online marketing within social media environments can produce vociferous consumer backlash. At the same time, there is other research to show that social media users do not always take kindly to overt attempts to promote brands through explicit advertising in social media. While some consumers will tolerate this activity, most feel that it is out of place in their online social world. Looking to the future, as noted earlier in this chapter, most consumers who used social media were found to be willing to accept advertising on these sites if it meant that they continued to get free access (Millward Brown, 2011). It is clearly important for brand marketers to get the balance right and ensure that they research their targeted digital market-ing environment first before launching into a campaign which, handled inap-propriately, could carry significant reputational risks.

Social media have emerged as having the greatest brand impact potential with consumers who are known to be enthusiastic brand users (or fans of the brand) already. Millward Brown (2011) reported that in a study conducted for the World Federation of Advertisers, a sample of nearly 3,700 fans across 24 brand pages were asked about how the brand's social media presence had made them feel about the brand. More than four in ten (43%) said that the brand became more appealing to them after visiting its social media sites. Brand fans compared to consumers who were classified in this way held more positive opinions about brands, regarded their favourite brand as offering good value for money and were more likely to say they would buy it.

Consumers have also been found to use social media to find and share information about brands. Research conducted in the United States by Nielsen and NM Incite found that 60% of consumers who researched for products online found out about specific brands or retailers through social networking sites. These consumers were also highly likely to read online product reviews and create their own reviews. Most women consumers who were active online in this way said they told other people about products that they liked. For the majority of social media users, their most preferred sources for product and service information were the ratings given by other consumers (63%) and consumer reviews (62%) (Nielsen, 2011).

Further research has confirmed that in a social media environment, consumers show an enthusiastic willingness at times to put their brand 'likes' on public display, and that this has been evidenced both through social network users talking about their brand preferences but also allowing others who visit their pages to see which brands they follow online (Burst Media, 2012). Burst Media conducted an online survey with 1,453 American internet users aged 18 and over. Overall, this research found that around half (49%) of all the people they surveyed said they 'liked' or 'followed' brands on social media sites. This percentage was far higher among those aged 18 to 34 (58%) In saying that they 'liked' their favourite labels or retailers on their social network pages consumers publicly allowed others to whom they gave access to witness these preferences. Many of these online consumers also said they made a point of tracking down and following bloggers who write about brands, with many of these people (66%) saying that this input could be influential in guiding their purchase decisions. In keeping with the child theme of this book, this survey also found that many more women who were mothers (50%) than who were not mothers (38%) said they offered personal comments about brands on social media sites (Burst Media, 2012).

Although social media sites can offer brand marketers competitive tariffs for the placement of advertising, overzealous advertising can irritate consumers when it appears on their social media sites (Pettey, 2008). This can pose risks for brands because their unwanted presence could trigger a lot of negative online chatter about them that is damaging to their reputations (Slavin, 2009). Used skilfully, in ways that are more consistent with the discourses that characterise these sites, social networks could provide economical channels for reaching large numbers of consumers, unrestricted by geographical boundaries (Javitch, 2008).

The social element of online consumerism has emerged as being an integral aspect of the role played by social media in relation to cultivation of brand likes and dislikes. Research from the United States by ROI Research has shown that for most America social network users, social media are sources of price comparisons (59%), information about sales and special offers (56%), and an opportunity for them to provide feedback to a brand owner or retailer (53%) (eMarketer.com, 2011b).

Social media, branding, and purchase intentions

Personal recommendations of brands can often carry far more weight than the appeals of even the most creative advertising campaigns. This is because of the importance for consumers of the trust they can place in sources of persuasion. This interpersonal factor emerges during childhood during the period when children orient themselves more towards their peer groups than their immediate families. In one study of social media carried out by Knowledge Networks and MediaPost Communications among a sample of more than 2,200 American internet users aged 13 to 80, it was found that one in seven (15%) said they would be more inclined to buy brands promoted through social media (Scott-Thomas, 2010).

Further research by US market research firm, Chadwick Martin Bailey, involved an online survey of over 1,500 consumers and found that 60% of Facebook brand fans and 79% of Twitter brand followers said they would be more likely to recommend a brand to other consumers since becoming a fan or follower in a social media setting. More than half of Facebook brand fans (51%) and two-thirds of Twitter brand followers (67%) also stated that they would be more likely to buy the brand they liked in this way themselves since following it online in this way (Chadwick Martin Bailey, 2013).

Following a brand on social media sites can be influenced by whether a consumer is already a brand user. Many more brand users (68%) than non-brand users (48%) said they followed brands on Twitter for information about discounts and other premium offers. Many brand followers (50%) also stated that after following a company's tweets about a brand, they were more likely to purchase from that supplier (eMarketer.com, 2011a). Although the impact on purchase intentions has been found in a study by Ipsos OTX/Ipsos Global @dvisor to vary across different national markets, significant minorities of internet users around the world have indicated that seeing a brand 'liked' or 'followed' by a personal friend would make them want to buy that brand (eMarketer.com, 2012).

Finding new customers through social media

Brands can proactively take advantage of online social media for self-promotion purposes by establishing a presence on the major sites such as Bebo, Facebook, MySpace, and Twitter. Does this social media presence generate more business? The evidence that branding on social media can find new customers has so far been based on indirect indicators, or derives from specific case studies. In one analysis of social media users, only a small proportion (13%) claimed to keep up with brands via their social networks, but these brand followers did so to get information about the brands and about discounts or giveaways (Hollis, 2011).

In a case example of the potential of social media to contribute to growth of new business, the Meerkat puppet Aleksandr Orlov – featured at the centre of a long-running and award winning marketing campaign for a price comparison site, comparethemarket.com – had almost 800,000 followers on his Facebook page in 2011. While this presence represented part of a wider integrated marketing campaign that used offline and online media, much increased traffic was measured to the company's website, and quotes increased year on year by 45% (Hollis, 2011).

Cultivating customer loyalty through social media

Having found new customers, it is then essential for brands that they keep them. Social media can draw consumers' attention to brands, but whether they can hold this attention over time is another matter. One analysis by market research company Millward Brown examined the fan bases on Facebook of 12 well-known brands and other brands within their respective product categories. The brands in question included: Southwest (airline); Honda, VW (motor vehicles); McDonald's, Pizza Hut, Subway, KFC, Dunkin' Donuts, Krispy Kreme (fast food outlets); Starbucks (coffee shops); Coca-Cola and Red Bull (non-alcoholic sugared drinks) (Hollis, 2011).

Fan bases varied dramatically between brands and product types, with soft drinks attracting far more than airlines. There was also a major difference between brands and product types in levels of consumer satisfaction, with far more consumers saying they were satisfied with soft drinks brands than with airline brands. What also seems to be important is that there is far from a level playing field for brands that establish a social media presence in a setting such as Facebook. Their fan base and the sentiments they attract could well be linked with their popularity and reputation in the offline world. Whether online social media have a specific impact on customer loyalty, therefore, remains an open question. Given that brand-related sentiments posted on social media sites resonate with the opinions of customers following their experience with the brand in the offline world, the digital world could magnify either positive or negative sentiments, with the outcome depending upon where the brand stands in general with its customers.

Other research conducted around the world with social media site users has found that those who regularly follow the sites of specific brands (called 'fans') were much more likely than other social media users (non-fans) to rate followed brands as being superior to their competitor brands. Fans of a brand also spent four times as much on the brand they were a fan of compared with other brands within the same product category (Millward Brown, 2011).

In using social media, however, it is important that brands understand the kinds of expectations consumers have of them. Although most social media fans or followers of brands are incentivised by coupons, discounts, and offers of free products or services, they also seek more general information and advice about products and services and want to be involved in providing feedback about brands that is used, and even to contribute creatively to future brand development. Any failure on the part of brands to communicate enough or in appropriate ways with consumers can result in consumers taking a more critical stance towards the brand (Cone Communication, 2010).

Children, brands, and social media

We have already seen that the debate concerning how much children are aware of, understand, and react to brands promulgated by more traditional marketing activities has disputed whether consumer socialisation research has adopted appropriate psychological models of child development, or used such models effectively. The nature of young consumer engagement via online social media invokes a different approach to branding in which the consumer is 'empowered' to contribute to brand design and promotion. Does this approach disguise marketing activity to an extent that children are less likely to become aware of what is happening than they would in the case of more transparent branding activities – even when they have reached a more advanced stage of cognitive development?

One review of this issue in the UK, conducted by the Committee for Advertising Practice (CAP), acknowledged immediate concerns about the use of children as brand ambassadors in peer-to-peer marketing activities in encouraging them 'to think about their friendships in a commercial and manipulative way that would exacerbate bullying and peer pressure' (CAP, 2012, p. 3). Children recruited to this role would be incentivised to use their existing online social network links and to make new ones to champion brands. This review concluded that academic expert opinion about whether this practice caused harm to those taking part was divided. The fact is that experts would be restricted to extrapolation from consumer socialisation literature derived from research on children's engagement with and understanding of other forms of marketing usually carried out in the offline world. Even much of that literature has been challenged for its failure to integrate cognitive development models effectively within analyses of children's reactions to different brand promotion activities.

Outright rejection of social media promotions that used children in active ambassadorial roles was not deemed necessary nor indeed in everyone's best interest, given a belief that this approach could be effective in getting positive health messages across to children in 'public interest' social marketing campaigns. Where marketing applications had purely commercial objectives, however, there was a need to ensure that young consumers were not abused or put in harm's way. CAP's conclusions included an undertaking to tighten its own codes of practice for advertisers to ensure that marketing in the online social media world was made explicit to all concerned, that no techniques should be used that could cause any kind of harm to children, and that children should be encouraged to behave in socially responsible ways in these campaigns and never infer that not owning the promoted brand will render them socially inferior or less popular (CAP, 2012).

The concern raised about branding in social media, especially when it involves children, is that marketing professionals have switched to more subtle methods of brand promotion and consumer persuasion. The use of 'other consumers', whom target consumers might regard as people like themselves could mean that brand promotions will be received less sceptically than they would when presented via clearly identified marketing campaigns. The key vehicle in this context is word-of-mouth. While word-of-mouth recommendations spread gradually in the offline world because people must engage in direct one-to-one conversations, in the online world, a single person can speak to many at the same time.

Moreover, while in the offline world we can see who we are speaking to when we meet people face-to-face, in the online world we cannot see them and so messages can be posted by sources pretending to be someone they are not. While online consumer recommendations can be highly influential in our brand choices, we might usually presume that these messages have been produced by ordinary consumers like ourselves when in fact they were written and posted by brand manufacturers, suppliers, or their agents. Even adults, with fully-formed cognitive abilities, could be fooled into accrediting disguised sources with authenticity. What then does this mean for the way children might be taken in by these subtle marketing techniques?

Debates about whether children understand what branding is about or what advertising tries to do have called upon evidence that has not always told the same story. One complication is that children cannot be conceived as a single homogenous consumer category. While young people can be differentiated in terms of their demography and in terms of their personality characteristics in the same ways as adult consumers, there is a further important factor and that is their ability to understand the world around them and the influence that their cognitive abilities can have on their information processing styles. Children are not fully formed human beings and at the early stages of childhood they do not think about things in the same way as adults.

In the early parts of this book, we examined what has been discovered so far about the effects of child development on the way children engage with advertising and with brands. Scholars who specialise in the study of marketing have enthusiastically adopted a stage model of child development, largely derived from the work of Jean Piaget. This model has been challenged by developmental psychologists as failing to explain comprehensively the way children's cognitive abilities mature over time or to account for evidence that the timing of the emergence of some cognitive abilities can vary from one child to the next (Smith et al., 2003).

The movement away from a stage model of development, in which different levels of cognitive development were identified with specific age groups, to a process-oriented model that envisaged a more gradual, fluid, and progressive nature to cognitive maturity throughout childhood means that it becomes difficult to divide young consumers into distinctive categories, aligned with the popular (in marketing research) age demographic (Kunkel, 2010).

Top brands on social media

The biggest social media brand in the world is Facebook. On Facebook, many hundreds of commercial brands for a wide range of products and services have established a presence. The biggest brand on Facebook in terms of numbers of fans of its own branded activities and promotion is Facebook itself. One audit of fan traffic to brands by Ignite (Tobin, 2013) reported that by the end of May 2013, Facebook had accumulated 93.1 million fans. In second place was YouTube with 74.6 million fans. The remaining brands in the top 20 were made up of soft drinks manufacturers, music brands, fast food outlets, a coffee shop chain, supermarkets, technology companies linked to computer games, telecoms operators, and food manufacturers (i.e. for candy, cookies, and potato chips). The top ten brands all had well over 30 million fans. In rank order after Facebook and YouTube they were Coca-Cola (65.9m), MTV (45.2m), Disney (44.3m), Red Bull (38.2m), Converse (36.5m), Starbucks (34.6m), Oreo (33.4m), and Playstation (32.7m). Many of these brands have a strong following among pre-teenage and teenage children.

For consumers, there may be a number of reasons why they follow brands on Facebook. In a survey of Facebook users by UPS and comScore, six out of ten respondents (60%) gave as their reason for 'liking' a retailer/brand on the site was that it offered special promotions. Just under half (47%) said that they endorsed a brand because it had provided them with a specific incentive to do so. Other reasons given were that it was a good way of keeping up to date with a retailer (36%), that they were a fan already (32%), and that they liked to voice their opinions about brands (25%) (Smith, 2013).

Children's exposure to mainstream social networks

Online social networking has emerged as a highly popular pastime for children and represents a central communications hub for today's 'digital native' kids through which they run their social lives (Clarke, 2009). Many of these sites are used by children perfectly innocently to keep in touch with friends and to post news about themselves. Not only can these sites provide cheap and convenient channels through which kids can keep up to date with developments in their friends' lives, they also serve the useful purpose of enabling last-minute social arrangements to be made. Concerns arise when children reveal too much about who they are and how they live their lives and open up this information to people they don't know and have never met. Although social network sites allow users to impose personal controls over how much information they reveal to others, children often forget or simply don't bother to apply any privacy settings to their personal profiles.

Such is the prevalence of social network site use among children in developed countries today, many kids simply don't see what the fuss is about when their parents voice concerns about the personal information they post about themselves. Social media use is the norm among today's kids. In the United States, for instance, nearly three out of four children who used the internet were estimated to use online social networks (Lenhart et al., 2010). Across Europe, research among 9–16-year-olds found that around six in ten children in this age bracket reportedly used social network sites (Livingstone et al., 2011). There are many social network sites that have been developed explicitly for kids. The most widely used sites, however, are those developed primarily for use by adults. While parents can take some reassurance from those sites designed for children that impose strict controls over membership and the way the site can be used, in the case of sites developed for adult users, the same level of safeguards generally does not exist.

The mainstream social network sites such as Facebook have minimum age limits. The usual threshold is 13. We already know that by this age, children have usually developed cognitively and socially to a stage where they can think in the abstract, empathise with other people's perspectives, and understand the persuasive purpose of advertising. Any branding that occurs on the most popular sites that were developed originally for adults could therefore be defended on the grounds that children at less advanced stages of cognitive development ought not to be there anyway. In fact, there are many under-age users of the major social networks.

Sites such as Facebook have become extremely popular with children (Livingstone & Brake, 2010). American research reported that over half of young people aged 15–18 have a social network profile, dropping to over four in ten of those aged 11–14 and around one in five of those in the 8 to 10 years age bracket (Rideout, Foehr & Roberts, 2010). In Europe, a year or so later, four in ten youngsters aged 9–12 claimed to have a social network profile, as did three quarters (77%) of those aged 13–16 (Livingstone, Olafsson & Staksrud, 2011). In countries such as Brazil and India, it was estimated that around 12–13% of Facebook users were aged between 13 and 17 years (Socialbakers. com, 2011).

Reflecting its position with other age groups, the most popular social media site among children is Facebook. Across Europe, one in three children aged 9 to 16 years claimed to be registered on the site. Despite its lower age limit of 13, the same research recorded one in five children aged under 13 saying they had a Facebook profile (Livingstone et al., 2011). In some countries, such as Australia, the proportion of under-13s claiming to be on Facebook has been found to be considerably higher (Green et al., 2011). Brands have established a major presence on Facebook as well. How children respond to these promotional sites is unknown in terms of their abilities cognitively to identify their true purpose. Such research might be difficult to construct in the field in any case because children aged below 13 are not supposed to use this site.

6

Brands and advergames

Advergames are electronic games children are invited to play that contain a product or brand. The name comes from a conflation of 'advertisement' and 'game'. The games provide a platform for very subtle forms of advertising because brands are integrated with the entertainment content. Hence the entertainment aspects of the game are not simply a background on top of which the advertising is placed, but are used as features of the brand promotion. Earlier mention has been made that advergames, as a marketing platform, pre-date the internet. The earliest forms of advertising in game environments occurred in console based computer games in the 1980s. Brands were presented within games in stand-alone spots. Eventually, brands and games became more closely inter-twined as the brand became embedded in the game narrative as components of game play.

Two principal manifestations of this phenomenon appeared. With 'in-game' advertising, brands sought to purchase space or locations within pre-existing interactive games. Brands had to negotiate positions within the game with the game owner/producer. This was much like a conventional product placement arrangement between a brand and movie or television show (Nelson, Yaros & Keum, 2006). With 'advergames', electronic interactive games were established by commercial brands themselves and the brands did not simply appear as static on-screen promotions, but were integrated with the game itself, with branded objects being manipulated by players as an aspect of game play (Youn & Lee, 2004; Lee & Youn, 2008).

Initially, games were regarded as a secondary platform for brand promotion by marketers. This changed as expansion of broadband connections meant that brands had access to a wider community of consumers, including children, via the internet. At the same time, there was a massive expansion of online gaming (Burns, 2006). There were questions about its so-called 'stickiness' or ability to attract and then hold the attention of consumers. Advergame producers soon discovered a range of techniques which could ensure that not only were players attracted to them but that their attention to the brand was held effectively enough to ensure that valuable marketing impacts followed (Winkler & Buckner, 2006; Lee & Youn, 2008). Among the different features that are strategically deployed by marketers in advergames are: the degree of integration between brand and game; viral marketing invitations to players to send emails to friends to encourage them to play; allowing players to customise specific aspects of games to make them personally more relevant; providing scores and feedback on game performance and allowing players to compete against other players rather than just playing by themselves. Advergame producers were also sensitive to the probable level of involvement of consumers with the type of product represented by the featured brand or brands. With products that were conventionally regarded as high involvement (i.e. more expensive to buy, occasional rather than regular purchases) advergames provided opportunities for players to learn about the specific attributes and benefits of the featured brand whereas for low involvement products much more emphasis was placed on the entertainment qualities of the game (Lee & Youn, 2008).

A number of brands have enjoyed considerable success in attracting consumers to their games, particularly those that can be played online on corporate websites or sites operated by game producing agencies. Wrigley's Candystand site, for instance, attracted five million visitors per month. This site offers players a range of games including arcade games (mainly racing), card games, puzzle games, sports based games, and multi-player games. Some games give players the chance to win cash prizes if they finish among the top points scorers.

As marketing devices, advergames represent an extension of the longer established phenomenon of product placement (Winkler & Buckner, 2006; Lee & Faber, 2007). In this case, brands have been deliberately embedded in movies, television programmes, and video games and are featured as seamless aspects of the ongoing dramatic narrative. Hence, a fictional character may be depicted in a movie driving a certain brand of car, drinking a branded beer, or using a well-known computer brand. The presence of the commodity strikes no one as unusual because we might expect the character's behaviour to be perfectly natural.

Under the typical product placement arrangement, a brand owner will have paid the producers to ensure that the camera dwells long enough on a brand name or logo to ensure that it registers with the audience. Advergames tend to take this marketing idea a step further by building a game around the brand and inviting players to engage in on-screen interactivity in which a branded product is manipulated as an integral part of the game itself. While under other product placement scenarios, the video production is made by a third party; with advergames, the brand owners produce their own video narratives and have far greater control over the way in which the entertainment elements of the game are directed in relation to the promotion of the brand (Wise, Bolls, Kim et al., 2008).

One of the main concerns about this form of advertising – a concern shared with product placement in mainstream media – is that persuasion processes are not sufficiently differentiated from the entertainment attributes of the media environment (Shrum, 2004). This characteristic, of course, is the whole point because it is designed to counteract difficulties experienced with more standard forms of advertising associated with websites.

Advergames have proliferated during the second generation web era, which has been defined by the growth of increasingly sophisticated interactivity on the internet, enabling users to engage in diverse and more dynamic ways with online communications systems and information repositories. This interactivity has manifested itself in a wide variety of ways. The migration of stand-alone computer games onto the internet where they can be played by multitudes of players at once has encouraged technology developments that have created a large number of computer-generated or 'virtual' realities.

Many of these virtual worlds have adopted gaming formats or evolved out of simpler electronic games and allow players to enter pretend realities where they can wear different identities. The power of these computer-generated environments to invoke deep psychological involvement from players was not lost on marketing professionals who saw an opportunity to develop a new platform for promoting commercial brands.

These new branding environments had the added advantage of being very attractive to young consumers. They were already enthused adopters of computer games, and the advergame concept emerged as a potentially effective method for reaching this consumer demographic. Advergames tend to have short playing times and therefore do not demand a lot of a player's time. They also tend to be made for different technology platforms and can be played through virtually any device that can gain website access (Cauberghe & Pelsmacker, 2010). Furthermore, the disguised nature of brand advertising in this setting might also mean a lower risk of rejection by young consumers irritated by online advertising formats (banners and pop-ups) that were underpinned by more traditional (pre-digital era) ideas about advertising. The disguised nature of brand promotions in advergame settings is also one of the principal sources of public concern, in that it does not display the kinds of cues children learn to recognise in regular advertising as they learn about persuasion (Panic et al., 213; An et al., 2014)

Advergames have become an increasingly prominent aspect of online brand marketing. This approach has been enthusiastically adopted by brand market-ers that target children and has been particularly prevalent among food brands. The Kaiser Family Foundation investigated a sample of websites operated by food brands that were prominent advertisers on television and found that nearly three quarters of these sites (73%) had advergames. They discovered 546 games on 77 sites representing 107 brands. Virtually all these games (97%) contained a 'brand marker' such as an image of the food item or product pack, a brand character, or a brand logo. For two-thirds of the brands (64%), their associated brands incorporated the brand as an integral feature of the game, that is, something that was manipulated within game play or was a prize outcome of the game (Kaiser Family Foundation, 2006).

Better than click-through

This integration of brands with entertainment content has been tested as an alternative approach to more conventional forms of brand promotion such as banner advertising, which have been found to have questionable effectiveness in the online environment (Dahlen, Rasch & Rosengren, 2003). Banner advertising was supposed to work by encouraging consumers to click-through to more information behind the banner. Click-through rates have been consistently registered as very low and this has led questions to be asked about whether banner advertising is a useful way to influence purchase patterns (Chatterjee, Hoffman & Novak, 2002; Moe & Fader, 2003).

Other researchers have questioned whether click-through rates provide an effective measure of banner adverts' influences on consumers (Dreze & Hussher, 2003, Yoon & Lee, 2007). There is evidence that banner adverts can raise brand awareness, brand attitudes, and purchase intentions (Cho, Lee & Tharp, 2001). One of the problems for advertisements presented as stand-alone messages on websites is that with many sites, visitors browse for only short durations per page and little time is left over for attention to advertising messages (Filloux, 2009). In online games, visitors can often spend an average of half an hour playing and, in the case of advergames, experiencing brand exposure (Fattah & Paul, 2002).

Evidence has emerged that repeat exposure to banner advertisements on a single website or across many websites is related to increased likelihood of making a purchase of the advertised product over time, even though immediate click-through rates are low. However, even with this research, no data were collected about the types of consumers, whether specific types of advertising message were effective, or indeed about the potential effects of other variables such as price and other promotions (Manchanda, Dube, Goh & Chintagunta, 2006).

Industry research has emerged that has questioned the efficacy of banner advertising compared with more interactive forms of advertising on the internet. In this case, advertisements that had animated elements and interactive components proved to be twice as effective as banner advertisements (Dynamic Logic, 2002).

Griffith and Chen (2004) found that combining an interactive virtual experience with an online advertisement resulted in consumers developing higher regard for the brand, having a stronger intention to purchase, and perceiving less risk associated with making a purchase decision. Where interactive formats are used online to produce three-dimensional visual representations of products that consumers can twist and turn so as to examine in a virtual space from all angles, this gives rise to better product knowledge, more favourable brand attitudes, and a stronger intention to purchase (Li, Daugherty & Biocca, 2002).

Interactive brand advertising might generate greater emotional arousal in consumers that could also play a part in promoting a positive brand attitude. In following up this hypothesis, one study found that the greater the level of interactivity displayed by web advertisements the better appreciated they were by consumers (Raney, Arpan, Pashupati & Brill, 2003).

In an early theoretical analysis of advergames, three levels of brand integration were distinguished (Chen & Ringel, 2001). These were called: associative, illustrative, and demonstrative. With associative integration, the brand appears in an online game but as a background feature. It is important that it represents a good fit with the virtual setting, but beyond being visible to the consumer, there is no further interaction opportunity. Thus, a beer brand might be seen in a virtual bar, but does not form an active ingredient of any game narrative.

With illustrative integration, the brand is present in a virtual situation and is featured as an aspect of the on-screen action that is controlled by the consumer. The brand's presence, however, tends to be supportive or peripheral to the central narrative of the game. Thus, a virtual character that is controlled by the consumer/player might be seen eating a branded food item or choosing from among branded clothes before embarking on their principal quest in the game.

Finally, at the highest level of brand integration – demonstrative – a virtual character is seen with a branded item that represents a repeat feature of the game narrative. In the context of the virtual character competing in a sports competition, he or she might be seen wearing branded sportswear or using branded equipment that plays an integral part in the game narrative, and to which the character's success could be attributed. This taxonomy could represent a useful heuristic device for classifying brand representations in advergames and also generate distinct hypotheses about potential effects of different levels of brand-game integration for further analysis.

Empirical evidence has emerged that the level of integration between a brand and an advergame is critical to the impact of the brand. In particular, the degree to which a brand has congruity with the surrounding entertainment content in an advergame has been found to make a difference to its impact on consumers. As with product placement, if the surrounding entertainment content resonates meaningfully with an embedded brand, congruency between brand and game content can render the brand more memorable. Furthermore, if the game is enjoyed by players, this positive attitude towards the game can transfer onto the brand (De Pelsmacker, Geuens & Anckaert, 2002; Nelson, 2005).

A positive outcome for brand image is enhanced when a brand is thematically related to game content (Nelson, Keum & Yaros, 2004). In contrast, if the flow of the game is interrupted by the presence of the brand, the image of the brand can suffer (Hernandez, Chapa, Minor et al., 2004). Congruity of brand and game does not always work in the same direction and can vary across different types of outcome. This has been found in relation to the impact of brands embedded in advergames on memory for brand. In regard to explicit memory, in which consumers are tested for their memory of a brand in a game they have just played, brand–game congruency promotes more confidence in their perception that they did witness the brand within the game. When memory is measured in a more implicit way, without making reference to the occasion on which the brand was experienced, brand–game incongruity has been found to work better but only when the brand was peripheral rather than a central feature of the game (Peters & Leshner, 2013).

Examples of advergames

There are many hundreds of online games linked to brands. Advergames can be accessed via companies' own websites, on social media sites, and as downloadable content or applications for mobile phones and other portable technologies. Some companies produce their own games, while many sub-contract out the creative aspect of game production to specialist agencies. These agencies sometimes produce games that are accessed via the brand owners' websites or play host themselves to these games. Games are made for different platforms such as the internet, consoles, and mobile phones. Many early games were tied to specific platforms, but over time marketers have realised that they need to ensure they use advergames that can be played over a range of platforms.

Many of the biggest brands that are consumed by children have been the most active producers of electronic games as marketing devices. Perhaps the most active have been Cadbury/Kraft, Kellogg's, McDonald's, M&Ms, Red Bull and Walkers. These games allow for solo play although many have multiplayer aspects. Some games promote team play and are linked to social media sites, through which online communities are created, from which rival teams emerge. The games have end-goals and many are competitive, often involving some kind of racing activity.

Kellogg's Rice Krispie website has a multitude of games that are aimed at pre-school children. You can play games in which you move your virtual cereal bowl so that branded breakfast cereals fall into it rather than over the table or onto the floor, or where you help branded characters fire cereals into a bowl. In Kellogg's Olympics (www.behance.net/gallery/Advergame-Concept-Kelloggs-Olympics/4054403) kids aged between 6 and 14 are invited to control on-screen characters to play a series of games inspired by Olympics events for which premium product offer rewards are offered to winners. Kids are invited to play online against their friends. The games include: 'Triple Jump' with the three Kellogg's characters, Snap, Crackle, and Pop; 'High Jump' with Smacks the Frog; 'Basketball' with Tony the Tiger; 'Rope Climbing' with Coco the Monkey; and 'Relay Race' with Pops the Bee. Kellogg's Froot Loops (www.frootloops.com) is a site with a number of advergames. The home page of the site does state that 'this is advertising from Kellogg's'. Click on Adventures and you are taken through to a treasure hunt game.

From St Patrick's Days (17 March 2013) General Mills' Lucky Charms site gave kids a chance to download a game in which they can chase eight marsh-mallow charms hidden inside Lucky Charms packs. Prizes can be won for each charm that is captured and players are also entered into a draw for a large money prize, (www.blog.generalmills.com/2013/03/a-chase-for-the-charms).

McDonald's introduced its first video game in 1988, called 'Donald Land', which was released in Japan at first. In this game, your on-screen character collects hamburgers. If you can complete this task successfully, you can progress through a number of levels. There are barriers to task completion, and failure to clear these can result in a player being sent back to a lower level where they must start over. The game also features a character called the Hamburglar who can steal a player's burgers. McDonald's entered a partnership with Virgin Games to produce further video advergames. Further games were released in the early 1990s, including 'Mick and Mack: Global Gladiators' and 'McDonald's Treasure Land Adventure'. All these games were permeated with McDonald's branding.

Cadbury/Kraft launched 'Spots versus Stripes', an augmented reality game in which you smack ducks as fast as you can for points. The game can be downloaded to mobile devices and is activated via Cadbury chocolate bar wrapping. As we saw in the last chapter, this game was also connected to a social media site that further promoted the game among consumers, and created consumer-led brand promotional environments on Facebook, Twitter, and YouTube (Stratman, 2010).

M&M's launched numerous video games from the turn of the twenty-first century. These games have included 'The Lost Formula', 'Minis Madness', 'Shell Shocked', 'Kart Racing', 'Break Em', and 'Beach Party'. These games were characterised by having different levels of difficulty, and in one instance different types of simulated sports activities ('Beach Party'). The company launched a team game ('Red versus Green') titled after and featuring two of its six animated candy caricatures called 'Red' and 'Green' (the others being

'Blue', 'Orange', 'Yellow', and 'Miss Brown'). In this game, players can choose to control either 'Red' or 'Green' in playing a number of puzzle games against the other character.

Red Bull launched a game called 'Red Bull Soapbox Racer' (www.red bullsoapbox.com) where you can race cars which you can build for yourself and compete against other players or against 'the bull' in a variety of races and challenges. Walkers Crisps released a free racing game called 'Flavour Races', which can be downloaded onto mobile devices, based around a novelty flavoured snack collection. Cars were given the names of flavours of crisp such as Builder's Breakfast, Chilli and Chocolate, Fish and Chips, Cajun Squirrel, Crispy Duck & Hoi Sin, and Onion Bhaji.

Consumers' engagement with advergames

In advergames, consumers often engage in direct interaction with a brand as an integral part of playing the game (Arnold, 2004). One of the main reasons why advergames are attractive to brand marketers is that they can elicit significant levels of brand exposure. This is true of both adults and children, where keen game players have been observed to devote many hours at a time to playing games, and to play the same game over and over many dozens of times (Gunn, 2001; Nelson, Keum & Yaros, 2004). Playing games can also bring great enjoyment and this positive emotion can become associated with the brand (Hirschman & Thompson, 1997; Raney, 2004).

Players may devote extended periods of time to playing with online games, and their interactive nature means that they are psychologically absorbing. Where games are used as brand promotion vehicles, therefore, and the brands themselves are integral features of the game, there are opportunities not only for extended and repeat brand exposure but also for generating high levels of attention to brands (Ferrazzi & Benezra, 2001). As we will also see, because this type of exposure to the brand is interpreted by consumer-players as an entertainment experience rather than a marketing experience, the usual defences that literate consumers deploy against the persuasive tactics of marketing professionals are not invoked (Klein, 2003). Hence consumers' psychological defences may be down when playing advergames (Li, Daugherty & Biocca, 2003). Yet, advergame producers utilise a range of marketing techniques designed specifically and strategically to draw consumers' attention to the featured brand (Lee & Youn, 2008).

Game playing online is an established and widespread behaviour among children. In some developed countries, a majority of children claim to have played these kinds of games on the internet even before their teens (Mediamark Research & Intelligence, 2007; Lee, Choi, Quilliam & Cole, 2009; Purswani, 2010; Quilliam, Lee, Cole & Kim, 2011). One study found that between the ages of 2 and 17 years, around half of children sampled reported playing online games at least six hours a week, with many playing more than twice this amount (Lee et al., 2009).

These games have been very popular on websites for food brands targeted at children (Dahl, Eagle & Fernandez, 2006; Lee & Youn, 2008; Lee et al, 2009; Culp, Bell & Cassady, 2010; Cicchirillo & Lin, 2011). One analysis of food marketing on websites identified as being the most popular among American kids aged 8 to 11 years found that advergames used branded characters to draw young players' attention to brand names and logos (Alvy & Calvert, 2008).

Another US study found over 600 games on the websites of 47 companies that marketed food products mostly for children (Lee et al., 2009). These food-related games would depict brand names, products and their packaging, and other brand-related content as integral elements within games. A study by researchers from the Kaiser Family Foundation identified 540 advergames on food company websites, with some sites containing multiple games (Moore & Rideout, 2007). Another audit of food manufacturer websites, on this occasion for companies that had advertised on children's television networks, the Cartoon Network and Nickelodeon, confirmed that advergames were widely used as promotional platforms (on 81% of sites). A sample of 19 food company websites here yielded 247 different advergames (Culp et al., 2010).

As part of playing these games children tend to be repeatedly required to engage with branded elements (Weber, Story & Harnack, 2006; Moore & Rideout, 2007). In other words, young game players can manipulate branded foods that would often form the focus of the game's objectives (Lee et al., 2009). The entertaining and interactive nature of these games has meant that children not only enjoy playing them but will also actively seek them out (Wise et al., 2008). This technique has worked especially well for food manufacturers, with research showing that advergames can generate much increased child traffic to their websites (Harris, Speers, Schwartz & Brownell, 2012).

One further worrying aspect that has been identified with these games is that many of the food brands that are promoted in this format could be classed as products of low nutritional value (Lee et al., 2009). This has raised concerns about the wider health implications for children of their exposure to this attractive and disguised form of brand marketing (Moore & Rideout, 2007). One review of websites of 15 major food manufacturers found that few incorporated nutritional information in their advergames. Their games were focused on getting the brand name across to players and a few even had links to additional advertisements that players could download, as well as providing opportunities to play the game offline. A few games also include viral marketing components that encouraged players to persuade others to play (Dahl, Eagle & Baez, 2009).

One example of this type of game is 'Spaceship Adventure', produced by Chewitts and accessible via its website (www.chewitts.co.uk/adventure games). Players help a monster find Chewitts inside a spaceship by clicking on objects depicted in a cabin.

Research by Elizabeth Quilliam and her colleagues constructed a sample of websites from organisations that manufacturer, prepare, and sell food to children, including major domestic food products, fast foods, and restaurant chains (Quilliam et al., 2011). Among the top companies in the market in these categories, they discovered 420 online games offered by 31 companies in relation to 87 brands. Following further trails and filtering of sites, a sample of 166 games judged to be targeted at children was selected for detailed analysis. The vast majority (88%) of these games contained brand identifiers.

The researchers found differences between advergames offered by companies signed up to a voluntary code of practice created by the Children's Food and Beverage Advertising Initiative, and others who had not done this. These included the use of clearly signalled advertising breaks, provision of healthy lifestyle information, and the extent to which high nutritional value brands were featured. All these features were more likely to occur in the advergames of companies who observed this code of practice. Having said that, a significant proportion of the latter advergames did not differentiate advertising from the entertainment content of the games (39%) and most featured nutritionally poor value products (79%).

Impact of advergames

Despite their growing appeal to marketers, more evidence is needed about the extent to which advergame enjoyment translates into increased sales and market share and, on the part of regulators, that children recognise these games as advertisements. A lot of theoretical thinking about advergames has focused on their interactive nature and the way they integrate branding elements seamlessly with entertainment content. This can mean that children are not able immediately to identify the source of the advergame. It might also mean that they don't recognise the persuasive intent that lies behind the game in relation to the featured brand (Mallinckrodt & Mizerski, 2007; Moore & Rideout, 2007). Another aspect to these games is that their popularity among children means that children are often motivated to share the games with their friends and often tell friends about them with forwarded links via social media sites (Clarke & Svanaes, 2012).

There is research evidence that advergames can attract the attention of children. The presence of these games on food brand websites did not necessarily bring more pre-teenage or teenage children to those sites, but sites with advergames tended to have a far greater proportion of users who were children.

Hence, the overall popularity of food brand websites was determined by a range of factors, but by including advergames, more of its users were drawn from among the ranks of kids. What was even more interesting, children explored sites with advergames far more extensively and spent more time on them (Harris et al., 2012).

In advergames, the brand is integrated into the game and the child's attention is focused on playing the game while at the same time experiencing, often without consciously thinking about it, exposure to the brand (Moore, 2004). As such, advergames represent a form of disguised advertising. In terms of exposure to brand, these games can be effective because the child's attention can be captured for much longer than would occur with traditional forms of advertising (Mallinckrodt & Mizerski, 2007; Dahl, Eagle & Baez, 2009). These games are believed to give children an enjoyable experience and this in turn rubs off on the integrated brand (Hernandez & Chapa, 2010). If the game is seen as fun, this sentiment also comes to be associated with the brand (Bailey, Wise & Bolls, 2009). By drawing in the attention of children through an enjoyable play experience, during which repeat brand exposure occurs, a brand can be rendered more memorable (Hernandez & Chapa, 2010).

Advergames often present challenges to players, for which they receive scores. The games provide opportunities for players to develop greater skill at playing and are constructed in a way that allows players to see, through their scores, the extent to which they have improved with experience and practice. This kind of feedback was known to encourage game playing long before the online game era (Holbrook, Chestnut, Oliva & Greenleaf, 1984). It is known that contemporary computer game players seek a challenge, and that performance feedback indicates how well they are performing in comparison with other players, as well as motivating them to want to do better (Garris, Ahlers & Driskell, 2002; Sherry, Lucas, Greenberg & Lachlan, 2006). In this way, these games encourage players to return again and again, and in doing so, of course, they also experience repeat exposure to integrated branding.

There is an understandable concern about the disguised nature of the brand promotions in advergames. The promotion aspect is subtly combined with an activity that is perceived as entertainment content rather than as marketing content. This disguised aspect to the form of advertising that advergames represent can be seen as a critical factor that underpins their persuasive power. There is evidence, for example, that when consumers know they are confronted with a promotional message that has persuasive intent, they raise cognitive defences against it and resist its appeals (Friestad & Wright, 1994). This understanding has been referred to as 'persuasion knowledge', and the resistance to a message that is perceived as being designed to make us do something we might otherwise choose not to do is known as 'psychological reactance' (Brehm & Brehm, 1981).

From a commercial perspective, there are good reasons why advergames represent an attractive platform for advertisers and why the branding is integrated with games in a subtle fashion. Advertisers have learned that 'in your face' advertising does not go down well with consumers in the online world. The same principle applies to advergames (Davidson, 2008). The embedded nature of brand presence in advergames means that it is not so readily identified by consumers as 'advertising' or 'marketing' content (Hertz, 2002; Keaty, John & Henke, 2002; Yang & Wang, 2008; Yang, Raskos-Ewoldsen, Dinu & Arpan, 2006). This is a good thing from the perspective of avoiding consumer irritation. Nevertheless, this can also place children at particular risk of susceptibility to this form of brand promotion (Moore, 2004). If game players are not aware of the true nature of advergames their usual defences in the presence of known persuasive marketing will be lowered and they could be more accepting of the brands featured in these games (Raney et al., 2003).

Supporters of this form of advertising can point to evidence from adult players that the presence of known brands in interactive games is perceived to add to their realism and this is regarded as a positive element of these games (Faber, Lee & Nan, 2004; Nelson, Keum & Yaros, 2004). With children, however, their relative cognitive immaturity means that they are not able to make sophisticated judgements about advertising of any kind, and these more subtle forms of brand promotion will not be recognised for what they are.

We need to know about whether any failure to identify the advertising and branding purposes of these games places already vulnerable young children at further risk of influence. Advergames represent a form of subtle and disguised promotion that is manifest in the offline world as product placement (Turnipseed & Rask, 2007). In that product placements tend to form a part of multi-faceted marketing initiatives that are located across a number of promotional platforms, any specific impact of advergames would need to be separated out from other parts of these campaigns. Some initial evidence has emerged that children may not grasp the commercial intent of advergames (Nairn & Hang, 2012). This insight is unlikely to emerge until children have developed cognitive skills that enable them to understand the persuasive purposes of branding in these games. Given that they are often aimed at children who have not yet reached a sufficient level of development to comprehend these more complex concepts, then we must ask whether there is a risk that they will be misled by advergames.

Is there any evidence that advergames can exert an influence over children's food choices? One of the key concerns has been that advergames tend to be associated with 'unhealthy' food products. Do they therefore encourage children to eat products of poor nutritional value? Research conducted with young adult online gamers has reported that the presence of banner advertisements when playing a game can result in better subsequent recall and recognition of advertised brands, and also better 'implicit' memory of brands, as measured by word completion tests where the banner advertisements serves as a prime and can affect propensity to complete brand names correctly. High performing game players exhibited even stronger effects on their explicit and implicit brand memories (Yeu, Yoon, Taylor & Lee, 2013). Do these effects also appear among children?

One study of children playing with the Fruit Loops Toss game, produced by Kellogg's, found some evidence that this experience influenced young consumers' liking of the brand. Perhaps more significantly, however, in relation to the concerns of critics of these games, it also emerged that the children who played this game were not encouraged to believe that the brand was healthier than natural fruit (Mallinckrodt & Mizerski, 2007). This research was conducted in Australia and invited children aged 5 to 8 years to play with and give their reactions to this game. An average of one in four of these children had grasped that this game had been produced by Kellogg's but only after a lot of prompting. This ability increased with age and by age 8, around four in ten understood that Kellogg's was behind this game. After prompting, an average of just over one in two (54%) said they understood that the purpose of the game was to get them to buy the cereal, with two-thirds (66%) of 8-year-olds saying they knew this (Mallinckrodt & Mizerski, 2007).

It has been further observed that this particular game had a high production quality but a poor narrative structure. This meant that although it was entertaining at a superficial level for the kids playing it, there was no lasting psychological absorption. For this reason, while it may have enhanced brand recognition, it did not generate brand loyalty (Purswani, 2010).

Research conducted among teenagers in Mexico found that brand recognition of snack product brands that had been featured in advergames could be enhanced by playing these games. An important mediating factor here was how much game playing also created greater liking of the brand and of the game. If a game was enjoyed and produced a favourable attitude towards the featured brand, that brand was better recognised and was also more likely later on to be selected over other brands when the teenage participants were given the opportunity to show their brand preferences (Hernandez & Chapa, 2010).

Evidence has also emerged that advergames can shape children's brand attitudes, although their effectiveness in relation to how well a brand is subsequently recalled can depend upon how involved consumers are with the brand in question. Furthermore, the effects on brand attitude may not always be in the direction desired. In one experimental study young consumers were invited to play an online game either two or four times. Repeat playing had little effect on brand recall, but did affect attitudes to the brand, but in a negative direction. This negative effect on brand attitude was more pronounced for high than for low involvement products (Cauberghe & Pelsmacker, 2010).

The significance of high versus low consumer involvement in products has been known for a long time. 'Involvement' in this context really means how much consumers are likely to give careful thought to making specific purchases. Such decision making is often linked to the price of the product. Expensive items, such as major household purchases (e.g. electrical goods, furniture, etc) and motor vehicles, along with premium branded purchases (e.g. designer clothes and accessories, cosmetics, jewellery, etc) will usually be given more thought because the financial outlay is considerable. Everyday items such as the regular food shopping, household cleaning products, and other so-called 'fast-moving consumer goods' are given less thought, and often consumers stick with tried-and-tested brands which are bought habitually. The degree of 'involvement' with the product can also translate into the amount of cognitive effort invested in evaluating advertising messages about brands.

One important theory that was developed to explain this phenomenon is the 'elaboration likelihood model' which posited that consumers' attitudes towards brands could be shaped by their exposure to advertisements, but that the effectiveness of advertising messages would depend upon the approach they took to promoting specific products. If the product represents a high involvement item, consumers are likely to seek specific product-related information that confirms why a specific variant or brand should be bought above others. Such information would often refer to product-related attributes, such as its functionality, reliability, and value for money. This approach would work best for high-status and high-value commodities incurring significant financial outlay. For everyday products, in contrast, consumers' decisions would involve less detailed weighing up of specific features, and these types of brands could be more effectively promoted by cosmetically appealing advertisements that were successful at grabbing consumers' attention through the production techniques they used (see Petty & Cacioppo, 1981, 1986).

With high involvement products, consumers seek credible, relevant, and sufficiently detailed arguments to persuade them to buy a specific brand. They also need sufficient opportunity to apprehend these arguments so that they can weight them up at their leisure. This means that such brand promotions may need to be repeated a few times to get all the relevant information across to consumers (Peracchio & Meyers–Levy, 1997). With repetition of advertisements, however, there is always a risk of 'wear out' whereby consumers get bored with seeing the same message over and over. There is also a risk, where arguments that are made in support of a brand are weak, that consumers will more readily recognise brand flaws and turn against it (Cacioppo & Petty, 1989).

The elaboration likelihood model applies not only to adult consumers but is applicable to child consumers. It is also a theory that has been tested and supported across a variety of advertising media. It remains to be seen whether excessive engagement of young consumers in advergames produces wear out effects for many brands. It may be an advantage that for many children, advergames are not perceived as advertisements. Their interactivity and entertainment value are key features that draw young consumers to them. Nevertheless, brand names receive repeat exposure in advergames and this can affect the nature of the psychological impact of the brand name which could change over time.

Jennifer Harris of the Rudd Centre for Food Policy and Obesity at Yale University and her colleagues reported an experimental study with boys and girls aged between 7 and 12 years. They divided these children into three groups, and in each group the children played with two advergames. In one group, the kids played with two advergames that represented healthy fruit and vegetable products; in a second group, they played two advergames for sweet snack foods (Pop-Tarts and Oreo Cookies); while the third group played advergames for non-food products.

The children in all groups were first put into a room on their own where they were seated in front of a computer screen that provided the interface with advergames. They were then each told that they could play with two games for as long as they liked but that they had to play with each game at least once. After 12 minutes, the researcher entered the room again and told the child to stop playing. Each child was then taken into a second room for a 'snack break' where they were confronted with a number of servings of sugary snacks, potato chips, cookies, fruit snacks, and fresh fruit and vegetables (carrots and grapes). They were told they could eat as much as they wanted of any of the snacks and were left for five more minutes while the researcher left them to it. The researcher then returned to the snack room and asked the child to compete a questionnaire saying how much they enjoyed each food and how healthy they thought it was. The children were allowed to continue snacking while completing the questionnaire.

A number of short-term effects on children's food choices were observed that were associated with the type of advergame they played. Those children that played the advergames for healthy foods consumed 50% more carrots and grapes than did children who played the advergames representing unhealthy foods. Children who played advergames not connected to food products fell in between the other two groups in terms of the amount of healthy food they consumed. Children who consumed the greatest amount of snack food classified as 'unhealthy' were those who played advergames for foods of this type.

Harris and her colleagues collected additional data through the children's parents about the regularity with which their kids played advergames at home. The results from this survey confirmed the data from the experiment. Children who reportedly had a history of playing advergames linked to unhealthy foods were more likely to consume these snacks foods and were less likely to consume healthy foods compared to children who played more often with advergames for healthy foods.

The children generally rated carrots and grapes as healthy foods and potato chips and cookies as unhealthy. Hence they knew the differences between these foods in terms of their nutritional value. Some foods that were made available were rated as 'moderately healthy' by the children (and also by the researchers). It is also interesting that the amount of consumption of these foods in the snack room was influenced by the type of advergames played beforehand. The researchers concluded therefore that advergames can influence children's food choices and that they probably do this by priming the consumption of specific foods types that are featured in the games. Thus, games that feature fresh fruit and vegetable products 'may trigger 'reminders' to eat fruits and vegetables as well as 'permission' to eat the unquestionably unhealthy snacks, but not increase generalized snacking behaviours' (Harris et al., 2012, p. 62).

Use of avatars

It is apparent that with advergames, the level of enjoyment produced by playing the game is an important factor, not only in terms of the popularity of the game but also in relation to how effective it proves to be as a vehicle for promoting a brand. One other distinctive and increasingly prevalent feature of online gaming worlds is the use of avatars.

The presence of avatars can make a difference to children's experience with online games, including advergames, Research carried out with 10- to 12-year-olds found not only that avatars can trigger stronger emotional reactions while playing, but also that enabling children to create their own avatars as opposed to being assigned off-the-shelf figures enhanced the experience even further. Customisation of avatars led children to register stronger psychophysiological responses during game play and to verbalise more positive opinions about the game and the way it made them feel afterwards (Bailey, Wise & Bolls, 2009).

Children's understanding as mediation of advergame effects

Researchers have used a number of methodologies to explore children's understanding of advergames. Research into this type of marketing has been guided by theories and methods developed and applied more generally to try to understand children's socialisation as consumers. Although some research has relied upon the ability of children or their parents to recall information about their use of advergames, many studies have invited children to play with these games and then questioned them afterwards about the experience.

In some instances, researchers have engaged children in open-ended conversations about advergames and brands. In other cases, children have been tested beforehand on their perceptions of brands and then tested again after playing with advergames that featured specific brands. The aim of these 'experiments' is to find out whether the experience of brand-centred advergames can change children's impressions of brands or even simply their ability to recognise or remember a particular brand. Some experiments have also measured behavioural responses by inviting children to choose between different brands in a product range to find out whether they are more likely to choose a brand that was featured in an advergame they had just played.

Collectively, the research that has accumulated so far has confirmed that children are familiar with advergames, although their understanding of the true purpose of these games is not always clearly articulated. Many commentators and reviewers of the evidence have been critical of advergames and have raised concerns that they place children at a disadvantage by disguising their true purpose from already vulnerable consumers (Dahl, Eagle & Baez, 2009; Nairn & Hang, 2012).

In-depth interviews with children aged 8 to 15 were used to explore children's perceptions of advergames, with games for a main release movie (*Chicken Little*) and a well-known deodorant (Sure) being used as exemplars to prompt discussion. By their mid-teens, a view emerged among some of these participants that you can be tricked into playing an advertisement by embedding it into a game format (Fielder, Gardner, Nairn & Pitt, 2007).

Further evidence from the UK has indicated that advergames represent quite a distinct form of advertising from other types. Much of the past research on children's developing abilities to recognise advertising has derived from studies of televised advertising. In a direct comparison of children's comprehension of advertising in different media environments, understanding of the persuasive commercial intent of brand promotions was higher for television advertisements and for programme sponsorship than for advergames. The only forms of brand promotion that scored significantly lower than advergames were in-game advertising and product placement in films (Owen, Lewis, Auty & Buijzen, 2012).

In an experimental study carried out in the United States, children aged between 8 and 11 years were assigned to two conditions (An & Stern, 2011). Both groups played with an advergame for Honey Comb breakfast cereal called 'Be A Popstar' which was located on the Postopia website (www. postopia.com) operated by Kraft. The two groups were differentiated by the nature of the brand advertising in the game. For one group the brand was contained within an advertising break in the game (as well as being a feature of the game itself), while for the other group, they played the game without the advertising break. The idea here was that by separating off from the game the brand name with an advertising break, it would draw children's attention to the marketing and persuasion purpose of the game.

Out of the sample of 112 children in this study, only one child spontaneously identified the purpose of the game as being to sell breakfast cereal. Many (40%) though that the game's real purpose was to teach you how to become a pop star, while many others (35%) thought it was simply a game to be played for fun. Only one in ten (10%) made reference to the advertising break, and even then it did not prompt them to identify the persuasive purpose of the game.

We saw earlier that consumers' level of involvement with a product can mediate the amount of attention they pay to advertising and the type of information they need to make up their minds about brands. A further variable that seems to underpin this process is whether they believe that what they are experiencing represents an attempt to persuade them to do something. The concept of persuasion knowledge has been developed to explain the importance of this kind of brand and advertising literacy to consumers.

Research with children has found that with advertising that occurs on television, having developed a degree of advertising literacy grounded in the idea that adverts are designed to persuade you to like and buy brands can influence the extent to which young consumers accept and are persuaded by televised advertising. In relation to advergames, however, persuasion knowledge is less important and how much a game is liked emerged as a more significant predictor of brand attitudes. If further cues are added to an advergame to signal the fact that it is being used to promote a brand, this can reduce the effect of the game on attitudes to the brand – although the game itself may still be enjoyed (Panic et al., 2013).

Other evidence has emerged from work done with 9- to 12-year-olds in The Netherlands that children in this age bracket demonstrate a growing awareness of brand advertising in online social games and its purpose. The children tended not to exhibit any significant level of concern about the presence of brands in these games. The influence of brand promotions in online games was enhanced when children were less critical of them and also if they perceived that peer groups rated specific brands highly. Relatively inexperienced game players were found to be more susceptible to brand influences than more regular players (Rozendaal, Slot, van Reijmersdal & Buijzen, 2013).

In a review of research from around the world carried out for the Family and Parenting Institute in the UK, Professor Agnes Nairn and her colleague Dr Haiming Hang concluded that children have difficulty recognising advergames as advertisements. This difficulty is experienced not simply by very young children but also by youngsters in their mid-teens who have reached levels of cognitive maturity similar to those of adult consumers. Advergames can shape children's behaviour without them being aware of it. This raises important ethical questions for advertisers and for advertising regulators. There are additional health-related concerns because many of the offending brands are for food products of dubious nutritional value (Nairn & Hang, 2012).

Towards more effective advergame marketing

Advergaming has been conceived as a form of product placement. However, a further debate has been enjoined that considers whether it might also be regarded as having some of the attributes of regular advertising. Both spot advertising and product placement have been found to affect brand awareness, which is often measured through tests of consumers' brand recall (Gupta & Lord, 1998; d'Astous & Chartier, 2000; Russell, 2002; Montgomery & Unnava, 2007).

In a very simple model of promoting brand awareness, it was assumed that mere exposure repeatedly over time could eventually cause a brand to become imprinted on the minds of consumers. This presumes that advertising messages only need to keep showing off the brand name and any related symbolism to have impact on consumers. This simplistic idea does not entertain the perception that the message is ineffective nor matter how often it is shown to people. In an increasingly crowded marketplace, brands fight for supremacy in terms of consumer awareness and must find ways of standing out. Brands must stand out not only at the point of reception when consumers are exposed to them; they must also be readily available for future use once stored in memory. Ensuring not only that a brand stands out in the marketplace but that it can also be readily retrieved from memory amidst the many others can be enhanced by cultivating brand distinctiveness and also by creating more than one cognitive route to brand recall

One strategy that can be adopted is to present the brand to consumers in different ways so that brand information is variably stored in memory. Specific concepts, such as brands, are believed to be organised in a networked fashion in memory according to different categories. Thus, specific brands of soaps might be stored as cleaning products. These might in turn be divided between personal cleaning products (e.g. hand wash, hair shampoos, shower gel) and household cleaning products (e.g. dish washer tablets, carpet cleaner, washing up liquid). Within these sub-categories are various branded products that are marketed with their distinctive qualities that derive from advertising campaigns, product placement links, celebrity endorsements, and advergames. By placing brands in different promotional settings and associating them with varied experiences for consumers, specific attributes become attached to them that provide additional routes to retrieval from memory in addition to those linked to their generic conceptual category (Meyers-Levy, 1989).

What also happens is that consumers may grow accustomed to experiencing brands being linked to specific settings, characterisations, and narratives, and expect specific brands to be presented in particular ways. The generic category to which a brand belongs may also determine a set of norms concerning the ways consumers believe that brand should be presented to them. Violation of those norms may mean that the brand attracts greater attention for a time, but the outcome is that consumers' attitudes towards the brand change in a negative way because it is seen to have abandoned the norms it was expected to adhere to (Meyers-Levy & Tybout, 1989; Sujan & Bettman, 1989).

When new products come to market, consumers need to be able to position them within an appropriate product category in order to understand the functions that the new product can perform. This information in turn helps consumers to decide whether this product has any relevance for their needs as well as whether it fits any related social image of themselves they believe it could reinforce. Associating a new product, such as a digital camera, with an older version of that product type (e.g. a standard film camera) can help consumers understand what type of product is being introduced to market (Moreau, Markman & Lehman, 2001).

Having presented a new product as a specific product type, consumers may then expect to see that product presented in an appropriate way in marketing campaigns. By featuring the product in a narrative context that is deemed relevant to it, given its intrinsic functions and uses, consumers can draw upon established social scripts internalised in their permanent memory stores to help them position the product (and brand) still further. This internal positioning of brands creates further access routes for retrieval of the brand and sets up a wider array of potential external triggers that can serve as reminders of the brand (Smith & Houston, 1985).

Problems can arise for brands that utilise many different associated attributes when other brands use overlapping attributes. While variable encoding of brands through association with many different attributes can potentially open up many different routes to memory, it also exposes a brand to the possibility that some of its linked attributes will be used by other brands. When this happens, it can cause confusion among consumers and even result in memory for one brand interfering with memory for another. This can happen not just when two brands are from the same product category – and therefore in direct competition for the same consumers – but also when they are from two different product categories and thus not competing within the same marketplaces. Examples of this 'competitive interference' effect might be when two brands use the same celebrity endorser or when they are placed within similar physical settings in advertisements (Kumar, 2000; Kumar & Krishnan, 2004).

Another important aspect of marketing and brand awareness among consumers is that advertisements can trigger a change of belief or attitude about a brand from one that has developed through direct experience. Hence, consumers can develop memories about brands that include knowledge about the functions and uses of the brand, attitudes about the quality of the brand compared to others, and so on. These memories can derive from direct experience of the brand, but these memories could change as a function of exposure to an advertising campaign for the brand. Such campaigning can resonate with and confirm the memories of actual brand experience, or they can cause those memories to change through a process that psychologists have called 'reconstructive memory' (Schachter, Norman & Koustaal, 1998; Koriat, Goldsmith & Pansky, 2000; Braun-La Tour & La Tour, 2004, 2005).

The importance of these cognitive processing factors is that in the context of using advergames for brand promotion, it is important to ensure that the brands are embedded within a setting and narrative framework that is deemed to be relevant to the featured brand in consumers' minds. There must be a degree of congruency between the meaning of the brand for consumers and the nature of the game that is being played around it.

Research has shown that thematic congruity between a brand and surrounding content in a movie or television programme can shape consumers' subsequent thoughts and feelings about the brand in product placement settings (Russell, 2002). The same principle is expected to apply with brand placements in online games (Lee & Faber, 2007). In the case where a number of distinct brands were placed in an online car racing game, those brands that exhibited a degree of semantic fit with the game were subsequently the ones best remembered by players (Lee & Faber, 2007).

In comparisons of consumers' memories for brands featured in video games and ones featured in advergames, it is the branded advergames that produce the best results (Chaney, Lin & Chaney, 2004; Winkler & Buckner, 2006). One explanation proposed for this difference is that with advergames, brands are more closely integrated with the game around them. This is because the game was developed for the explicit purpose of promoting brand awareness. While the placement of brands in standard video games is also intended to promote brand awareness, the brand owners did not control the production of the game and may not therefore be able to achieve the same degree of brand-entertainment content congruence as they can with home-made online games. We know from other research with more standard forms of internet advertising, that placement of brands on websites where the site content has greater thematic relevance to the product type represented by the brand, can enhance positive consumer attitudes towards the brand and even raise purchase intentions (Shamdasani, Stanaland & Tan, 2001).

Kevin Wise, of the Missouri School of Journalism, and his colleagues constructed a study of advergames in which consumers were recruited to play with games designed to promote the brand of a travel company called Orbitz (Wise et al., 2008). Participants were recruited from a small mid-west town in the United States and divided randomly into conditions in which some played with thematically relevant advergames and others played with thematically non-relevant advergames. The relevant advergames had travel and holiday themes. One game, called 'Find Your Hotel', required players to negotiate their way through a number of obstacles to find a hotel. Another game, called 'Gondoliero' comprised a series of gondola races. The games with low thematic relevance to the brand were 'Paper Football' and 'Sink the Putt'. The first game was based on an offline table football game in which the player must flick a folded paper triangle through a set of goalposts. The other game was a computerised miniature golf game.

Participants completed a pre-test of their attitudes towards travel brands that included the featured brand. They then took part in an unrelated experiment for 30 minutes before being invited to play either with two games of high thematic relevance or two games of low thematic relevance. After five minutes of playing with the games, they completed further paper-and-pencil measures in which they evaluated the games and provided brand attitudes again. Overall, attitude toward the game predicted attitude toward the brand. The more the participants said they liked the game, the more their attitude towards the travel brand changed in a positive direction. When separate analyses were carried out on participants who played with the brand relevant games and those who played with the non-relevant games, greater liking for the games being played predicted improved brand attitudes only among those in the brand relevant condition. The results showed that enjoyment of an advergame is important to the attitudes consumers develop about featured brands. It also confirmed that the thematic relevance of a game to the brand is also a critical factor in this context.

In an interview about the research, Kevin Wise remarked:

> While games that related to the brand were not inherently more enjoyable than unrelated games, the transfer of enjoyment from the game to a positive attitude toward the brand was stronger when the game and brand were thematically related. Game enjoyment led to positive attitude toward the brand when a high thematic connection existed between the game and the brand. This was not the case when the participants played games with a low thematic connection. (News Bureau, University of Missouri, 2008).

Turning advergames around – social and health benefits

There has been a lot of criticism of advergames, not simply because they represent a disguised form of marketing, but also in relation to the product fields in which they have been applied. One of the biggest child markets is for foodstuffs. The types of foods that are most active in terms of their marketing are products deemed as having poor nutritional value and associated with various health problems among young people. One of the most significant social problems stemming from consumption of unhealthy foods is the prevalence of obesity in childhood. This condition is linked in turn with a wide range of other short-term and long-term health problems. Yet, if marketing techniques such as advergames can be used with some effect to promote unhealthy foods, there is nothing to stop them being used to promote consumption of healthy foods. There is no reason to believe either that advergames, as marketing devices, can only be effective when they are used with commercial products believed to cause harm to consumers.

The power of advergames is grounded in their production qualities and in particular in the way they convert brands into attractive on-screen characterisations or focal points of challenging or intriguing narratives with which children can relate and with which they want to play. These production techniques can be applied to games that promote healthful or socially positive behaviours. A study by Jennifer Harris and her co-workers from Yale University, already reviewed earlier in the book, found that when children play advergames which feature healthy fruit and vegetable brands, they are encouraged to choose these types of foods over sugary snack foods and do so, at least when given an opportunity to choose between such foods within minutes of playing this type of game (Harris et al., 2012).

What seems to be important is that the game itself must be pitched at a level that children can understand and relate to and that it uses play techniques that draw in the active attention of kids. Thus, a game that preaches nutritional values to children may be less successful than one that gets kids to play with fruits and vegetables in an interactive and goal directed fashion (Baranowski, Baranowski, Thompson et al., 2011). Other attempts at developing video games with health-related messages have also had some success in promoting healthier consumer behaviour among children (Lu, Baranowski, Cullen et al., 2010).

The correct pitching of advergames is crucial. We know already that the cognitive abilities of children mature gradually over time, and at any one point before they reach full cognitive maturity they may be limited in their capacity to comprehend particular types of promotional message. These cognitive limitations can mean an inability to process specific types of messages or a tendency to focus their attention on particular aspects of an advertisement, such as its colours, characterisations, and other production effects rather than on the central message about the brand (Moore & Rideout, 2007; Cicchirillo & Lin, 2011).

The commercial imperative

As the game industry has grown to become a premier entertainment platform that captures vast numbers of players, many of whom devote substantial amounts of time to game playing, it is understandable that the marketing world has identified games as potentially important and effective brand promotion environments. Large corporations behind the big commercial commodity and service brands have not simply explored opportunities to place their brands within existing games, but have also created their own online games in which the game narrative is built around a specific brand. These advergames have the appearance of regular electronic games and provide players with entertainment but they also have a specific commercial agenda and that is the promotion of the featured brand.

Whether advergames are effective has been widely debated and investigated. Market research has shown that adult players get a lot of enjoyment from these games and that the presence of brand names and symbols – even when contained within explicitly identified advertisements – does not detract from their entertainment value. One study found that most players (61%) exhibited more favourable opinions about featured brands after playing these games than they had beforehand. For a significant minority of players (44%), brand recall also improved after playing the game, compared with pre-game exposure (Brightman, 2008).

As advergames become more numerous, brand owners will also need to become more creative in the games they produce. Consumers will expect advergames, as with all other electronic games, to evolve with better production quality, more involving narratives and greater challenges for players (Parrotta & George, 2008). One question that arises from such developments is whether this will make advergames look less like advertising than they already do. For experienced consumer gamers who are familiar with these games, this might not be a problem. For inexperienced consumers, such as children, who will undoubtedly be enticed to play these games even more if the games become more challenging (and hence enjoyable), this could be a serious issue. Moreover, the child market is a target of growing significance for advergame marketers.

In-depth interviews with communications professionals have confirmed that brand marketing experts place more and more value on techniques such as advergames to reach consumers – and especially young consumers. The major objective of these games is to raise brand awareness and to encourage players to return to a game time after time. An advergame must therefore be brightly packaged, contain interesting characters and objects and a challenging competitive narrative that takes time to master but allows players to enjoy success through repeat play. There must be tangible signs of success in terms of becoming better as a player by using scoring systems that tell players how well they are performing and enabling them to track how their skills at playing the game have improved. All these different elements must be in place for any successful electronic game and in the case of the advergame they must be integrated with a target brand (King, 2012).

For the agencies behind advergames, success can be measured in terms of the numbers of consumers who sign up to the game, the extent to which the game attracts visitors to a website, the amount of time players devote to the game, and whether the advergame triggers viral marketing whereby players communicate to others about the game and attract more players to it. In the future, these games are expected to evolve to become more sophisticated in production and narrative terms and to provide more complex, interactive scenarios for consumers to engage with brands. These games must never lose sight of their final objective, however, and that is to promote the brand and ultimately to contribute to its position in the market. Advergames will therefore need to develop techniques to enable consumers to translate their brand perceptions in the online world to their perceptions and eventually their behaviour in the offline world (King, 2012).

The use of advergames to reach young consumers is understandable given their popularity with children of different ages. Video games have established a worldwide presence and are known to engage children more deeply than most other forms of advertising. The games' interactive nature gives children game players control over events on screen, and the integration of brands with game narratives and objectives encourages a deeper level of processing of the featured brand in each case. These games can evoke strong emotional connections with brands, which stem from the enjoyment and other emotions experienced with the game itself, but which can transfer onto the brand itself (Montgomery & Chester, 2011). Through their immersion in a game, children lose sight of the fact that it is a brand promotion and regard the brand as an aspect of the game rather than as a stand-alone item they are expected to like. This experience can produce a change of attitude towards the brand without the young consumer realising it. This new psychological disposition might then in turn encourage future brand purchase.

7

Brands and adverworlds

We have seen that social media sites have expanded exponentially during the twenty-first century, and the most popular sites, such as Bebo, Facebook, MySpace, Twitter, and others, now have billions of subscribers. On these sites, users can post biographical and up-to-date information about developments in their lives, as well as images of themselves, their family and friends, and many other things. This content can be published to the entire world or reserved for selected visitors. These sites can also give them one-to-one communications channels for more private correspondence. In addition, growing numbers of websites have emerged that contain electronic games of varying degrees of complexity. Many of these games have provided sites of integrated branding – in effect a form of interactive product placement. They have also become highly popular with young consumers who turn to them for entertainment, but at the same time receive a significant dose of brand exposure.

On a smaller scale, but one that is expanding all the time, there has been a parallel development of so-called 'virtual worlds'. These formats combine many of the elements of social media sites and online games. Virtual worlds provide three-dimensional environments in the two dimensional space of a computer screen in which the user is represented as an avatar. An avatar is a cartoon-like character that can take on human or animal form and represents the virtual world presence of the user. Through their avatars, 'players' or 'users' can communicate and engage with others in the virtual environment. They can play games against other players or simply exchange pleasantries with them. They can also establish new friendships and sometimes even romantic relationships that may remain 'virtual' and confined to the virtual world or sometimes venture into the offline or 'real' world.

In the more advanced online worlds, users have a wide range of choices of avatar forms and they can dress their avatar from extensive wardrobes. They can decide on the gender and ethnicity of the avatar and give it mannerisms. They can also speak through the avatar (in text form) to other users' avatars. Virtual worlds can be independently produced but include product placements or they can be branded worlds that offer a virtual space in which occupants engage from time to time with branded items. Virtual worlds have not yet captured the user populations of the most used social media sites, but they are collectively growing rapidly, especially among children. Hence they present an opportunity to brand marketers by offering a new platform to reach young consumers, and a challenge to researchers to find out what impact these branded environments might have on the consumer socialisation of children, and more acutely on their brand choices.

Marketing and virtual worlds

There are two broad types of online world. The most widely used are those that have arisen out of combat games. The best known include EverQuest, Lineage, and World of Warcraft. These games have attracted many millions of players from all over the world. The second type of online world consists of online social communities that can contain game elements but which are primarily focused on creating social networks. There are versions of these virtual worlds that have been developed for adult users and for child users. The most widely adopted adult virtual worlds are Entropia Universe and Second Life, and the most popular virtual worlds for teenagers are Habbo Hotel, Sims Online, and There. In all these games, users are represented on sites as avatars and are also able to obtain their own personal spaces which they can develop as they see fit. While the combat game worlds offer fantasy settings of the kind normally associated with science fiction scenarios, the social virtual worlds adopt a more realistic, everyday environment (Hemp, 2006, O'Brien, 2012; Seifert, 2012).

Users of these worlds who seek access to the full range of features and services must pay subscription charges, but the companies that operate these worlds also allow people to explore them, within limits, for free. Online virtual worlds have their own monetary systems which people can use to make purchases of virtual goods and services. Real money must usually change hands between the user and operator to obtain virtual currencies, as in any offline currency exchange. It is also possible to create virtual merchandise for sale to other users and change the Second Life currency, known as Linden Dollars, into real world currency via internet exchanges.

In Second Life, users include private corporations and public organisations as well as individuals. Users can move around the Second Life world via their avatars and visit the sites developed by other users. Users can purchase virtual land and erect virtual buildings of their own design on this. Virtual businesses exist in this world developed both by individual users and by organisations. Second Life has virtual houses and apartment complexes, shopping malls, banks, offices, car showrooms, restaurants, take-away food outlets, bars, clubs, hotels, amusement parks, and so on. Some of these sites have been developed by commercial organisations and feature real brands from the offline world.

Second Life and other virtual worlds have seen a number of major commercial brands take up a presence and establish virtual operations in spaces purchased on these sites. Adidas, BMW, Budweiser, Coca-Cola, Dell, IBM, Microsoft, Reebok, and Reuters have all set up shop in Second Life. It is possible, for example, to purchase virtual Coke from virtual Coke machines in Second Life. McDonald's has fast food kiosks in Sims Online, with avatar employees serving up virtual burgers and fries to customers' avatars for free. Brands such as Levi's and Nike have a presence in There, the teens' virtual world, selling virtual jeans and virtual sports shoes to avatars using the in–world currency.

These online worlds have therefore become sites of brand placement that not only give brand exposure to consumers but also engage consumers by allowing them to make (virtual) brand purchases. The companies behind brands can also organise other events within the virtual worlds that users can take part in. Such sponsored virtual occasions provide further opportunities for brand exposure. Major brands have entered virtual worlds to enhance their brand awareness and also to explore new ways of getting consumers to engage with their brands. Although virtual worlds have their own currencies that cannot always be exchanged for real world money, major brands nevertheless hope that consumer exposure in virtual worlds will eventually translate into purchases in the real world (Arakji & Lang, 2008; Barnes & Mattsson, 2008).

Virtual businesses that are set up in these virtual worlds can make virtual commodities that can be sold to other users. Hence, a consumer market can be established in virtual worlds that mirror those in the real world. Occasionally, opportunities can be created for virtual brands that exist only in a virtual world to migrate into the real world. This has happened with virtual clothes designs which have been picked up by real world designers and enabled the virtual world designers to enter the fashion industry in the offline world (Hemp, 2006).

In another manifestation of this platform, some large companies have created their own virtual worlds. Going beyond 'advergames' that comprise branded online games (see Chapter 6), some companies have developed 'adverworlds', where participants are represented by avatars and can interact with others in a range of virtual scenarios. Interestingly, a number of these adverworlds have been launched by adult brands for child markets. Thus, the Wells Fargo bank launched Stagecoach Island, while Daimler Chrysler developed Mokitown for teenagers and pre-teenagers respectively. These sites have combined entertainment with educational applications.

Coca-Cola introduced Coke Studios, which was designed for teenagers; as with sites such as Second Life, users were represented by avatars, were given personal spaces to furnish, and could make in-world purchases using virtual currency, including virtual cokes from virtual vending machines. Users could also take part in activities with other users and earn points – which comprised the in-world currency. The main theme of this world – hence its name Coke Studios – was a music studio environment in which users could produce compilations of music tracks for others to hear. Audiences would then be invited to rate these productions, and users would receive points called 'decibels' which they could then use to exchange for studio equipment. We will examine children, social media and virtual world brand marketing further in the next section.

Whether consumer activity in virtual worlds can provide an accurate indication of how they might behave as consumers in the real world remains uncertain. There is some evidence that consumers are more likely to behave similarly to the real world in brand purchase settings for virtual worlds that present more realistic settings. In other words, the more a virtual world mirrors the real world in its appearance and in the way users behave in it, the less its users' behaviours depart from habits established in the real world (Suntornpithug & Khamalah, 2010). Another factor that can shape virtual world behaviour and ensure it remains close to real world behaviour is the adoption by users of their real world identity in a virtual world (Arakji & Lang, 2008).

Some research has emerged that lends support to the hope of virtual marketers that their brand presence in virtual worlds will pay dividends in the offline world. In this case, brand experiences and consumer behaviour online have been found to influence consumers' brand decision making in the real world (Kwon & Lennon, 2009). People increasingly shop for products across different channels and platforms and as these multi-model consumer experiences become more widespread and ingrained, we might expect to find that consumers will approach and respond to brands in similar ways regardless of where that experience takes place. Brand experience is known to shape consumers' brand perceptions and purchasing decisions, and increasingly this experience takes place in a number of different environments (Chattopadhyay & Laborie, 2005; Brakus, Schmitt & Zarantonello, 2009).

There are other important factors that come into play in the context of whether eventual purchase decision is driven by brand marketing. One factor is how close is exposure on the brand marketing platform to an eventual purchase setting? A second factor is the degree of congruence between the image of a brand and the self-concept held by the consumer. In a virtual world setting in which consumers often adopt a new persona via their avatar, or even several different avatar identities, the match between brand image and self-identity could become more problematic. Of course, adult users might return to their real identity cognitively when appraising a brand experienced in a virtual world setting if they have it in mind to make a real world purchase. With children, who adopt pretend online identities during a period of development when their self-identity is still under construction, the position becomes even more complicated.

Many consumers in markets where internet presence is firmly established already make online brand purchases from brand manufacturers' or suppliers' websites. The inability to evaluate products seen in website shop windows in the same way as would be possible in a real retail setting in which consumers can examine products up close can inhibit consumers from making some online purchases. Brand image could hypothetically counteract this social distance effect if a brand's reputation is so high that consumers trust that a purchase represents a low risk. Virtual worlds may be able to contribute further to the breakdown of the inhibiting effects of no direct contact with products by enabling some degree of virtual inspection of brands in simulated brand handling settings (Levin, Levin & Weller, 2005; Suh & Chang, 2006). Enriching the online brand shopping experience in this way could hold the key to mass adoption of this form of consumption across a wide array of products (Jahng, Jain & Ramamurthy, 2000; Choi, 2008; Brunelle, 2009).

Interaction with brands in virtual settings can enhance not only how much consumers know or feel they know about a brand but can also cultivate positive brand attitudes and an intention to purchase (Schlosser, 2003; Fiore, Kim & Lee, 2005). For these positive effects to occur, however, it is essential that virtual brand experiences are congruent with real world brand experiences (Urban, Hauser, Qualls et al., 1997; Kaltcheva & Weitz, 2006).

The transference of brand influences in virtual worlds to the real world is the critical factor in terms of the marketing applicability and usefulness of these computer-generated environments. If experiences with brands in interactive virtual worlds can serve effectively to promote consumers' attitudes and beliefs about brands and through these psychological factors trigger purchase intentions or actual purchases in the real world, then it raises important questions about how children might be affected by virtual worlds in relation to their socialisation as consumers. Much of the evidence so far on brand marketing influence transference from the virtual to the real world has been obtained with adult samples. Although this research does not provide direct insights into the consumer socialisation influences of virtual world marketing, it does at least demonstrate the possibility that real effects can derive from what at first sight appear to be unreal, play environments.

The evidence of relevance has derived from two types of investigation. The first type has used controlled experimental methodologies in which participating adults interact with virtual environments manipulated by the researchers. The second type of study has surveyed known users of established virtual worlds to find out about their in-world experiences with real-world brands.

In one interesting experimental study, Terry Daugherty of the University of Texas at Austin and his colleagues found that exposure to a brand of digital video camera in a virtual world setting promoted consumers' attitudes towards the brand and enhanced their intention to make a future purchase of this item (Daugherty, Li & Biocca, 2008). The researchers had hypothesised on the basis of past evidence that allowing consumers to examine a product will better inform their decision to purchase than mere exposure to advertising. In this context, even an interactive experience with a brand in a virtual world setting could be better than no pre-purchase inspection experience (Biocca, Li & Daugherty, 2001).

The researchers provided three types of experience with the product: a standard print advertisement, a three-dimensional, virtual advertisement, and inspection of the product itself. In the three-dimensional advertisement condition, participants could examine the camera on screen, rotate it in every direction, and zoom in and out to examine both exterior and interior features in detail. These three types of product experience were paired in every combination and order of presentation. After controlled exposure to the product, participants were tested for their product knowledge, attitude toward the product, and intention to purchase. Virtual world experience had a specific effect all of its own and also worked well in combination with both exposure to product advertising and with product trial experience in the real world.

Virtual exposure to the product, when it preceded exposure to the print advertisement or actual product inspection, produced more positive attitudes towards the product and a stronger intention to purchase than did conditions in which virtual interaction was not used. The virtual experience also enhanced product knowledge but not always to a significantly greater extent than did conditions not using this type of experience. The authors emphasised the exploratory nature of this study and called for further research to confirm and extend its findings. Nevertheless, it was indicative of psychological mechanisms involving product-related knowledge, attitude, and belief formation that could be shaped through interactive virtual experiences with products which could in turn create the conditions following which likelihood of actual purchase was enhanced (Daugherty et al., 2008).

As well as the nature of advance brand promotions – whether they occur in a virtual world or the real world – there are other factors concerning the way consumers relate to brands and to virtual environments that come into play to mediate whether virtual exposure to brands has a transferable impact in the real world. Self-concept and brand image congruence is known to be important in the offline world. There is every reason to believe this will also be a factor in virtual worlds where brands are marketed. Consumers will often take the lead from important others in their social environment in the real world (Chebat, Sirgy & St James, 2006). We also know that with children, the perspective of the 'other' emerges during the 'tween' years (especially around 10 to 12 years) and blossoms during their teens. On this evidence, therefore, we might hypothesise that in virtual worlds, brand appeal can be enhanced if it is seen to attract the attention of virtual people with which the consumer identifies. The problem with this hypothesis – and with proving it – is that people often tend to assume bogus identities in virtual worlds. Although some people may choose to stick closely to their offline identity, others will opt for an avatar that is not only different from their real selves in terms of physique or socio-economic class, but go even further and choose to be a different gender or even take on a non-human form.

These issues were explored by Jason Gabisch and Kholekile Gwebu, who conducted a survey with a sample of people who used Second Life (Gabisch & Gwebu, 2011). They surveyed only people aged over 18 and ended up with a small sample of 158 respondents. Over half of these people registered their residency as being within the United States, while others were from Canada, France, Italy, Germany, the Netherlands, and the UK. Respondents were asked to think about real life brands they had encountered in Second Life, to list five brands, and then to choose one of these brands they had had 'the most memorable experience with' (p. 308). The specific brands that were singled out most often were IBM, Adidas, Coca-Cola, Dell, and Nike.

As testimony for marketing effects, two-thirds (66%) of the respondents said they often purchased virtual products in Second Life and more than one in three (36%) said they had purchased products related to their selected brand. As evidence of some marketing effect transference from the virtual world to the real world, one in four respondents (26%) claimed to have bought a product in real life after being exposed to branding in Second Life.

In more complex statistical tests, Gabisch and Gwebu explored relationships between three variables that had previously been identified by researchers as having effects on brand choices. These variables were called 'perceived diag-nosticity', 'self-image congruence', and 'behavioural congruence'. Perceived diagnosticity measured the extent to which respondents felt that experiences with brands in a virtual world are helpful in terms of assessing the quality of a brand in the real world. Self-image congruence was a measure of the extent to which respondents perceived themselves as similar to other people who used a brand in a virtual world. Behavioural congruence indicated the degree to which respondents believed that the actions of their avatar in a virtual world reflected how they would behave in similar circumstances in the real world.

All three of these variables emerged as statistically significant predictors of real world purchase intentions. They were found to have a direct and signifi-cant relationship to purchase intentions relating to respondents' most preferred brand from Second Life and also, in the case of self-image congruence and behavioural congruence, an indirect effect via their influence on attitudes towards brands. These effects were found to operate independently of any effect of previous purchase experiences with the specific brand each respondent singled out (Gabisch & Gwebu, 2011).

Brand marketing on children's social networks and virtual worlds

While many children have illegally signed up to social network sites with a minimum membership age of 13, there are many other sites that have been designed specifically for teenagers and pre-teens. These sites generally contain many of the features of Facebook, MySpace, and Twitter. They permit members to create personal profiles which can be regularly updated. Users can post messages and images of themselves as photographs and videos, make links with 'friends', exchange files, listen to music, watch movies, play games, and join chat rooms in which they can talk about all kinds of topics. In addition to micro-blogging and social networking sites in the Facebook and Twitter mould, many virtual worlds targeted at children have been launched. In these sites kids can link with other users, as they can through standard online social networks, but they can also wander a virtual world in the form of an avatar, engage in a wide range of activities on their own or with others, and also conduct transactions involving trades of virtual items or online purchases using in-world currencies.

Some sites have been developed with educational objectives in mind, while others are focused on entertainment and social communication. Among the most widely used sites are Club Penguin, Edmodo, Everloop, Fanlala, GiantHello, Imbee, Kazaana, Kidswirl, Kidzworld, Nicktropolis, Scuttle Pad, Skid-e-Kids, Stardoll, Sweety High, Togetherville, What's What, and Yoursphere. Some of these sites engage minimally in what we might call 'consumer-related activities', whereas others readily allow commercial brands to have a presence and encourage users to engage in brand-related activities and purchase transactions. Let us take a look at a few of these sites to get a flavour of what they have to offer.

One of the most widely used is Club Penguin, a site operated by Disney. It has an international membership and allows kids from all over the world to link to each other, exchange information, to chat, and play collectively with interactive games. The site has features on topics of interests to kids as well as interactive games. One feature that has become increasingly prevalent is that members have a visual on-screen representation in the form of an avatar, in this case in the form of a penguin.

There are several sites, such as Edmodo, Giant Hello, Togetherville, and What's What, that look a lot like Facebook. They contain all the core components of Facebook, such as personal profiles, tools to post messages and upload photographic images and video sequences, access to chat rooms and group activities, file swapping, and game playing activities. Togetherville was actually tied to an adult site and children can only gain access to this site via their parents, provided mum or dad is already registered with Facebook. Edmodo has an educational application that allows kids to interact with their teachers to talk about school topics. Giant Hello has a lot of consumer-related content, with celebrity fan pages and brand pages with embedded advertising sitting alongside those sponsored by commercial organisations such as fashion magazines and fast food chains.

Some sites are more direct in their involvement of kids in commercial activities. Everloop offers a social network for kids aged 7 to 13. Users can connect with friends, play games, join groups, and post messages and pictures. In addition, the site has its own currency and kids can buy 100 'Evercredits' for $1. These credits can be directly purchased or earned in other ways, such as by referring friends to the site or winning advertising-embedded interactive competitions and games.

Kazaana is a social network targeted at children aged 6 to 12 years. It has personal profiling, email, image and video exchange, chat, and interactive elements. Users can also follow Fan Pages provided by approved organisations, some of which have shops integrated within their pages, from which site users can make purchases.

On Kidzworld, which is aimed at 9- to 15-year-olds, members can create personal profiles, establish links with friends, send and receive emails, upload and send photographs and videos to friends, enter chat rooms, and play interactive games. The site also contains a lot of embedded advertising for toys, games, other products, and competitions.

In Nicktropolis, launched and run by children's television channel Nickelodeon, kids can play games, replay clips from TV shows, and enter competitions. They can also upload their own video material. The site contains extensive commercial merchandising with well-known brands. In the site's shop, kids can link through to retail brands such as Amazon, Argos, Toys R Us, and others.

Stardoll is operated by a Swedish based company and allows pre-teens and teens to engage in a range of online activities centred on fashion. Members get a doll to dress and accessorise and their own room space to decorate. Once assigned a doll, a member can dress him or her any way they like, take decisions about their doll's hairstyle and clothes, and situate their doll in spaces that can also be furnished. Members can also dress up celebrity dolls – both female and male. A visit to the site in June 2013 by the author found opportunities to dress up such diverse public figures as the singer Dido, Harry Styles (of the boy band One Direction), actress Kate Winslet, soccer player Frank Lampard, fashion model Giselle Bundchen, Camilla Parker-Bowles (wife of Prince Charles), and even Queen Elizabeth II.

The Stardoll site provides merchandise for dressing the doll and furnishing personal space. There are opportunities to acquire designer brands (with real labels being featured) and for members to dress their own doll like their favourite celebrity. Purchases can be made using the site's own currency called 'starcoins'. The site runs a wide range of clubs linked to specific celebrities (e.g. Hannah Montana), animals and fashion and a variety of other themes, in which they can make contact with other members. The site has a social networking facility and members can have their dolls and spaces rated by other members.

Sweety High is a site just for girls, aged between 10 and 17 years. Members can connect with each other, upload photos and videos and earn rewards for different activities. The site hosts a competition called 'Be a Star', which girls can enter to display talents in fields such as fashion design. There is also a teen-hosted 'Food Star' web feature that gives cooking tips and has celebrity guests. Although there are no adverts, brands are regularly featured in relation to competitions.

One of the most popular sites dedicated to children is Yoursphere, which takes members aged under 18. Kids can link with each other, start a blog, join virtual groups in multiplayer games and take part in chat rooms. The site has interactive games, a virtual world and a currency system. Members are represented in the site through personal avatars. In the currency system, credits can be earned for taking part in various on-site activities, which can then be exchanged for prizes such as consoles, iPhones, and other products. For fixed monthly payments Gold membership can be acquired for individuals or entire families, which then provides access to premium events and activities, allowing further credits to be earned.

Habbo is a social networking site aimed at teenagers and developed in Finland. Started in 2000 and expanded to 150 countries, the site takes the form of a virtual hotel environment. Users can obtain their own rooms in the hotel which they can customise and there are public spaces in the 'hotel' in which users can intermingle. Members join online communities in which they are represented as avatars. Habbo is also heavily commercialised and enables users to make purchases with the site currency to furnish their rooms and clothe their avatar. Many mainstream brands have a presence on the site and use it for promotional purposes.

The site attracted controversy when an investigation into its practices by Channel 4 News found that there had been lapses in its safety systems and in particular in controlling the kinds of content to which its young members were exposed. These concerns centred on the nature of online chat in its chat room facility, where pornographic and violent messages were found. A news reporter had posed as an 11-year-old girl and engaged in explicit sexual talk

(O'Brien, 2012; Seifert, 2012). The company subsequently suspended all chat. Some UK retailers stopped selling Habbo gift cards.

Habbo has two currencies which comprise 'credits' or coins that can be used to buy furniture from a catalogue and 'Pixels' which are a free currency. There is a premium subscription service called the Habbo Club which contains upgraded features and costs more. It is targeted at teenagers, and 90% of its users are aged 13–18, who spend an average of 41 minutes on the site each visit. It has 273 million users worldwide (Sulake.com, 2012). The site attracts a lot of external sponsorship interest especially from the music and entertainment sectors. There are direct links to the site and links via Facebook.

There has been a lively debate about the potential impact on children of internet marketing campaigns and brand promotions. This has polarised between those commentators who envisage children as active consumers taking advantage of a new marketing environment that both empowers them and expands their choices as consumers, and critics who believe that digital marketing manipulates vulnerable youngsters to seek material goods before they are able to differentiate good purchases from bad (see Linn, 2004; Buckingham, 2007). Given the kinds of concerns that have been debated previously about the way children, at different points in their development, are able to cope with consumerism when promoted by explicit advertising and, in the context of the theme of this book, how they understand and engage with brands, it is important to consider these concerns again here because the online world has triggered the use of more subtle brand promotion methods.

Theories of branding have increasingly focused on the ways in which consumers mentally engage with brands, and the significance of brands in forming part of personal identity (Belk, 1988). Brands can become an integral part of consumers' lives and lifestyles (Fournier, 1998). They can also be used to grow group identity as well as individual identity (Cova & Cova, 2001; Muniz & O'Guinn, 2001).

Research by Skaar (2009) investigated the way Norwegian children aged 11 and 12 years got involved with Piczo. Children's use of this site was monitored once a week for two three-month periods and a further twelve-month period. The children were interviewed about the site. In addition, Piczo pages were downloaded and analysed during these periods. Individual users can produce self-representations on the site through the use of text descriptions, photographs, videos and music. Brands can also present themselves on the site using similar tools and formats. Children who use this site can utilise the non-commercial tools and facilities provided by Piczo when producing their personal image or 'brand', or they can purchase commercially branded items in this context. Users can also extract elements, including commercially branded items or backgrounds, from the page of a friend to use on their own page.

When developing their own page, users are invited to provide some personal details about their physical characteristics, family background, place of residence, and personality. They describe their hobbies and interests and also their likes and dislikes in fields such as books, films, music, and sport. In doing so, they are given opportunities to make reference to branded items and build these into their personal identity.

Skaar distinguished between 'collectors' and 'elaborators' among Piczo users. Elaborators tended to build a personal page using branded materials, whereas collectors did not. Elaborators continue to upgrade their personal page in imaginative ways, whereas collectors quickly give up doing this. Hence, some users of this social network integrated branded items with non-branded items in defining their personal identities. The use of brands in creating a self-image for others to see was often accompanied by evaluative comment which assessed the value of specific brands. In some instances, the kids on this site would replace original descriptive text they had produced about themselves with co-opted branded material.

Membership of Piczo had social currency also in the offline world. The kids who joined this site tended to be the most self-confident and popular. Belonging to this site reinforced a view they and others like them had formed about themselves in the offline world as being confident to express their identities freely and openly to others and publicly to state their brand preferences. In offering public evaluations of brands they also became self-appointed brand opinion leaders, operating on an equal footing with professional marketers on this media platform. Interviews with children who used Piczo indicated that while personal descriptors might be a source of social ridicule or teasing, their openness with their associations with brands enhanced their social reputation.

The potency of this form of online brand marketing stems from the opportunities it presents to children, while their identities are still under formation, to engage with brands as part of a personal branding exercise. This approach goes beyond conventional advertising where young consumers can extract varying elements to inform their brand decisions and, during their early years, are protected in part by their own cognitive information processing limitations.

Sites that enjoin children to adopt commercial brands and to cut and paste them into montages of verbal descriptions and images that represent the way they see themselves cause a closer and more dynamic involvement with brands than passive exposure to advertisements ever could. As children become more sensitive to peer influences with age, the open publication of self-images to others on social networking sites provides a rich resource of image exchange grounded in commercial brands. In essence, children generate a viral marketing campaign for commercial brands such that those brands that are adopted by the most popular children will then be downloaded by others to be integrated with and re-presented as part of an evolving self-identity (Griffiths & Casswell, 2010).

We need to know much more about the impact of brand activities in social media and virtual world sites. It is clear that these sites have emerged as leading edge platforms for brands to engage with young consumers. Although research with traditional forms of marketing such as magazine and television advertising has indicated that children can display early abilities to distinguish physically between advertisements and surrounding media content and then gradually show insights into the persuasive purpose of brand promotions also from an early age, their understanding of brands and advertisements does not match that of adults until they reach their teens. Yet, they experience widespread and repeated exposure to brands and brand promotions during their early years of life.

Certainly 'tweens' display a growing awareness of brands and develop their own distinct tastes and preferences between the ages of 8 and 12 years. This emergent knowledge and understanding is helped by brand advertising taking on an explicit form that can be distinguished from its surroundings. Even then, children's judgements about brands are still bounded by self-centred perspectives on the world. Their abilities to take on board the perspectives of others are still far from fully formed. Increased interactions with peer groups at school, at each other's homes and elsewhere, gradually cultivate a broader understanding that their own personal view of the world is not the only one that exists and, more importantly, not the only one that counts. Their openness with personal brand preferences can be tempered by insights into what other people might think about their tastes and fashion sense.

When branding is more subtle and disguised, fresh questions can be asked about how children might be conditioned as young consumers. Psychological models of child development have provided conceptual frameworks for the analysis of children's understanding of brands and brand promotions in the offline world. The body of research that has emerged over half a century has shed light on children's awareness of brands and their changing involvement with brands as they grow up.

This research has also helped us to understand more about how children engage psychologically with different kinds of brand marketing activity in the offline world and their understanding of a key concept such as 'persuasion'. Children's abilities to identify and talk about brands, to know what advertising is and what it is designed to achieve, and to embrace and yet control consumerist urges have been measured in relation to explicit brand representations in different real world settings. Can the conceptual models and theories of children's cognitive and social development also shed light on how they are influenced by the more subtle forms of brand marketing that have surfaced in the twenty-first century in the online world?

8

Regulation and control of branding to children

In today's consumer world, children become aware of brands from an early age. As we have seen, there is evidence that even before they start school, 3- and 4-year-olds can identify brand names and refer to specific brands when making requests to their parents to buy them things (Valkenburg & Buijzen, 2005). Brands continue to have a strong presence in children's lives as they grow up. The range of brands that kids can name and comment upon increases year on year (Achenreiner & John, 2003). Concerns have been raised about this phenomenon in that it seems to demonstrate an unhealthy preoccupation with consumerism. In particular, questions have been raised about the focus it places on self-definition in terms of consumption and brands used, rather than on more worthy qualities (Chaplin & John, 2005; Oyserman, 2007).

For sceptics, childhood has become overly commercialised, and this in turn can have harmful effects on children by cultivating a value system whereby self-worth is determined by commodities owned and by undermining self-confidence among those unable to afford premium brands (Palmer, 2006). The use of sexual themes to define child-oriented products – even from an early age – introduces a further set of concerns about the sexualisation of childhood which brings with it a range of further concerns about risks this can cause for children's physical and psychological well-being (Papadopoulos, 2010).

Some commentators and researchers have regarded the commercialisation of childhood to have reached a point that proactive intervention in warranted on the part of governments to bring commercial brand owners and distributors to heel and to ensure that they do not engage in marketing practices likely to harm children (Palmer 2007; Hawkes & Harris, 2011; King, Hebden, Grunseit et al., 2011). In the UK, even the Prime Minister, David Cameron, has spoken out repeatedly on this issue and threatened legislative action where industry self-regulation is absent or slow moving (Morris, 2010; Curtis, 2011; Wintour, 2011). In this context, the concept of 'harm' is an emotive term and also denotes a serious outcome for children following from repeated exposure to brands and associated promotional messages. For any new public policies and accompanying marketing restrictions to be fair and effective, however, it is important that 'harm' is clearly defined, measured, and proven to exist.

Research evidence of brand marketing to children has been cited by critics to substantiate their claims. Calls for tighter regulation over the marketing activities that are aimed at children in different product and service sectors have been backed by reviews of empirical research and original studies (see Palmer, 2006; Mayo & Nairn, 2009; Mothers' Union, 2010; Papadopoulos, 2010; Family Lives, 2012). It is essential that the reviews provide comprehensive critiques of the evidence and not biased diatribes designed to support a pre-determined policy position. It is equally important that any new research presents evidence of relevance to arguments about cause–effect relationships between the activities and outputs of agents of commercialisation and children's cognitive, emotional, and behavioural responses.

This book has examined the evidence concerning children and engagement with brands and the processes of branding. It has indicated that the nature of children's relationships with, perceptions of, and uses of brands is not a simple matter. Furthermore, the nature of children's reactions to brand promotions in the form of advertising or other types of marketing is also complex and fluid. Although there is evidence that children can demonstrate brand awareness at the ages of 15, 10, 5, and even earlier, it would be wrong to assume that the 'meaning' of brands to kids is the same at these different ages (Valkenburg & Cantor, 2001). There is ample evidence to show that kids relate to brands in qualitatively different ways as they pass through various levels of psychological development (Laczniak & Palan, 2004; Nelson & McLeod, 2005). Such changes tend to be linked not just to cognitive development but also to the changing nature of children's social relationships with their parents and peers (Bartsch & London, 2000; Dotson & Hyatt, 2005). It is important to understand this developmental process and how it shapes the ways children perceive and behave in the world around them.

What does 'harm' mean?

It is also important to define what is meant by 'harm'. There are harms that refer to specific behaviour patterns than could put a child at risk. There are harms that are concerned with the creation of needs that undermine a child's ability to get along with others or that represent sources of tension. There are also harms that arise from the lessons learned from branding whereby social status becomes defined by material possessions rather than by the individual's personal achievements and relationships with others. When we introduce sexual themes into commercialisation, there are potential harms that derive from the treatment of children as sexual commodities or as having sexual attributes long before they have reached full physical maturity (Buckingham, Willetts, Bragg & Russell, 2010; Mothers' Union, 2010; Papadopoulos, 2010; Gunter, 2014).

Sometimes a reaction to brands or the various activities that are used by marketing professionals to promote them can be deemed harmful simply because a child fails to understand what is going on. In other words, an advertisement for a brand has the ultimate objective of persuading consumers to buy the brand. There is nothing inherently wrong about this activity in an open, consumer society, provided consumers are aware of what is happening. Then, consumers – young or old – can make informed judgements about whether to allow themselves to be persuaded or not. Psychologically mature consumers can usually cope with persuasive messages and not be swayed by marketers' claims without further considering their veracity. Less mature consumers, such as children, can be less well equipped cognitively to weigh up brand promotions in terms of whether they choose to believe them and may be more likely to take them at face value or at least to take a lead from them in terms of uncritical brand requests they make to parents or others who might be in a position to buy things for them.

All these observations lead us to ask whether a 'harm' that might be caused by commercial branding activities at one point in a child's development is likely to be present at a later point, once a child's level of development has advanced to a position that he or she becomes internally inoculated against it. From the review of research in this book, we have seen that how children respond to brand promotions, as well as what brands mean to children, are processes that are in a state of flux. What this means is that brands (and associated advertisements) mean one thing to a 4-year-old, something else to an 8-year-old, and something else again to a 14-year-old (Achenreiner, 1997; John, 1999). This also means that the nature and meaning of 'harm' in this context might also vary across the age span.

The fluidity of childhood in terms of a child's psychological development is multi-faceted. There are cognitive, emotional, social, cultural, and physical components. A child's ability to process and store information, to interpret their experiences, to relate to other people, and to cope with physical changes that occur as they grow up all come into play at different times and mediate their reactions to brands (Young, 1990; Gunter et al., 2005; McAlister & Cornwell, 2010). It is important for brand marketers, regulators, consumers, and those of us who conduct research into children's consumerism to understand the nature of these processes and how they work.

While accepting that child development is fluid and that children's understanding of brands is in flux, there remains a concern about whether early harms stay with the child, even though they may eventually not elicit a reaction from the child as he or she reaches a high plain of understanding. If we accept the concept of reconstructive memory, and if this concept applies in this context, then earlier forms of interpretation of brands could be changed and displaced by later ones that accompany a higher level of cognitive development (see Roediger & McDermott, 1995; Braun-La Tour & La Tour, 2004; Braun-La Tour & Zaltman, 2006; Roediger, Wixted & DeSoto, 2012). This does not mean there is no cause for concern about brand promotions once children get beyond a certain age or level of development. As this happens, children could engage with brands in new ways that bring their own negative side-effects. It does invite the prospect of an accumulation of 'harms', where earlier ones derive not from intrinsic qualities of advertisements or brand symbolism per se, but more from the ways that children are able to interpret these stimuli.

Brand dispositions and personal identity

There are also interesting variations in the cycles of developments that different types of child psychological maturation display, with important implications for how children respond to brands. Children's cognitive abilities underpin their comprehension of brands and brand promotions. These abilities are clearly important to the way kids think about brands and understand what they mean. Cognitive interpretations of brands also underpin emotional reactions to brands – or brand attitudes (Stewart, Morris & Grover, 2007). Cognitive abilities show progressive maturation year after year, moving forward more swiftly in some kids than in others, but generally becoming more sophisticated with age (John, 1999).

Turning to certain aspects of personality development, however, this forward moving cycle is not always replicated. When we consider brands against the backdrop of children's orientations towards materialism, for instance, we can witness one type of engagement with brands during pre-teen years, a different (and perhaps regressive) orientation in early teens years, before seeing a return to pre-teen patterns in later adolescence. This U-shaped cycle occurs because of the varying effects of different mediating variables at different points in a child's development (Achenreiner & John, 2003).

Brands and materialism have been linked to self-concept or self-identity. However, the importance of brands to self-identity does not emerge until children have reached a point in their cognitive development where they understand a brand's social or cultural symbolism. This understanding emerges by early teen years when there is also an emergent uncertainty about personal image. Very often, young teens develop negative thoughts about themselves at this time of life. Their orientation towards brands is then very much driven by a need to find ways of bolstering self-esteem. Once they have traversed this delicate stage in their development, their self-identity settles down and stabilises and during their late teens their attention turns to activities and personal achievements as symbols of esteem while brand purchases are less important in this context (Chaplin & John, 2007). Thus, in examining how kids engage with brands, we need to take into account a variety of factors that underpin brand involvement, and know which factors are most significant mediators of children's relationships with brands at different ages.

Transparency of branding

Concerns about branding and children stem not only from the mere presence of marketing in the child's environment, but also from the way it is presented. Children are vulnerable consumers. Their vulnerability is not the same throughout childhood, however, assuming that marketing professionals play fair. As children's cognitive, emotional, and social development takes place, their internalised abilities to make sense of brand advertising, for instance, also grows (Fielder, Gardner, Nairn & Pitt, 2007). The effective emergence of this greater understanding and the protection it affords them against persuasive brand promotions is predicated on an assumption that brand promotions are explicit and visible to consumers (Hirschman & Thompson, 1997).

With advertisements in a medium such as television, for example, children's recognition of these messages can be detected even at the age of 3 or 4, provided researchers use sufficiently sensitive measurements (Levin, Petros & Petrella, 1982). Shifts in basic perceptual orienting responses can be measured between programmes and commercial breaks. This does not prove that children can articulate complex distinctions between programmes and advertisements (Gunter et al., 2005). It does nevertheless represent the beginnings of differential psychological responding that will eventually blossom into more sophisticated descriptions and then explanations of differences between programmes and advertisements. Children are assisted in this context by the physical divide between programmes and advertisements (Zuckerman et al., 1978; Kunkel & Roberts, 1991).

If the visible divide between advertisements and surrounding media content is removed, the net result will be to render the advertising less physically distinct. Although there are other clues to the nature of advertising that experienced consumers can identify to help them recognise when they are confronted with a persuasive message, this type of advertising literacy takes a while to develop. Confusion can surface when advertisements share many content and format features with surrounding media content. Then, perceptual differentiation can become clouded. This might happen for instance if an advertisement uses cartoon-like animation to promote a brand and is then embedded in a cartoon programme (Kunkel, 2001).

Distinguishing commercial from non-commercial content can be rendered even more difficult when brands are integrated into entertainment content. This happens partially in the case of programme sponsorship and more completely in the case of product placement. In the online world, this phenomenon has become even more widespread with the emergence of social media sites, advergames and adverworlds as brand promotion platforms. The latter can be regarded as disguised forms of advertising. In relation to the traditional marketing media, this type of marketing has seen a growth of product placement in movies and television programmes. In the online world, a whole range of new brand marketing techniques have been developed, involving social networks, virtual worlds, and video game environments (Nairn & Hang, 2012).

These developments have raised concerns not simply because of the difficulties they may cause to young consumers in terms of recognition of persuasive messages but also because of the commodity fields that have adopted this form of marketing most enthusiastically. Where children are concerned, social media and electronic gaming platforms have been extensively used by food and drinks manufacturers, and most especially by those brands that are deemed to represent products of relatively poor nutritional value (Henry J. Kaiser, 2006; Nairn & Hang, 2012).

There has been an ongoing debate about the role played by food advertising in shaping poor eating habits that have in turn resulted in rising obesity levels among children (e.g. Montgomery & Chester, 2007; Corbett & Walker, 2009; Hunter, 2009; Hawkes & Harris, 2011). If this form of marketing can promote poor dietary habits among children, argue its critics, then the manufacturers of these food products must take some of the responsibility for the growing obesity epidemic observed in many western countries. There have been a number of major reviews of research evidence concerning the nature and effects of food marketing (Hastings et al., 2003, 2005, 2006; Livingstone & Helsper, 2004, 2006; Livingstone, 2005, 2006a, 2006b; Institute of Medicine, 2006; Cairns, Angus & Hastings, 2009; Cairns, Angus, Hastings & Caraher, 2013). These reviews recognised that children's food preferences and dietary habits can be influenced by a variety of social and psychological factors. In amongst these factors, however, food marketing activities were determined to have a part to play. Leaving aside the possible effects of food promotions on food choices, dietary habits, and overall health and well-being, they can raise brand awareness among children from an early age and convey beliefs about a brand (Lindstrom, 2008). Before they start school, many kids can recall brand names they have seen (Macklin, 1996). Repeated exposure to brand names and logos can encourage specific brand choices (Baker, 1999) and this effect can occur without consumers being consciously aware of it (Ferraro, Bettman & Chartrand, 2008).

Children's reactions to brands can also depend upon whether they recognise a commercial promotion when confronted by one. In the digital world, commercial product promotions have become increasingly subtle and disguised. Such trends have implications for how readily young consumers are able to identify brand marketing when it occurs. Brand promotions on the internet that have used subtle marketing techniques which embed brands seamlessly within social network, virtual and gaming environments need to be better understood in terms of their potential impact on children. Many leading food companies have utilised their websites as primary platforms for their marketing (Moore & Rideout, 2007; Lee, Choi, Quilliam & Cole, 2009). The use of advergames in particular is a popular technique in this setting and has been found to attract children's attention (Harris et al., 2012).

Research has found that when children are exposed to food brands in game playing settings (e.g. advergames) this experience can influence their food choices immediately after they finish playing. Such embedded branding can raise children's awareness of the featured brands compared with its status before they played a brand-featured game. It can also encourage children to choose the featured brand over other non-featured brands in the same product range (Mallinckrodt & Mizerski, 2007). What we have less information about is whether such experiences can cultivate longer-term effects on food choices and preferences (Jones, Wiese & Fabrianesi, 2008).

Product categories such as breakfast cereals, fast food, and sugary drinks have been vigorously promoted through social media and advergames. Some of the biggest and best known brands in the world have been behind these developments, such as Burger King, Coca-Cola, Kraft, McDonald's, Pepsi Co, and Subway (Harris et al., 2009; Schwarz, Brownell et al. 2010, 2011). In addition, brands for product ranges that are targeted at adult consumers but which nonetheless appeal to children have caused concern. This concern has centred on alcoholic beverage brands, which have been found initially to intrigue pre-teenage children with their frequently humorous advertising campaigns, but then become important signs of social status in teen years.

During the twenty-first century, increasing social concerns about underage drinking and youth binge drinking have encouraged many governments to tighten their regulations on alcohol marketing, which initially focused on brand marketing through mainstream media (Gunter, Hansen & Touri, 2010). Growing recognition of the popularity and prevalence of digital media marketing platforms such as online social networks and online computer games has drawn increased attention to these new marketing forms.

Major international bodies such as the World Health Organization have called for tighter regulations to control food marketing activities targeted at children (Hawkes, 2004, 2005, 2006, 2007a). Responsibility for such action has been laid at the doors both of governments and the food and drinks industries. Some major food and drinks companies have proactively crafted their own codes of practice to take personal control in a potentially restrictive regulatory climate. In the United States, the Children's Advertising Review Unit is an industry-sponsored body tasked with drafting and implementing codes of practice for food and drinks marketing. This body has acknowledged that food and drinks marketers should be especially cautious about how they market their brands to children. In yet another US initiative, the Children's Food and Beverage Advertising Initiative was established in 2006 by leading American companies in the sector and the Council of Better Business Bureaus. This body made a pledge to encourage the adoption of healthier lifestyles through dietary choices made by children. Yet, despite such actions, there is evidence that food and drinks companies continue to target children with their brands (Hawkes, 2007b; Hawkes & Harris, 2011).

As some areas of brand marketing have been challenged by tighter regulations, other areas have been opened up. These fresh opportunities for brand marketers have often represented recognition on the part of regulators that consumer markets have become increasingly crowded and competitive and also that certain media technologies have empowered consumers in terms of their reception of brand promotions (Quilliam et al., 2011).

The role of cognitive defences and consumer literacy

Despite the concerns that have long been raised about the influences of advertising on children, it has also been recognised, with empirical support, that children's vulnerability to brand promotions can be reduced through education. It is feasible to create interventions from relevant adults, such as parents or teachers, when children are exposed to brand advertising to encourage youngsters to think more reflectively and critically about what they are seeing (or hearing) and to begin to challenge the accuracy and honesty of commercial messages (Roberts, Christenson, Gibson et al., 1980). The cultivation of this type of literacy has been found to work effectively in relation to children's reactions to televised advertising (Bijmolt, Claassen & Brus, 1998). Children's susceptibility to advertising can operate through their limited cognitive abilities to work out what advertisements are really designed to do and also by a willingness to enjoy advertisements uncritically, especially when they tell an interesting story or use entertaining production techniques (see Phelps & Hoy, 1996; Derbaix & Bree, 1997; Gunter et al., 2005).

Proactive steps can be taken to enhance children's critical orientation towards advertising, which in turn can reduce their susceptibility to the brand appeals that advertisements make. Some interventions have entailed finding ways to reduce advertising exposure levels by controlling children's media diets (Robinson, Saphir, Kraemer et al., 2001). Another approach is for an adult to talk to children while they are looking at advertisements or just afterwards and offer either informative or critical comments about the advertising and the techniques it uses (Bijmolt et al., 1998).

Research has found that both informational interventions that comment on the techniques used by advertisements and affective interventions that entail negative evaluations of advertisements can be effective in helping children become better informed consumers, more sceptical about advertising, and more inclined to dislike advertisements. Buijzen (2007) tested out a series of interventions of these kinds with children aged 5–6 years, 7–8 years, and 9–10 years. The children in each age group were randomly assigned to conditions in which they watched televised advertisements and received informational or evaluative interventions or no interventions immediately after each commercial message. They were tested for their advertising knowledge (e.g. 'Do you think commercials try to sell things to people?') and their scepticism about it (e.g. 'Do you think television commercials tell the truth?'). They were also asked how much they liked each advertisement.

The findings indicated that the factual or information interventions had the desired effect of enhancing children's knowledge about advertisements and increasing their scepticism towards advertising. The latter effects in turn fed into a shift in evaluation of advertisements which tended to be liked less. Evaluative interventions could also influence children's subsequent attitudes towards advertisements in the expected (negative) direction. These effects occurred to some extent across all three age groups. One exception to this general rule was that the youngest children were not sensitive to or influenced by negative evaluative interventions. Nonetheless, they did exhibit increased scepticism about advertisements after receiving factual interventions, and this scepticism in turn tended to lead them to become more critical of advertisements and to like them less.

More generally, it has long been observed that children acquire an understanding of advertising over time through experience in consumer settings, as a result of repeat exposure, and through conversations with other people in their lives, especially their families and friends, and develop what has been termed 'persuasion knowledge' (Friestad & Wright, 1994). In earlier chapters that examined the role of children's cognitive development, we saw that as children pass through different phases in their maturation, they come to see the world differently. These emergent cognitive abilities underpin evolving insights into the nature and purpose of advertising and the meaning of brands (Rozendaal, Buijzen & Valkenburg, 2011). As their persuasion knowledge becomes more firmly established through this developmental process, children also acquire specific cognitive defences against the influences of advertising. These defences can represent important internalised protection against the persuasive effects of advertising messages (Livingstone & Helsper, 2006). These defences need to be appropriately cued during advertising exposures to be brought into play.

One of the issues that arises with forms of advertising that are less explicit, such as the embedding of brands in social media or online gaming environments, is that so much else is going on that children may not recognise when promotional messaging on behalf of commercial brands is taking place. Interactive games can be especially potent in this respect because children can become cognitively and emotionally highly involved in the action. This experience is driven by the sense of control they have over what takes place on screen (Williams & Clippinger, 2002). As such, the experience of playing these games can be very enjoyable and cultivates favourable attitudes towards the games themselves (Hsu & Lu, 2004; Waiguny & Terlutter, 2011). While there is nothing intrinsically wrong about this, it does create a set of conditions in which the commercial intentions of game-embedded branding does not become immediately apparent (Mallinckrodt & Mizerski, 2007).

Put simply, children who have 'persuasion knowledge' or who are, in other words, advertising literate also tend to possess internalised defences against the persuasive effects of advertising. These defences will only usually be invoked, however, when the children know they are confronted with advertising. When this awareness is missing because branding takes on a more disguised form, these defences are not as likely to be brought into play and the child could be rendered more susceptible to its persuasive appeals.

One empirical test of this observation confirmed that it can occur. When different groups of children were exposed to a brand of potato chips either in the form of television advertising or as an embedded brand in an advergame, they were more likely to recognise the televised promotion as 'advertising' and less likely to do this in the case of the advergame (Panic et al., 2013). The same study also showed that unless the presence of embedded branding was highlighted to children in the advergame, they were unlikely consciously to notice it but were more likely subsequently to display a purchase preference for the advertised brand. The latter effect was presumed to occur because in the condition in which their attention was not drawn to the brand in the advergame, their cognitive defences against persuasion were not aroused.

One further factor at play here was the degree to which the children experienced a positive affective or emotional reaction to playing with online games. This enjoyment level reached a point at which children had their attention distracted away from branding within the game and therefore perceived no reason to challenge the subtle brand messaging (Panic et al., 2013). Of course, specific cues can be inserted that draw consumers' attention to the presence of embedded branding, such as product placement within television programmes, movies, or video games, but these devices can sometimes trigger a negative reaction among viewers or players because such advertising or branding separation features can disrupt the flow of the entertainment (An & Stern, 2011). Consequently, there is a tension between taking steps to protect young consumers and the risk that in doing so the perceived enjoyment value of the entertainment content is jeopardised.

It is possible to design formal interventions in the shape of consumer literacy courses to educate children about the subtle persuasion techniques that are used by brands in advergames. Such interventions have been found to yield positive results for many young consumers just as their consumer awareness is emerging, and can ensure that they are not duped even by the more subtle forms of persuasion used by marketers in virtual environments where brands are positioned as aspects of computer games (An et al., 2014).

New forms of branding and new forms of regulation

In most parts of the world regulations exist that have been designed to protect the interests of child consumers. These rules and codes have acknowledged the vulnerabilities of children owing to their psychological immaturity. They have also largely been developed in relation to the pre-digital world. In that world, brand advertising was less diverse, more explicit, and more distinctly separate from other media content (e.g. TV programmes, movies, magazine articles, etc) in which it was embedded. In the digital era, as brand promotions have moved online on websites, social media settings, and online computer game-playing environments they have become less clearly and unequivocally distinguishable or separable from other content. Thus, questions have been asked about whether such promotions place immature consumers at a disadvantage in terms of being able to resist the diverse and subtle persuasive activities used by marketers via the internet. The digital marketing world has developed at a pace; the regulatory systems and codes associated with marketing regulation less so.

One important area of regulation relaxation has concerned product placement, especially in movies and on television. In the UK, the Office of Communication introduced new rules to permit product placement in television programmes from 28 February 2011. This initiative did not open up a free-for-all new marketing environment for brand owners. There are restrictions on the type of products that can be placed, the types of programmes in which placements can occur, and limits on the way in which products can be presented in programmes. Product placements were restricted to films, television drama series and serials (e.g. soap operas), entertainment shows, and sports programmes. They were not allowed in children's programmes, news programmes, current affairs, consumer affairs, and religious programmes. Product categories such as alcohol, baby milk substitutes, foods and drinks high in fat, salt, or sugar, gambling, medicines, and tobacco were all prohibited (Ofcom, 2010).

Despite the restrictions, product placement opportunities were opened up for a wide range of product and service markets in respect of much of the mainstream television schedules. Given the subtle nature of product placement as a brand marketing technique, this regulatory change will mean that many children will be exposed to examples of it on a regular basis when watching television. Even in those households in which live television viewing has been replaced by viewing of self-recorded or online repository playback viewing – where spot advertising can be avoided with the fast-forward button – this new form of brand marketing will still be seen. It will be important to conduct further research into the impact of such marketing exposure experiences on children's brand awareness and consumer socialisation.

There is no doubt that some brand marketers have been fleet of foot and moved onto new digital platforms both because they know they can reach young people there and also because by doing so they can circumvent legal restrictions of their activities in the mainstream advertising media. The use of sites such as Facebook for brand promotion purposes is a primary example of this strategy. On Facebook, brand marketers can engage in transparent advertising if they wish, but they can also simply stimulate public 'chat' about brands. In the latter case, once the chat has been triggered, it is maintained by consumers themselves. One consumer will post a comment about a brand, which then triggers responses from others. The problem these kinds of online activities cause for advertising regulators is that they are not technically classed as 'advertising' even though they do in effect raise the public profile of a brand and may also bring about a modification of the brand image.

There have been some cases where this type of online brand chat is not only transparently serving as a brand promotion, but also can go beyond this and create discourses that have socially worrying side-effects. In Australia, the Advertising Standards Bureau took an important decision in September 2012 to classify the Facebook pages of two alcohol brands – Smirnoff vodka and Victoria Bitter beer as marketing communications tools and therefore as falling under the industry self-regulatory code of ethics. These brands had used Facebook as a space within which consumers engaged in online talk about the products and about alcohol consumption, during which they were invited to think creatively about the brands themselves. This activity led to the appearance of inappropriate chatter about drinking that could have been seen by children, and which in the context of regular advertising would not be permitted. The policing of this activity, given the subtle nature it can take, will be difficult, but the ASB had made a start by making it clear that brand owners would be held responsible for the contents appearing on their own social media pages (Brodmerkel & Carah, 2013).

The need for this extension of legislation in regard to social media brand promotion initiatives was underlined by research conducted By Antonia Lyons and her colleagues of the School of Psychology, Massey University, among young adults aged 18 to 25 in New Zealand. The researchers interviewed these young consumers in 19 friendship groups, and found that social media use and alcohol consumption were closely linked (see Lyons, Goodwin, Niland et al., 2012; Davidson, 2013).

Although these consumers were not children, they were not far out of childhood and displayed strong orientations both towards the use of social media and the consumption of alcohol in their social lives. For these young adult consumers, social media and alcohol brands and their consumption had become intertwined. Social media sites were used to organise drinking events or other social occasions at which some alcohol consumption would occur. It was also recognised as a useful platform to receive information about alcohol brands, both through brands' own promotional activities, such as premium offers, sponsored events, and competitions, and via the chatter of consumers about alcohol consumption.

These young people also engaged in this online talk about booze, and their own posts became seamlessly integrated with marketing content posted by alcoholic beverage manufacturers. Because this 'marketing' was not as explicit as in other media, it was less likely to trigger consumers' socialised defences against marketing influences. Moreover, this chatter was openly available for child users of social media sites to witness (Lyons et al., 2012).

Recognising key concerns with branding

Branding is a part of all of our lives. It is unlikely that many of us would wish to return to a society in which commodity and service choices were radically reduced. Not only do we, as consumers, welcome choices for ourselves, but also for our children. Brands have an important role to play in a crowded marketplace in helping consumers to decide between product variants. Professional brand marketers have the job of creating these distinctive qualities in brands to enable us to make informed decisions in terms of what and what not to buy. Children learn about consumerism as a natural part of their lives.

While accepting all of this, we cannot trust that all brand marketers will play fair. Commercial pressures, which have grown in increasingly competitive consumer marketplaces, encourage marketers to use all the tools in their armoury to reach consumers with information about their brands and messages designed to persuade consumers that advertised brands are the best. When standard marketing techniques are thought to be insufficient to get the results they seek, some marketers might be tempted to make exaggerated claims that, in effect, mislead consumers.

The main areas of concern have focused both on traditional forms of marketing and newer techniques that have emerged in the digital age. We do need to be watchful over the sheer volume of brand activity, especially when this is targeted at children. Moreover, we need to be concerned about the attachment to brands of specific social, cultural, and psychological themes that may be inappropriate for naïve young consumers. The association with child-targeted commodities of sexualised themes represents one aspect on this concern (see Gunter, 2014).

In addition, in a world in which digitised communications have increasingly empowered consumers to pick and choose which brand messages they wish to pay attention to, it is understandable that marketing professionals will seek to extend their brand promotion methods using the same technologies and communications networks that consumers have adopted. There is nothing inherently wrong about this except where marketers adapt non-marketing formats – classed by consumers, for example, as 'entertainment' – for marketing purposes and create disguised forms of marketing. There are particularly acute concerns with this trend where children are concerned because they already have limited understanding of the more transparent forms of branding.

Children can be very resilient psychologically in relation to attempts to persuade them. They cannot all be treated as a single homogeneous demographic however. Psychologically, children pass through a continual and fluid period of cognitive, emotional, and behavioural development between birth and adulthood, and their abilities to understand what brands mean and how marketing works also evolve gradually over time. Transparent forms of brand marketing that can be clearly and distinctly recognised can assist children to identify and understand brands and branding especially when their cognitive abilities are limited (Wright et al., 2005; Verhellen et al., 2014).

Less transparent forms of brand promotion are much less helpful in this respect and can be so subtle that even mature consumers can be duped. Even though children may have developed a level of cognitive understanding that enables them to discern the primary objectives of many brand marketing techniques, they sometimes need to be prompted to use it. This prompting may be particularly important in relation to subtle marketing methods that do not immediately appear to be what they really are (Terlutter & Capella, 2013; An et al., 2014).

As marketers are encouraged by the availability of these new platforms, by the shifting mediated behaviours of consumers, and by commercial pressures to use any methods they believe will give them an advantage, the temptation to engage in unscrupulous forms of branding might also increase. No blame can be attached to marketers for adopting new methods of reaching consumers accorded to them by digital media developments. The important point to make here is that the same legal and ethical principles should apply with new brand promotions platforms as ones adopted with advertising in conventional mainstream mass media.

People as consumers need information to help them make brand choices. As citizens they also deserve protection from unscrupulous brand sales operators whose primary motives are to sell rather than provide high quality merchandise and services and deliver exactly what it says on the tin. The growth of brand markets has led to more crowded and competitive marketplaces in which there will always be temptations for marketers to use sharp practices to stay ahead of their rivals. Understanding these practices and how to cope with them requires acknowledgement and awareness of the interplay between a range of different professional, social, and psychological factors (Terlutter & Capella, 2013)

As consumers increasingly adopt new digital media platforms to communicate with each other about brands, inevitably commodity and service suppliers will seek to join these conversations. In doing so, they will also seek to influence those conversations to benefits their own brands. The big question now is whether consumers recognise that there is persuasion going on in these contexts. Will the persuasion knowledge they acquire as young, developing consumers sensitise them to the more subtle and disguised persuasion techniques being deployed by commercial brands in the digital world? How vulnerable will children be in this setting given that their persuasion knowledge will often be only partly established? These are important questions that will require action, as well as cooperation, between a number of stakeholders – children, their parents or guardians, educators, governments and their regulators, and commercial business and industry and their advertising and brand design agencies and advisors.

It will continue to be important for governments and their regulators to create a legislative framework to set the boundaries for brand manufacturers and suppliers in terms of how they promote their products and services to children. The official agencies must also devise relevant codes of practices to underpin tools and procedures for monitoring brand marketing activities and trends and to take action as and when appropriate. In fairness to marketers, however, any such action must be informed by a thorough understanding of relevant evidence about young consumers and their responses to brands.

The corporate sector must deploy its own professional codes that resonate with prevailing consumer protection legislation and related official codes of practices, ensuring that its marketing executives and any external agencies it uses are fully cognisant of these codes and how to comply with them. At the same time, codes of practice must be informed by research about young consumers and how they respond to different types of brand promotion. It is unlikely that there can be a 'one size fits all' style of regulation for all brand promotion platforms. The diverse nature of digital communications platforms and their distinctiveness compared with traditional mass media mean that old regulatory frameworks are unlikely to be fit for purpose in relation to new forms of digital media and styles of brand promotions they have created. Brand marketing and advertising regulations therefore need to be updated and fully informed by the latest research into children's comprehension of digital as well as analogue advertising.

Finally, consumers can and probably must take steps to protect themselves and their children in the world of digital marketing. This world has empowered consumers in so many ways in terms of ease of searching for brands to buy, sources of brand-related information, and by providing convenient forms of shopping and engaging in purchase transactions. Such empowerment cannot be granted without consumers recognising that they are active stakeholders in this new world of consumerism, who must also take on some degree of personal responsibility in relation to safeguarding their own interests. As citizens they are likely to expect centralised protection, while as consumers they want more choice and convenience, as well as good value for money. Those who take responsibility for guiding children through their early stages of social and psychological development – parents/carers and educators – must ensure they play their part in the socialisation and protection of these fledgling consumers, imparting to them the persuasion knowledge they need to cope with all the new forms of brand marketing and not just the old ones.

Bibliography

3A Media (2013, 22 February) *Branding Your Kids*. Available at: www.3amediaonline. com/branding-your-kids. Accessed 4 June 2013.

Aaker, D. (1991) *Managing Brand Equity: Capitalising on the Value of a Brand Name*. New York: Free Press.

Achenreiner, G. B. (1997) Materialistic values and susceptibility to influence in children. In M. Brucks & D. J. MacInnis (Eds.) *Advances in Consumer Research*, 24, pp. 82–88. Provo, UT: Association for Consumer Research.

Achenreiner, G. B. & John, D. R. (2003) The meaning of brand names to children: A developmental investigation. *Journal of Consumer Psychology*, 13(3), 205–219.

Adams, J. (2006) Striking it niche – extending the newspaper brand by capitalizing on new media niche markets: Suggested model for achieving consumer brand loyalty. *Journal of Website Promotion*, 2(1–2), 163–184.

Aitken, P. P. (1989) Television alcohol commercials and under-age drinking. *International Journal of Advertising*, 8, 133–150.

Aitken, P. P., Eadie, D. R., Leathar, D. S. et al. (1988) Television advertisements for alcoholic drinks do reinforce under-age drinking. *British Journal of Addiction*, 83, 1399–1419.

Aksoy, L. & Bloom, P. (1999) The effects of cultural orientation and trust toward marketers on the level of consumer deception. *Proceedings of the Cross-Cultural Research Conference,* Association for Consumer Research, Cancun, Mexico.

Ali, M., Blades, M., Oates, C. & Blumberg, F. (2009) Young children's ability to recognise advertisements in web page designs. *British Journal of Developmental Psychology*, 27(1), 71–83.

Alvy, L. & Calvert, S. (2008) Food marketing on popular children's websites: A content analysis. *American Dietetic Association*, 108(4), 710–713.

American Marketing Association Dictionary (2013). Available at: www.marketing power.com/_layouts/Dictionary.aspx?dLetter=B. Accessed 11 December 2013.

An, S. & Stern, S. (2011) Mitigating the effects of advergames on children: Do advertising breaks work? *Journal of Advertising*, 40(1), 43–56.

An, S., Jin, H. S. & Park, E. H. (2014) Children's advertising literacy for advergames: Perception of the game as advertising. *Journal of Advertising*, 43(1), 63–72.

Anderson, E. (1998) Customer satisfaction and word-of-mouth. *Journal of Service Research*, 1(1), 5–17.

Andronikidis, A. & Lambrianidou, M. (2010) Children's understanding of television advertising: A grounded theory approach. *Psychology & Marketing*, 27(4), 299–322.

Arakji, Y. R. & Lang, K. R. (2008) Avatar business value analysis: A method for the evaluation of business value creation in virtual commerce. *Journal of Electronic Commerce Research*, 9(3), 207–218.

Araujo, T. & Neijens, P. (2012) Friend me: Which factors influence top global brands participation in social network sites. *Internet Research*, 22(5), 626–640.

Ariely, D. (2000) Controlling the information flow: Effects on consumers' decision-making and preferences. *Journal of Consumer Research*, 7 (September), 233–248.

Arnold, C. (2004) Just press play. *Marketing News*, 38(9), 1–15.

ATL (2008, 11 August) Children are highly influenced by brands and logos – ATL. Available at: www.atl.org.uk/media-office/media-archive/children-influenced-brands-logos-ATL.asp. Accessed 22 July 2013.

Auty, S. & Lewis, C. (2004) Exploring children's choice: The reminder effect of product placement. *Psychology and Advertising*, 21(9), 697–713.

Babin, L. & Carder, S. T. (1996) Viewers' recognition of brands placed within a film. *International Journal of Advertising*, 15(2), 140–151.

Bailey, R., Wise, K. & Bolls, P. (2009) How avatar customizability affects children's arousal and subjective presence during junk food-sponsored online video games. *Cyberpsychology & Behavior*, 12(3), 277–283.

Baker, W. E. (1999) When can affective conditioning and mere exposure directly influence brand choice? *Journal of Advertising*, 28(4), 31–46.

Balasubramanian, S. K. (1994) Beyond advertising and publicity: Hybrid messages and public policy issues. *Journal of Advertising*, 23, 29–46.

Baldwin, C. (2009, 12 June) Twitter helps Deli rake in sales. Available at: www.reuters.com. Accessed 14 July 2013.

Baranowski, T., Baranowski, J., Thompson, D. et al. (2011) Video game play, child diet and physical activity behaviour change: A randomized clinical trial. *American Journal of Preventative Medicine*, 40(1), 33–38.

Barnes, S. & Mattsson, J. (2008) Brand value in virtual worlds: An axiological approach. *Journal of Electronic Commerce Research*, 9(3), 195–206.

Baron-Cohen, S., Leslie, A. M. & Frith, U. (1985) Does the autistic child have a 'theory of mind'. *Cognition*, 21, 37–46.

Barry, T. E. & Gunst, R. F. (1982) Children's advertising: The differential impact of appeal strategy. In J. H. Leigh & C. R. Martin, Jr. (Eds.) *Current Issues and Research in Advertising*, pp. 113–125. Ann Arbor, Graduate School of Business Administration, University of Michigan.

Bartholomew, A. & O'Donohue, S. (2003) Everything under control: A child's eye view of advertising. *Journal of Marketing Management*, 19(4), 433–457.

Bartsch, K. & London, D. (2000) Children's use of mental state information in selecting persuasive arguments. *Developmental Psychology*, 36(3), 352–365.

Batra, R. & Ray, M. L. (1985) How advertising works at contact. In L. F. Alwitt &

A. A. Mitchell (Eds.) *Psychological Processes and Advertising Effects*, pp. 13–43. Hillsdale, NJ: Lawrence Erlbaum Associates.

Belk, R. W. (1985) Materialism: Trait aspects of living in the material world. *Journal of Consumer Research*, 12 (December), 265–280.

Belk, R. W. (1988) Possessions and the extended self. *Journal of Consumer Research*, 15 (September) 139–168.

Belk, R. W., Bahn, K. D. & Mayer, R. N. (1982) Developmental recognition of consumption symbolism. *Journal of Consumer Research*, 9 (June), 4–17.

Belk, R. W., Mayer, R. & Driscoll, A. (1984) Children's recognition of consumption symbolism in children's products. *Journal of Consumer Research*, 10 (March), 386–397.

Bell, R. A., Berger, C. R., Cassady, D. & Townsend, M. S. (2005) Portrayals of food practices and exercise behaviour in popular American films. *Journal of Nutrition Education and Behavior*, 37(1), 27–32.

Berg, P. (2009, 27–28 May) *Southwest Airlines Nuts About Online Communication*. Presentation at the Inbound Marketing Summit, Boston, MA.

Berger, J. & Milkman, K. L. (2012) What makes online content viral? *Journal of Marketing Research*, 49(2), 192–205.

Bergstrom, A. (2000) Cyberbranding: Leveraging your brand on the Internet. *Strategy & Leadership*, 28(4), 10–15.

Bernoff, J. & Li, C. (2008) Harnessing the power of the oh-so-social web. *MIT Sloan Management Review*, 49(3), 36–42.

Bever, T. G., Smith, M. L., Bengen, B. & Johnson, T. G. (1975) Young viewers' troubling response to TV ads. *Harvard Business Review*, 53 (November) 109–120.

Bhatnagar, N., Aksoy, L. & Malkoc, S. A. (2004) Embedding brands within media content: The impact of message, media, and consumer characteristics on placement efficacy. In L. J. Shrum (Ed.) *The Psychology of Entertainment Media – Blurring the Lines Between Entertainment and Persuasion,* pp. 99–116. Mahwah, NJ: Lawrence Erlbaum Associates.

Bijmolt, T. H. A., Claassen, W. & Brus, B. (1998) Children's understanding of TV advertising: Effects of age, gender, and parental influence. *Journal of Consumer Policy*, 21, 171–194.

Biocca, F., Li, H. & Daugherty, T. (2001) *Experiential Ecommerce: Relationship of Physical and Social Presence to Consumer Learning, Attitudes and Decision Making.* Presented at Presence, 4 Annual International Workshop on Presence in Philadelphia, PA, 21–23 May.

Blatt, J., Spencer, L. & Ward, S. (1972) A cognitive developmental study of children's reactions to television advertising. In G. Comstock and E. Rubinstein (Eds.) *Television and Social Behavior, Vol. 4.* Washington, DC: US Government Printing Office.

Boush, D. M., Friestad, M. & Rose, G. M. (1994) Adolescent scepticism toward TV advertising and knowledge of advertiser tactics. *Journal of Consumer Research*, 21 (June), 165–175.

Boyland, E., Harrold, J., Kirkham, T. et al. (2011) Food commercials increase preference for energy-dense foods, particularly in children who watch more television. *Journal of the American Academy of Pediatrics*, 128(1), 93–100.

Brady, J., Farrell, A., Wong, S. & Mendelson, R. (2008) Beyond television: Children's engagement with online food and beverage marketing. *Clinical Medicine: Pediatrics*, 2, 1–9.

Brakus, J. J., Schmitt, B. H. & Zarantonello, L. (2009) Brand experience: What is it? How is it measured? Does it affect loyalty? *Journal of Marketing*, 73(3), 52–68.

Brand Domain (2013) The history of branding. Available at: www.branddomain. wordpress.com/2013/03/31/the-history-of-branding. Accessed 5 July 2013.

Brand Republic (2011) Kids Brand Index. Available at: www.brandrepublic.com/ kidsbrandindex. Accessed 14 August 2014.

Brandt, K. S. (2008) You should be on YouTube. *ABA Bank Marketing*, 40(6), 28–33.

Braun, O. L. & Wicklund, R. (1989) Psychological antecedents of conspicuous consumption. *Journal of Economic Psychology*, 10 (June), 161–187.

Braun-La Tour, K. A. & La Tour, M. S. (2004) Assessing the long-term impact of a consistent advertising campaign on consumer memory. *Journal of Advertising*, 33(2) 49–61.

Braun-La Tour, K. A. & La Tour, M. S. (2005) Transforming consumer experience: When timing matters. *Journal of Advertising*, 34(3), 19–30.

Braun-La Tour, K. A. & Zaltman, G. (2006) Memory change: An intimate measure of persuasion. *Journal of Advertising Research*, 46 (March), 57–72.

Brehm, S. & Brehm, J. (1981) *Psychological Reactance*. New York: Academic Press.

Brennan, B. (2012, 12 March) Why kids and parents now aspire to the same brands. Forbes. Available at: www.forbes.com/sites/bridgetbrennan/2012/03/12/why-kids-and-parents-now-aspire-to-the-same-brands. Accessed 4 June 2013.

Brightman, J. (2008) Gamers embracing contextual in-game ads, says Nielsen and IGA. GameDaily (Online), 17 June. Available at: www.gamedaily.com/articles/news/ gamers-embracing-contextual-ingame-ads-say-nielsen-and-iga?biz=1. Accessed 4 June 2013.

Bristow, F. & Asquith, J. A. L. (1999) What is in a name? An intercultural investigation of Hispanic and Anglo consumer preferences and the importance of brand name. *Journal of Product and Brand Management*, 8(3), 183–203.

Brodmerkel, S. & Carah, N. (2013) Alcohol brands on Facebook: The challenges of regulating brands on social media. *Journal of Public Affairs*, online preview. Doi:10.1002/pa.1466.

Brucks, M., Armstrong, G. M. & Goldberg, M. E. (1988) Children's use of cognitive defenses against television advertising: A cognitive response approach. *Journal of Consumer Research*, 14, 471–482.

Brunelle, E. (2009) The moderating role of cognitive fit in consumer channel preference. *Journal of Electronic Commerce Research*, 10(3), 178–195.

Buckingham, D. (2007) Selling childhood? Children and consumer culture. *Journal of Children and Media*, 1(1), 15–24.

Buckingham, D. (2009) *The Impact of the Commercial World on Children's Wellbeing*. London: Department for Children, Schools and Families.

Buckingham, D., Willetts, R., Bragg, S. & Russell, R. (2010) *Sexualised Goods Aimed at Children: A Report to the Scottish Parliament Equal Opportunities Committee.* Edinburgh: Scottish Parliament Equal Opportunities Committee.

Buijzen, M. (2007) Reducing children's susceptibility to commercials: Mechanisms of factual and evaluative advertising interventions. *Media Psychology*, 9, 411–430.

Buijzen, M. & Valkenburg, P. M. (2000) The impact of television advertising on children's Christmas wishes. *Journal of Broadcasting & Electronic Media*, 44(3), 456–470.

Buijzen, M., Van Reijmersdal, E. A. & Owen, L. H. (2010) Introducing the PCMC model: An investigative framework for young people's processing of commercial media content. *Communication Theory*, 20, 427–450.

Burns, E. (2006) Online games market to hit $4.4 billion by 2010. Available at: www.clickz.com/showPage.html?page=3623306. Accessed 12 July 2014.

Burst Media (2012, June) Online insights: Let's get social – web user preferences, habits and actions in Spring 2012. Available at: www.burstmedia.com/pdf/burst_media_online_insights_2012_06. Accessed 8 July 2013.

Bussey, C. (2011, 10 August) Marketing to children – Kids Brand Index 2011. *PR Week.* Available at: www.prweek.com/uk/news/1084293. Accessed 10 June 2013.

Butter, E. J., Popovich, P. M., Stackhouse, R. H. & Garner, R. K. (1981) Discrimination of television programs and commercials by pre-school children. *Journal of Advertising Research*, 21 (April), 53–56.

Cacioppo, J. T. & Petty, R. E. (1989) Effects of message repetition on argument processing, recall and persuasion. *Basic and Applied Social Psychology*, 10, 3–12.

Cairns, G., Angus, K. & Hastings, G. (2009, December) *The Extent, Nature and Effects of Food Promotion to Children: A Review of the Evidence to December 2008.* Geneva: World Health Organization.

Cairns, G., Angus, K., Hastings, G. & Caraher, M. (2013) Systematic reviews of the evidence on the nature, extent and effects of food marketing to children: A retrospective summary. *Appetite*, 62, 209–215.

Calder, B. J. & Sternthal, B. (1980) Television commercial wearout: An information processing view. *Journal of Marketing Research*, 27, 173–186.

Calfee, J. E. & Ringold, D. J. (1988) Consumer scepticism and advertising regulation: What do the polls show? In M. J. Houston (Ed.) *Advances in Consumer Research*, Vol. 15, pp. 244–248. Provo, UT: Association for Consumer Research.

Calkins, S. D. & Hill, A. (2007) The emergence of emotion regulation: Biological and behavioural transactions in early development. In J. Gross (Ed.) *Handbook of Emotion Regulation*, pp. 229–248. New York: Guilford.

Calvert, S. L. (2008) Children as consumers: Advertising and marketing. *The Future of Children*, 18(1), 205–234.

Campbell, M. & Keller, K. L. (2003) Brand familiarity and ad repetition effects. *Journal of Consumer Research*, 30(2), 292–304.

CAP (2012, 20 December) *Review of the Use of Children as Brand Ambassadors and in Peer-to-Peer Marketing.* London: Committee for Advertising Practice. Available at: www.cap.org.uk/news-reports/~/media/Files/CAP/Reports. Accessed 11 June 2013.

Carah, N. & Brodmerkel, S. (2012, 21 August) Ruling on alcohol brands' Facebook sites will shake up social media marketing. The Conversation. Available at: www.

theconversation.com/ruling-on-alcohol-brands-facebook-sites-will-shake-up-social-media-marketing. Accessed 27 June 2013.

Carlson, S. M. & Wang, T. (2007) Inhibitory control and emotion regulation in preschool children. *Cognitive Development*, 22, 489–510.

Cauberghe, V. & Pelsmacker, P. D. (2010) Advergames. *Journal of Advertising*, 39(1), 5–19.

Chadwick Martin Bailey (2013) Consumers engaged via social media are more likely to buy, recommend. Available at: www.cmbinfo.com/press-center-content/46920/Consumers-Engaged-Via-Social-Media-Are-More-Likely-To-Buy-Recommend. Accessed 6 July 2013.

Chaney, I. M., Lin, K-H. & Chaney, J. (2004) The effect of billboards within the gaming environment. *Journal of Interactive Advertising*, 5(1). Available at: www.jiad.org/vol5/no1/chaney/index. Accessed 10 October 2013.

Chaplin, L. N. & John, D. R. (2005) The development of self-brand connections in children and adolescents. *Journal of Consumer Research*, 32(June), 119–129.

Chaplin, L. N. & John, D. R. (2007) Growing up in a material world: Age differences in materialism in children and adolescents. *Journal of Consumer Research*, 34 (December), 480–493.

Chatterjee, P., Hoffman, D. L. & Novak, T. P. (2002) Modeling the clickstream: Implications for web-based advertising efforts. *Marketing Science*, 22(4), 520–541.

Chattopadhyay, A. & Laborie, J. L. (2005) Managing brand experience: The market contact audit. *Journal of Advertising Research*, 45(1), 9–16.

Chebat, J., Sirgy, J. M. & St, James, V. (2006) Upscale image transfer from malls to stores: A self-image congruence explanation. *Journal of Business Research*, 59(12), 1288–1296.

Cheema, A. & Kaikati, A. M. (2010) The effect of need for uniqueness on word of mouth. *Journal of Marketing Research*, 47(3), 553–563.

Chen, J. & Ringel, M. (2001) Can advergaming be the future of interactive advertising? Working Paper. Available at: www.locz.com.br/loczgames/advergames.pdf. Accessed 10 October 2013.

Chen, M. J., Grube, J. W., Bersamin, M. et al. (2005) Alcohol advertising: What makes it attractive to youth? *Journal of Health Communication*, 10(6), 553–565.

Chernin, A. (2007) The relationship between children's knowledge of persuasive intent and persuasion: The case of televised food marketing. Ph.D. dissertation, University of Pennsylvania. (UMI Publication No AAT 3292015).

Chernin, A. (2008) The effects of food marketing on children's preferences: Testing the moderating roles of age and gender. *The Annals of the American Academy of Political and Social Science*, 615, 102–117.

Cheyne, A. D., Dorfman, L., Bukofzer, E. & Harris, J. L. (2013) Marketing sugary cereals to children: A content analysis of 17 child-targeted websites. *Journal of Health Communication*, 18(5), 563–582.

Cho, C., Lee, J. & Tharp, M. (2001) Different forced-exposure levels to banner advertisements. *Journal of Advertising Research*, 41(4), 45–56.

Choi, E. J. (2008) An exploratory study of the effect of shopping congruence on perceptions, attitudes, and purchase intentions in online and offline stores. Doctoral dissertation, Michigan State University.

Christenson, P. G. (1982) Children's perceptions of TV commercials and products: The effects of PSAs. *Communication Research*, 9(4), 491–524.

Churchill, G. A. & Moschis, G. P. (1979) Television and interpersonal influences on adolescent consumer learning. *Journal of Consumer Research*, 6 (June), 23–35.

Cicchirillo, V. & Lin, J. (2011) Stop playing with your food: A comparison of for-profit and non-profit food-related advergames. *Journal of Advertising Research*, 51(3), 484–498.

Clark, R. A. & Delia, J. G. (1976) The development of functional persuasive skills in childhood and early adolescence. *Child Development*, 47, 1008–1014.

Clarke, B. (2009) Early adolescents' use of social networking sites to maintain friendship and explore identity: Implications for policy. *Policy & Internet*, 1(1), 55–89.

Clarke, B. & Svanaes, S. (2012, May) *Digital Marketing and Advertising to Children: A Literature Review*. London: Advertising Education Forum. Available at: www.aeforun.org/gallery/8612144. Accessed 13 June 2013.

Colapinto, J. (2011, 3 October) Famous Names. *The New Yorker*. Available at: www.newyorker.com/reporting/2011/10.03/111003fa_fact_colapinto. Accessed 14 June 2013.

Coleman, J. C. & Hendry, L. (1990) *The Nature of Adolescence*, 2nd edn. London: Routledge.

Collins, A. M. & Quillian, M. R. (1969) Retrieval time from semantic memory. *Journal of Verbal Learning & Verbal Behavior*, 8, 240–247.

Collins, R. L., Ellickson, P. L. McCaffrey, D. F. & Hambarsoomians, K. (2007) Early adolescent exposure to alcohol advertising and its relationship to underage drinking. *Journal of Adolescent Health*, 37(1), 29–36.

Cone Communication (2010) *2010* Cone Communication new media study – fact sheet. Available at: www.conecomm.com/stuff/contentmgr/files/0/61d7fb20ef60d001b5b77a4308eeb986b/files/consumer_new_media_fact_sheet_final.pdf. Accessed 8 July 2013.

Consoli, J. (2004) Running in place(ment). *Brandweek*, 45(28), 4–6.

Constantinides, E. & Fountain, S. J. (2008) Web 2.0: Conceptual foundations and marketing issues. *Journal of Direct, Data and Digital Marketing Practice*, 9(3), 14.

Corbett, C. & Walker, C. (2009) Catchy cartoons, wayward websites, and mobile marketing – food marketing to children in a global world. *Education Review*, 21(2), 84–91.

Costa, M. (2010, 10 June) Brand awareness comes as part of growing up. *Marketing Week*. Available at: www.marketingweek.co.uk/brand-awareness-comes-as-part-of-growing-up/3014357.article. Accessed 28 May 2013.

Cova, B. & Cova, V. (2001) Tribal aspects of postmodern consumption: The case of French in-line roller skaters. *Journal of Consumer Behaviour*, 1(1), 67–76.

Covell, K. (1992) The appeal of image advertisements: Age, gender and product differences. *Journal of Early Adolescence*, 12(91), 46–60.

Cowley, E. & Barron, C. (2008) When product placement goes wrong: The effects of program liking and placement prominence. *Journal of Advertising*, 37(1), 89–98.

Coyle, J. R. & Thorson, E. (2001) The effects of progressive levels of interactivity and vividness in web marketing sites. *Journal of Advertising*, 30(3), 65–77.

Cragg, A. (2004) *Alcohol Advertising and Young People. Research Report for the Independent*

Television Commission and Ofcom, British Board of Film Classification, and Advertising Standards Authority, London: Cragg, Ross and Dawson.

Csikszentmihalyi, M. & Rochberg-Halton, E. (1981) *The Meaning of Things: Domestic Symbols of the Self*. Cambridge: Cambridge University Press.

Culp, J., Bell, R. A. & Cassady, D. (2010) Characteristics of food industry websites and 'advergames' targeting children. *Journal of Nutrition Education and Behavior*, 42(3), 197–204.

Curtis, P. (2011, 6 June) David Cameron backs proposals tackling sexualisation of childhood. *The Guardian*. Available at: www.guardian.co.uk/society/2011/jun-06/david-cameron-children-sexualisation-commercialisation. Accessed 26 July 2013.

Dahl, S., Eagle, L. & Baez, C. (2009) Analyzing advergames: Active diversions or actually deception: An exploratory study of online advergames content. *Young Consumers: Insight and Ideas for Responsible Marketers*, 10(1), 40–59.

Dahl, S., Eagle, L. & Fernandez, C. (2006) Analyzing advergames. In K. Podnar & Z. Jancic (Eds.) *Proceedings* 11 International Corporate and Marketing Communications Conference, Ljubljana, pp. 181–189.

Dahlen, M., Rasch, A. & Rosengren, S. (2003) Love at first site? A study of website advertising effectiveness. *Journal of Advertising Research*, 43(1), 25–33.

Dalton, M. A., Tickle, J. J., Sargent, J. D. et al. (2002) The incidence and context of tobacco use in popular movies from 1988–1997. *Preventative Medicine*, 34(5), 516–523.

Dammler, A. & Middelmann-Motz, A. (2002) I want one with Harry Potter on it. *International Journal of Advertising and Marketing to Children*, 3(2), 3–8.

d'Astous, A. & Chartier, F. (2000) A study of factors affecting consumer evaluations and memory of product placements in movies. *Journal of Current Issues and Research in Advertising*, 22(2), 31–40.

d'Astous, A. & Seguin, N. (1999) Consumer reactions to product placement strategies in television sponsorship. *European Journal of Marketing*, 33(9/10), 896–910.

Daugherty, T., Li, H. & Biocca, F. (2008) Consumer learning and the effects of virtual experience relative to indirect and direct product experience. *Psychology & Marketing*, 25(7), 568–586.

Davidson, I. (2013, 8 March) Alcohol 'hard to regulate on social media'. *The New Zealand Herald*. Available at: www.nzherald.co.nz/nz/news/article. Accessed 6 July 2013.

Davidson, R. (2008) Advergaming. Buckle in for a new era. In M. Ipe (Ed.) *Advergaming and Ingame Advertising*, pp. 128–146. Hyderabad: ICFAI University Press.

Deal, D. (2005) The ability of online brand games to build brand equity: An exploratory analysis. Paper in *Proceedings of the 2005 DIGRA Conference*. Available at: www. gamesconference.org/digra2005/viewabstract.php?id=46. Accessed 14 June 2013.

Dean, D., Digrande, S., Field, D. et al. (2012, January). *The Internet Economy in the G-20: The $4.2 Trillion Growth Opportunity*. Boston, MA: Boston Consulting Group.

DeLorme, D. E. & Reid, L. N. (1999) Moviegoers' experiences and interpretations of brands in films revisited. *Journal of Advertising*, 28(2), 71–96.

Dell'Antonia, K. J. (2010, 3 April) Preschoolers know all about brands. Doublex.

Available at: www.slate.com/articles/double_x/doublex/2010/04/preschoolers_ know_all_about_brands. Accessed 4 June 2013.

De Pelsmacker, P., Geuens, M. & Anckaert, P. (2002) Media context and advertising effectiveness: The role of context appreciation and context/ad similarity. *Journal of Advertising*, 31, 49–61.

Derbaix, C. & Bree, J. (1997) The impact of children's affective reactions elicited by commercials on attitudes toward the advertisement and the brand. *International Journal of Research in Marketing*, 14, 207–229.

Derscheid, L. E., Kwon, Y. H. & Fang, S. R. (1996) Preschoolers' socialization as consumers of clothing and recognition of symbolism. *Perceptual & Motor Skills*, 82, 1171–1181.

Divol, R., Edelman, D. & Sarrazin, H. (2012, April). Demystifying social media. Available at: www.mckinsey.com/insights/marketing_sales/understanding-social-media. Accessed 11 June 2013.

Donohue, T. R., Meyer, T. P. & Henke, L. L. (1978) Black and white children: Perceptions of TV commercials. *Journal of Marketing*, 42 (October), 34–40.

Donohue, T. R., Henke, L. L. & Donohue, W. A. (1980) Do kids know what TV commercials intend? *Journal of Advertising Research*, 20 (October), 51–57.

Dotson, M. J. & Hyatt, E. M. (2005) Major influence factors in children's consumer socialization, *Journal of Consumer Marketing*, 22(1), 35–42.

Doyle, S. (2007) The role of social networks in marketing. *Journal of Database Marketing & Customer Strategy Management*, 15, 60–64.

Dredge, S. (2012, 8 August) Digital brands spark thrills and fear in children's entertainment industry. *The Guardian*. Available at: www.guardian.co.uk/technology/appsblog/2012/oct/08/digital-kids-brands. Accessed 22 July 2013.

Dreze, X. & Hussher, F. (2003) Internet advertising: Is anybody watching? *Journal of Interactive Marketing*, 17(4), 8–23.

Duke, C. R. & Carlson, L. B. (1994) Applying implicit memory measures: Word fragment completion in advertising tests. *Journal of Current Issues and Research in Advertising*, 16(2), 29–40.

Dynamic Logic (2002) *Rich Media Campaigns Twice as Effective as Lifting Brand Message Association*. Research Report. Available at: www.dynamiclogic.com/beyond_0602. php. Accessed 4 November 2012.

Elliott, R. & Leonard, C. (2004) Peer pressure and poverty: Exploring fashion brands and consumption symbolism among children of the 'British poor'. *Journal of Consumer Behaviour*, 3(4), 347–359.

eMarketer.com (2011a) What Twitter users think about the brands they follow. Available at: www.emarketer.com/articles. Accessed 8 July 2013.

eMarketer.com (2011b) Consumers embrace social media for brand feedback. Available at: www.emarketer.com/articles. Accessed 8 July 2013.

eMarketer.com (2012, 10 July). The ripple effects of following a brand on social media. Available at: www.emarketer.com/Article/Ripple-Effect-of-Following-a-Brand-on-Social-Media. Accessed 8 July 2013.

Erftlier, T. & Dyson, A. H. (1986) 'Oh ppbbt!': Differences between oral and written persuasive strategies of school-aged children. *Discourse Processes*, 9, 91–114.

Ernst & Young (2012, May) Protecting and strengthening your brand: Social media governance and strategy. Available at: www.ey.com/Publication/VwLUAssets/ Protecting_and_strengthening_your_brand. Accessed 3 June 2013.

Escalas, J. E. & Bettman, J. R. (2003) You are what they eat: The influence of reference groups on consumers' connections to brands. *Journal of Consumer Psychology*, 13(3), 339–348.

Evans, D. (2011) *Social Media Marketing: An Hour a Day*. Indianapolis: Wiley.

Eysenck, M. W. (1977) *Human Memory: Theory, Research and Individual Differences*. Oxford: Pergamon Press.

Eysenck, M. W. (1984) *A Handbook of Cognitive Psychology*. Hillsdale, NJ: Lawrence Erlbaum Associates.

Faber, R. J., Lee, M. & Nan, X. (2004) Advertising and the consumer information environment online. *American Behavioral Scientist*, 48(4), 447–466.

Family Lives (2012, June) All of our concern: Commercialisation, sexualisation and hypermasculinity. Available at: www.TeenBoundaries.co.uk. Accessed 12 June 2013.

Fattah, H. & Paul, P. (2002, May) Gaming gets serious. *American Demographics*, 39–43.

Ferraro, R., Bettman, J. R. & Chartrand, T. L. (2008) The power of strangers: The effect of incidental consumer brand encounters on brand choice. *Journal of Consumer Research*, 35, 729–741.

Ferrazzi, K. & Benezra, K. (2001) Journey to the top. *Brandweek,* 16 April, pp. 28–36.

Fielder, A., Gardner, W., Nairn, A. & Pitt, J. (2007) Fair game? Assessing the commercial activity on children's favourite websites and online environments. National Consumer Council and Childnet International. Available at: www.childnet.com/ publications/policy/aspx. Accessed 12 June 2013.

Filloux, F. (2009) measuring time spent on a web page. Monday note. Available at: www.mondaynote.com/2009/05/24/measuring-time-spent-on-a-web-page. Accessed 8 August 2013.

Fiore, A. M., Kim, J. & Lee, H. (2005) Effect of image interactivity technology on consumer responses toward the online retailer. *Journal of Interactive Marketing*, 19(3), 38–53.

Fischer, P. M., Schwartz, M. P., Richards, J. W. et al. (1991) Brand logo recognition by children aged 3 to 6 years. *Journal of American Medical Association*, 266, 3145–3148.

Fisher, T. (2009) ROI in social media: A look at the arguments. *Journal of Database Marketing & Customer Strategy Management*, 16, 189–195.

Fournier, S. (1998) Customers and their brands: Developing relationship theory in consumer research. *Journal of Consumer Research*, 24(1), 343–373.

Fournier, S. & Richins, M. L. (1991) Some theoretical and popular notions concerning materialism. *Journal of Genetic Psychology*, 127 (December), 157–162.

Frank, T. (1997) *The Conquest of Cool: Business, Culture, Counterculture and the Rise of Hip Consumerism*. Chicago: University of Chicago Press.

Friestad, M. & Wright, P. (1994) The persuasion knowledge model: How people cope with persuasion attempts. *Journal of Consumer Research*, 21(1), 1–30.

Frye, D., Zelazo, P. D. & Palfai, T. (1995) Theory of mind and rule-based reasoning. *Cognitive Development*, 10, 483–527.

Funk, T. (2011) *Social Media Playbook for Business: Reaching Your Online Community with Twitter, Facebook, LinkedIn and More*. Santa Barbara, CA: Praeger.

Gabisch, J. A. & Gwebu, K. L. (2011) Impact of virtual brand experience on purchase intentions: The role of multichannel congruence. *Journal of Electronic Commerce Research*, 12(4), 302–319.

Gaines, L. & Esserman, J. F. (1981) A quantitative study of young children's comprehension of television programs and commercials. In J. Esserman (Ed.) *Television Advertising and Children: Issues, Research and Findings*, pp. 96–105. New York: Child Research Service.

Galst, J. P. (1980) Television food commercials and pro-nutritional public service announcements as determinants of young people's snack choices. *Child Development*, 51(3), 935–938.

Garris, R., Ahlers, R. & Driskell, J. E. (2002) Games, motivation, and learning: A research and practice model. *Simulation & Gaming*, 33, 441–467.

Gillin, P. (2007) *The New Influencers: A Marketer's Guide to the New Social Media*. Sanger, CA: Quill Driver Books.

Ginsburg, H. P. & Opper, S. (1988) *Piaget's Theory of Intellectual Development*. Englewood Cliffs, NJ: Prentice Hall.

Glass, Z. (2007) The effectiveness of product placement in video games. *Journal of Interactive Advertising*, 8(1), 1–27.

Goldberg, M. E. (1990) A quasi-experiment assessing the effectiveness of TV advertising directed to children. *Journal of Marketing Research*, 27, 445–454.

Goldberg, M. E. & Gorn, G. J. (1978) Some unintended consequences of TV advertising to children. *Journal of Consumer Research*, 5, 22–29.

Goldberg, M. E., Gorn, G. J. & Gibson, W. (1987) TV messages for snacks and breakfast foods: Do they influence children's preferences? *Journal of Consumer Research*, 5, 73–81.

Goldberg, M. E., Gorn, G. J., Peracchio, L. & Barnossy, G. (2003) Understanding materialism among youth. *Journal of Consumer Psychology*, 13 (September), 278–288.

Goldenburg, J., Libai, B. & Muller, E. (2001) Talk of the network: A complex systems look at the underlying processes of word-of-mouth. *Marketing Letters*, 12(3), 211–223.

Gorn, G. J. & Goldberg, M. E. (1978) The impact of television advertising on children from low income families. *Journal of Consumer Research*, 4, 86–88.

Gould, S. J., Gupta, P. B. & Grabner-Kraurer, S. (2000) Product placements in movies: A cross-cultural analysis of Austrian, French, and American consumers' attitudes toward this emerging international promotional medium. *Journal of Advertising*, 29(4), 41–58.

Grassl, W. (1999) The reality of brands: Toward an ontology of marketing. *American Journal of Economics and Sociology*, 58, 313–360.

Green, L., Brady, D., Olafsson, K. et al. (2011) *Risks and Safety for Australian Children on the Internet. Full Findings from the AU Kids Online Survey of 9–16 year Olds and their Parents*. Available at: www.exposedprojects.org/wp-content/uploads/2013/01/risk-and-safety-for-Australian-children-on-the-internet. Accessed 13 June 2013.

Griffith, D. A. & Chen, Q. (2004) The influence of virtual direct experience (VDE) on on-line ad message effectiveness. *Journal of Advertising*, 33(1), 55–68.

Griffiths, R. & Casswell, S. (2010) Intoxigenic digital spaces? Youth, social networking sites and alcohol marketing. *Drug and Alcohol Review*, 29, 525–530.

Gross, J. J. (Ed.) (2007) *Handbook of Emotion Regulation*. New York: Guilford.

Guest, L. P. (1942) The genesis of brand awareness. *Journal of Applied Psychology*, 26(6), 800–808.

Guest, L. P. (1955) Brand loyalty – twelve years later. *Journal of Applied Psychology*, 39(6), 405–408.

Guest, L. P. (1964) Brand loyalty revisited: A twenty-year report. *Journal of Applied Psychology*, 48(2), 93–97.

Gunn, E. (2001) Product placement prize. *Advertising Age*, 72(7), 10.

Gunter, B. (2014) *Media and the Sexualization of Childhood*. London: Routledge.

Gunter, B. & Furnham, A. (1998) *Children as Consumers: A Psychological Analysis of the Young People's Market*. London: Routledge.

Gunter, B., Hansen, A. & Touri, M. (2010) *Alcohol Advertising and Young People's Drinking: Representation, Reception and Regulation*. Basingstoke: Palgrave Macmillan.

Gunter, B., McAleer, J. & Clifford, B. (1992, 11–13 March). Children and television advertising: A developmental perspective. In: *Children and Young People: Are They the New Consumers?*, pp. 187–209. Amsterdam: European Society for Opinion and Marketing Research, Conference Proceedings. Milan, Italy.

Gunter, B., Oates, C. & Blades, M. (2005) *Advertising to Children on TV: Content, Impact and Regulation*. Mahwah, NJ: Lawrence Erlbaum Associates.

Gupta, P. B. & Lord, K. R. (1998) Product placement in movies: The effect of prominence and mode on audience recall. *Journal of Current Issues and Research in Advertising*, 20(1), 47–59.

Gupta, S., Armstrong, K. & Clayton, Z. (2011) *Social Media*. Harvard School Publishing, October, 1–14.

Ha, L. (1996) Advertising clutter in consumer magazines: Dimensions and effects. *Journal of Advertising Research*, 36, 76–83.

Hallerman, D. (2008) Behavioral targeting: Marketing trends. eMarketer.com. Available at: www.emarketer.com/Reports/All/Emarketer_2000487.aspx. Accessed 10 October 2013.

Hanna, R., Rohm, A. & Crittenden, V. L. (2011) We're all connected: The power of the social media ecosystem. *Business Horizons*, 54(3), 265–273.

Harris, J. L., Brownell, K. D. & Bargh, J. A. (2009) The food marketing defense model: Integrating psychological research to protect youth and inform public policy. *Social Issues and Policy Review*, 3, 211–271.

Harris, J. L., Pomeranz, J. L., Lobstein, T., Brownell, K. D. (2009) A crisis in the marketplace: How food marketing contributes to childhood obesity and what can be done. *Annual Review of Public Health*, 30, 211–225.

Harris, J. L., Schwarz, M. B. & Brownell, K. D. (2009) *Cereal FACTS: Evaluating the Nutritional Quality and Marketing of Children's Cereals*. Yale Rudd Center for Policy and Obesity. Available at: www.cerealfacts.org/media/Cereal_FACTS_Report. Accessed 10 October 2013.

Harris, J. L., Schwarz, M. B., Brownell, K. D. et al. (2010) *Fast Food FACTS: Evaluating Fast Food Nutrition and Marketing to Youth*. Yale Rudd Center for Policy and Obesity. Available at: www.fastfoodfacts.org/media/Fastfood_FACTS_Report. Accessed 10 October 2013.

Harris, J. L., Schwarz, M. B., Brownell, K. D. et al. (2011, October) *Sugary Drinks FACTS: Evaluating Sugary Drink Nutrition and Marketing to Youth*. Yale Rudd Center for Policy and Obesity. Available at: www.sugarydrinksfacts.org/media/Sugarydrinks_FACTS_Report

Harris, J., Speers, S., Schwartz, M. & Brownell, K. D. (2012) US food company branded advergames on the internet: Children's exposure and effects on snack consumption. *Journal of Children and Media*, 6(1), 51–68.

Hasebrink, U., Gorzig, A., Haddon, L. et al. (2011) *Patterns of Risk and Safety Online: In-depth Analyses From the EU Kids Online Survey of 9–16 Year Olds and their Parents in 25 Countries*. London: EU Kids Online, London School of Economics.

Hastings, G., McDermott, L., Angus, K. et al. (2006) *The Extent, Nature and Effects of Food Promotion to Children: A Review of the Evidence*. Technical paper prepared for the World Health Organization. Geneva: WHO. Available at: www.wholibdoc.who.int/publications/2007/9789241595247_eng. Accessed 8 August 2013.

Hastings, G., Stead, M., McDermott, L. et al. (2003) Review of research on the effects of food promotion to children. Available at: www.food.gov.uk/multimedia/pdfs/foodpromotiontochildren1. Accessed 8 August 2013.

Hastings, G., Stead, M., McDermott, L. et al. (2005, September) *Review of Research on the Effects of Food Promotion to Children. A Report Commissioned by the Food Standards Agency*. Available at: www.foodstandards.gov.uk/multimedia/pdfs/promofoodchildrenexec. Accessed 8 August 2013.

Hawkes, C. (2004) *Marketing Food to Children: The Global Regulatory Environment*. Geneva: World Health Organization.

Hawkes, C. (2005) Self-regulation of food advertising. What it can, could and cannot do to discourage unhealthy eating habits among children. *British Nutrition Foundation Nutrition Bulletin*, 30, 374–382.

Hawkes, C. (2006) Uneven dietary development: linking the policies and processes of globalization with the nutrition transition, obesity and diet related chronic diseases. *Globalization and Health*, 2, 4.doi:10.1186/1744-8603-2-4.

Hawkes, C. (2007a) *Marketing Food To Children: Changes in the Global Regulatory Environment 2004–2006*. World Health Organization, Geneva. Available at: www.who.int/dietphysicalactivity/regularory_enviroment_CHawkes07. Accessed 8 April 2014.

Hawkes, C. (2007b) Regulating food marketing to young people worldwide: Trends and policy drivers. *American Journal of Public Health*, 97(11), 1962–1973.

Hawkes, C. & Harris, C. L. (2011) An analysis of food industry pledges on marketing to children. *Public Health Nutrition*, 14(8), 1403–1414.

Haynes, J., Burts, D. C., Dukes, A. & Cloud, R. (1993) Consumer socialization of preschoolers and kindergartners as related to clothing consumption. *Psychology and Marketing*, 10 (March/April), 151–166.

Hemp, P. (2006) Avatar-based marketing. *Harvard Business Review*, June, 48–56.

Available at: www.vphil.stanford.edu/news/2006/hbr-avatar-based-marketing. Accessed 20 June 2013.

Henry J. Kaiser Family Foundation (2006) It's child's play: Advergaming and the online marketing of food to children. *Education and Health*, 24(3), 44–45.

Hernandez, M. D. & Chapa, S. (2010) Adolescents, advergames and snack foods: Effects of positive affect and experience on memory and choice. *Journal of Marketing Communications*, 16(1–2), 59–68.

Hernandez, M. D., Chapa, S., Minor, M. S. et al. (2004) Hispanic attitudes toward advergames: A proposed model of their antecedents. *Journal of Interactive Advertising*, 4, 116–131.

Hertz, L. M. (2002) Advertising regulation on the internet. *The Computer and Internet Lawyer*, 19(6), 18–26.

Hess, R. D. (1970) Social class and ethnic influences upon socialization. In P. H. Mussen (Ed.) *Manual of Child Psychology*, Vol. 2, 3rd edn, pp. 457–559. New York: Wiley.

Hirschman, E. C. & Thompson, C. J. (1997) Why media matter: Towards a richer understanding of consumers' relationships with advertising and mass media. *Journal of Advertising*, 26(1), 43–60.

Hite, C. F. & Hite, R. E. (1995) Reliance on brand by young children. *Journal of the Market Research Society*, 37(2), 185–193.

Hite, R. E. & Eck, R. (1987) Advertising to children: Attitudes of business vs. consumers. *Journal of Advertising Research*, 27(5), 41–53.

Ho, S-H., Lin, Y-L. & Yang, Y-T. (2011) In-game advertising: Consumers' attitude and the effect of product placements on memory. *African Journal of Business Management*, 5(24), 10117–10127.

Hobbs, R. & Frost, R. (2003) Measuring the acquisition of media literacy skills. *Reading Research Quarterly*, 38, 330–355.

Hoffman, D. & Fodor, M. (2010) Can you measure the ROI of your social media marketing? *MIT Sloan Management Review*, 50(1), 41–50.

Hoffman, D. L. & Novak, T. P. (1996) Marketing in hypermedia computer-mediated environments: Conceptual foundations. *Journal of Marketing*, 60, 50–68.

Hogg, M. K., Bruce, M. & Hill, A. J. (1999) Brand recognition and young consumers. In E. J. Arnould & L. M. Scott (Eds.) *Advances in Consumer Research*, Vol. 26, pp. 671–674. Provo, UT: Association for Consumer Research.

Holbrook, M. B., Chestnut, R. W., Oliva, T. A. & Greenleaf, E. A. (1984) Play as a consumption experience: The roles of emotions, performance and personality in the enjoyment of games. *Journal of Consumer Research*, 11, 728–739.

Hollis, N (2011) Social media: Fans and followers are an 'end', not a 'means'. Available at: www.millwardbrown.com/Insights/PointsofView/SocialMediaFansandFollowers Accessed on 8 July 2013.

Holt, D. B. (2003) Brands and branding. Cultural Strategy Group. Available at: www.culturalstrategygroup.com/wp-content/uploads/brands-and-branding-csg.pdf. Accessed 5 July 2013.

Houston, J. P. (1981) *Fundamentals of Learning and Memory*. New York: Academic Press.

Hsu, C-L. & Lu, H-P. (2004) Why do people play on-line games? An extended TAM with social influences and flow experience. _Information and Management_, 41(7), 853–868.

Hudson, S. & Hudson, D. (2006) Branded entertainment: A new advertising technique or product placement in disguise? _Journal of Marketing Management_, 22(5–6), 489–504.

Hudson, S., Roth, M. & Madden, T. (2012) Customer communication management in the new digital era. _Centre for Marketing Studies_, 1–28.

Hunter, N. E. (2009) Revisiting the regulation debate: The effect of food marketing on childhood obesity. _Pierce Law Review_, 7(2), 205–233.

HWZ/BV4 Brand Report (2012, January) The most valuable social media brands 2012. Available at: www.rankingthebrands.com/PDF/The%20Most%20Valuable%20 Social%20Media%20Brands%202012,%20HWZ. Accessed 3 June 2013.

HWZ/BV4 Brand Report (2013, January) The most valuable social media brands 2013. Available at: www.rankingthebrands.com/The-Brand-Rankings. aspx?rankingID=239&year=617. Accessed 3 June 2013.

Institute of Medicine (2006) _Food Marketing to Children and Youth: Threat or Opportunity?_ Washington, DC: National Academies Press.

ITU (2008) _Use of Information and Communication Technology by the World's Children and Youth: A Statistical Compilation_. Geneva: International Telecommunications Union.

Jahng, J., Jain, H. & Ramamurthy, K. (2000) Effective design of electronic commerce environments: A proposed theory of congruence and an illustration, _Systems and Humans_, 30(4), 456–471.

Jansen, B. J., Zhang, M., Sobel, K. & Chowdury, A. (2009) Twitter power: Tweets as electronic word of mouth. _Journal of the American Society for Information Science and Technology_, 60(11), 2169–2188.

Jarvis, J. (2005, 29 August) My Dell hell. _The Guardian_. Available at: www.guardian. co.uk/technology/2005/aug/29/mondaymediasection. Accessed 28 June 2013.

Javitch, D. (2008) Entrepreneurs need social networking. Entrepreneur.com. Available at: www.entrepreneur.com/humanresources/employeemanagementcolumnistda vidjavitch/article198178.html. Accessed 3 June 2013.

John, D. R. (1997, October) You are what you wear: The meaning of brand names to children. Paper presented at the Association for Consumer Research Conference, Minneapolis, MN.

John, D. R. (1999) Consumer socialization of children: A retrospective look at twenty-five years of research. _Journal of Consumer Research_, 26, 183–213.

John, D. R. & Sujan, M. (1990) Age differences in product categorization. _Journal of Consumer Research_, 16, 452–460.

Jones, S. C., Wiese, E. & Fabrianesi, B. (2008) Following the links: Food advertising and promotion on children's magazine websites. _Journal of Nonprofit and Public Sector Marketing_, 20(2), 165–190.

Kaiser Family Foundation (2006) _It's Child's Play: Advergaming and the Online Marketing of Food to Children_. Menlo Park, CA: The Henry J Kaiser Family Foundation. Available at: www.kff.org. Accessed 10 October 2013.

Kalehoff, M. (2013) Why consumers become brand fans. Syncapse. Available at: www. synapse.com/why-consumers-become-facebook-brand-fans. Accessed 1 July 2013.

Kaltcheva, V. D. & Weitz, B. A. (2006) When should a retailer create an exciting store environment? *Journal of Marketing*, 70(1), 107–118.

Kapferer, J. (1992) *Strategic Brand Management*. New York: Free Press.

Kaplan, A. M. & Haenlein, M. (2010) Users of the world, unite! The challenges and opportunities of social media. *Business Horizons*, 53(1), 59–68.

Kaplan, A. M. & Haenlein, M. (2011) Two hearts in three-quarter time: How to waltz the social media/viral marketing dance. *Business Horizons*, 54(3), 253–263.

Karrh, J. A. (1998) Brand placement: A review. *Journal of Current Issues & Research in Advertising*, 20(2), 31–49.

Kasser, T. (2002) *The High Price of Materialism*. Cambridge, MA: MIT Press.

Kasser, T., Ryan, R. M., Couchman, C. E. & Sheldon, K. M. (2004) Materialistic values: Their causes and consequences. In T. Kasser and A. D. Kanner (Eds.) *Psychology and Consumer Culture*, pp. 11–28. Washington, DC: American Psychological Association.

Keaty, A., John, R. J. & Henke, L. L. (2002) Can internet service providers and other secondary parties be held liable for deceptive online advertising? *Business Lawyer*, 58(1), 479–511.

Keller, E. (2005) Influentials inspire buyer confidence. *Advertising Age*, 76, 22–24.

Keller, E. (2007) Unleashing the power of word of mouth: Creating brand advocacy to drive growth. *Journal of Advertising Research*, 47(4), 448–452.

Keller, K. L. (2003) Brand synthesis: The multidimensionality of brand knowledge. *Journal of Consumer Research*, 29, 595–600.

Kelly, K. J. & Edwards, R. W. (1998) Image advertisements for alcohol products: Is their appeal associated with adolescents' intention to consume alcohol? *Adolescence*, 33(129), 47–59.

Kemler, D. G. (1983) Exploring and reexploring issues of integrality, perceptual sensitivity, and dimensional salience. *Journal of Experimental Child Psychology*, 36, 365–379.

Keng, C-J. & Lin, H-Y. (2006) Impact of telepresence levels on internet advertising effects. *CyberPsychology & Behavior*, 9(1), 82–94.

King, L., Hebden, L., Grunseit, A. et al. (2011) Industry self regulation of television food advertising: Responsible or responsive? *International Journal of Pediatric Obesity*, 6(2–2), e390–398.

King, S. (2012) The interactive indulgence: The use of advergames to curb childhood obesity. *The Elon Journal of Undergraduate Research in Communications*, 3(2), 31–41.

Klein, L. R. (2003) Creating virtual product experiences: The role of telepresence. *Journal of Interactive Marketing*, 17 (Winter), 41–55.

Klein, N. (2000). *No Logo*. Toronto, Random House.

Koriat, A., Goldsmith, M. & Pansky, A. (2000) Toward a psychology of memory accuracy. *Annual Review of Psychology*, 51, 481–537.

Kotler, P. (1965) Behavioural models for analysing buyers. *Journal of Marketing*, 29(4), 37–45.

Kuhn, M. & Eischen, W. (1997) *Leveraging the Aptitude and Ability of Eight-Year-Old Adults and Other Wonders of Technology*. European Society for Opinion and Marketing Research (ESOMAR) Seminar on Youth Research, Copenhagen, 22–24 October.

Kumar, A. (2000) Interference effects of contextual cues in advertisements on memory for ad content. *Journal of Consumer Psychology*, 9(3), 155–166.

Kumar, A. & Krishnan, S. (2004) Memory interference in advertising: A replication and extension. *Journal of Consumer Research*, 30 (March), 602–611.

Kunkel, D. (1988) Children and host-selling television commercials. *Communication Research*, 15(1), 71–92.

Kunkel, D. (2001) Children and television advertising. In D. G. Singer & J. L. Singer (Eds.) *Handbook of Children and the Media,* pp. 375–394. Thousand Oaks, CA: Sage.

Kunkel, D. (2010) Commentary: Mismeasurement of children's understanding of the persuasive intent of advertising. *Journal of Children and Media*, 4(1), 109–117.

Kunkel, D., McKinley, C. & Wright, P. (2009) The impact of industry self-regulation on the nutritional quality of foods advertised on television to children. Children Now. Available at: www.childrennow.org/uploads/documents/adstudy_2009. Accessed 13 July 2013.

Kunkel, D. & Roberts, D. (1991) Yong minds and marketplace values: Research and policy issues in children's television advertising. *Journal of Social Issues*, 47(1), 57–72.

Kunkel, D., Wilcox, B. L., Cantor, J. et al. (2004) *Report of the APA Task Force on Advertising and Children.* Washington, DC: American Psychological Association.

Kwon, W. & Lennon, S. J. (2009) Reciprocal effects between multichannel retailers' offline and online brand images. *Journal of Retailing*, 85(3), 376–390.

Laczniak, R. N. & Palan, K. M. (2004) Under the influence. *Marketing Research*, 16(1), 34–40.

La Ferle, C. & Edwards, S. M. (2006) Product placement: How brands appear on television. *Journal of Advertising*, 35(4), 65–86.

Lamb, S. & Brown, L. M. (2006) *Packaging Girlhood: Rescuing Our Daughters from Marketers' Schemes.* New York: St Martin's Press.

Lapierre, M. A., Vaala, S. E. & Linebarger, D. L. (2011) Influence of licensed spoke-scharacters and health cues on children's ratings of cereal taste. *Archives of Pediatric and Adolescent Medicine*, 165, 229–234.

Lavidge, R. & Steiner, G. (1961) A model for predictive measurement of advertising effectiveness. *Journal of Marketing*, 24(4), 59–62.

Lawlor, M. A. & Prothero, A. (2003) Children's understanding of television advertising intent. *Journal of Marketing Management*, 19, 411–431.

Lee, E. B. & Browne, L. A. (1995) Effects of television advertising on African American teenagers. *Journal of Black Studies*, 25(5), 523–536.

Lee, M., Choi, Y., Quilliam, E. T. & Cole, R. T. (2009) Playing with food: Content analysis of food advergames. *Journal of Consumer Affairs*, 43(1), 129–154.

Lee, M. & Faber, R. J. (2007) Effects of product placement in on-line games on brand memory: A perspective of the limited capacity model of attention. *Journal of Advertising*, 36(4), 75–90.

Lee, M. & Youn, S. (2008) Leading national advertisers' uses of advergames. *Journal of Current Issues and Research in Advertising*, 30(2), 1–13.

Leiber, L. (1998) Commercial and character slogan recall by children aged 9 to 11 years: Budweiser frogs versus Bugs Bunny. Center on Alcohol Advertising.

Available at: www.traumafdn.org/trauma/alcohol/ads/budstudy.html. Accessed 27 March 2010.

Lenhart, A., Purcell, K., Smith, A., Zikuhr, K. (2010) *Social Media & Mobile Internet Use Among Teens and Young Adults*. Washington, DC: Pew Internet and American Life Project. www.pewinstitute.org. Accessed 8 August 2013.

Leonhardt, D. & Kerwin, K. (1997, 30 June) Is Madison Avenue taking 'get 'em while they're young' too far? *Business Week*, pp. 62–67.

Levin, A. M., Levin, J. P. & Weller, J. A. (2005) A multi-attribute analysis of preferences for online and offline shopping: Differences across products, consumers and shopping stages. *Journal of Electronic Commerce Research*, 6(4), 281–290.

Levin, D. & Kilbourne, J. (2008) *So Sexy So Soon: The New Sexualised Childhood and What Parents Can Do to Protect Their Kids*. New York: Ballantine.

Levin, S. R., Petros, T. V. & Petrella, F. W. (1982) Preschoolers' awareness of television advertising. *Child Development*, 53 (August), 933–937.

Li, H., Daugherty, T. & Biocca, F. (2002) Impact of 3-D advertising on product knowledge, brand attitude and purchase intention: The mediating role of presence. *Journal of Advertising*, 31(3), 43–57.

Li, H., Daugherty, T. & Biocca, F. (2003) The role of virtual experience in consumer learning. *Journal of Consumer Psychology*, 13(4), 395–407.

Lieberman, L. R. & Orlandi, M. A. (1987) Alcohol advertising and adolescent drinking. *Alcohol Health and Research World*, 12(1), 30–43.

Lindstrom, M. (2008) Brand kids. *Young Consumers*, 9(1), 66–67.

Lindstrom, M. (2011) *Brand Child*. London: Kogan Page.

Linn, S. (2004) *Consuming Kids: The Hostile Takeover of Childhood*. New York: New Press.

Liu, Y. & Shrum, L. J. (2002) What is interactivity and is it always such a good thing? Implications of definition, person and situation for the influence of interactivity on advertising effectiveness. *Journal of Advertising*, 31(4), 53–64.

Livingstone, S. (2005) Assessing the research base for the policy debate over the effects of food advertising to children. *International Journal of Advertising*, 24(3), 1–10.

Livingstone, S. (2006a) *New Research on Advertising Foods to Children: An Updated Review of the Literature*. Media@LSE, Department of Media and Communication. Available at: www.lse.ac.uk/collections/media@lse/whoswho/sonialivingstone. Accessed 22 July 2013.

Livingstone, S. (2006b) Does TV advertising make children fat? What the evidence tells us. *Public Policy Research*, 13(1), 54–61.

Livingstone, S. & Brake, D. (2010) On the rapid rise of social networking sites: New findings and policy implications. *Children and Society*, 24(1), 75–83.

Livingstone, S., Haddon, L., Gorzig, A. & Olafsson, K. (2011) *Risks and Safety on the Internet: The Perspective of European Children. Full findings*. London: EU Kids Online, London School of Economics.

Livingstone, S. & Helsper, E. (2004) *Advertising 'Unhealthy' Foods to Children: Understanding Promotion in the Context of Children's Daily Lives. A Review of the Literature for the Market Research Department of the Office of Communication (Ofcom)*.

London: Ofcom. Available at: www.ofcom.org.uk/research/consumer_audience_research/tv/food_ads/appendix2.pdf. Accessed 12 October 2012.

Livingstone, S. & Helsper, E. (2006) Does advertising literacy mediate the effects of advertising on children? A critical examination of two linked research literatures in relation to obesity and food choice. *Journal of Communication*, 56, 560–584.

Livingstone, S., Olafsson, K. & Staksrud, E. (2011) *Social Networking, Age and Privacy*. London: EU Kids Online, London School of Economics.

Lu, A., Baranowski, J., Cullen, K. et al. (2010) Interactive media for childhood obesity prevention. *Health Communication*, 25(6/7), 581–582.

Lucas, K. & Lloyd, B. (1999) Starting smoking: Girls' explanations of the influence of peers. *Journal of Adolescence*, 22, 647–655.

Lyons, A., Goodwin, I., Niland, P. et al. (2012) *Mixing Alcohol and Social Media: Young Adults and Drinking Cultures*. European Health Psychology Society's 26th Conference, 21–25 August, Prague. Available at: www.ehps2012prague.com. Accessed 8 July 2013.

Macklin, M. C. (1983) Do children understand TV ads? *Journal of Advertising Research*, 23(1), 63–70.

Macklin, M. C. (1985) Do young children understand the selling intent of commercials? *Journal of Consumers Affairs*, 19 (Winter), 293–304.

Macklin, M. C. (1987) Preschoolers' understanding of the informational function of television advertising. *Journal of Consumer Research*, 14 (September), 229–239.

Macklin, M. C. (1996) Preschoolers' learning of brand names from visual cues. *Journal of Consumer Research*, 28, 251–261.

Mallalieu, L., Palan, K. M. & Laczniak, R. N. (2005) Understanding children's knowledge and beliefs about advertising: A global issue that spans generations. *Journal of Current Issues and Research in Advertising*, 27(1), 53–64.

Mallinckrodt, V. & Mizerski, D. (2007) The effects of playing an advergame on young children's perceptions, preferences and requests. *Journal of Advertising*, 36(1), 87–100.

Manchanda, P., Dube, J-P., Goh, K. Y. & Chintagunta, P. K. (2006) The effect of banner advertising on internet purchasing. *Journal of Marketing Research*, 43, 98–108.

Mangleburg, T. F. & Bristol, T. (1999) Socialisation and adolescents' scepticism toward advertising. In M. C. Macklin & L. Carlson (Eds.) *Advertising to Children: Concepts and Controversies*, pp. 27–47. Thousand Oaks, CA: Sage.

Mangold, W. G. & Faulds, D. J. (2009) Social media: The new hybrid element of the promotion mix. *Business Horizons*, 52, 357–365.

MarketingMagazine.co.uk. (2006, 11 January) Available at: www.marketingmagazine.co.uk/news/534969/Mark-Ritson-branding-Norder-fire-smokers-bland-brands.

Markham, E. M. (1980) The acquisition and hierarchical organization of categories by children. In R. J. Spiro, B. C. Bruce & W. F. Brewer (Eds.) *Theoretical Issues in Reading Comprehension*. pp. 371–406. Hillsdale, NJ: Lawrence Erlbaum.

Markham, E. M. & Callahan, M. A. (1983) An analysis of hierarchical classification. In R. Sternberg (Ed.) *Advances in the Psychology of Human Intelligence*, Vol. 2, pp. 325–365. Hillsdale, NJ: Lawrence Erlbaum.

Marshall, C. (1997, September) Protect the parents: Exploiting parents and children through advertising. *Management Today*, p. 6.

Martinic, M. & Measham, F. (Eds.) (2008) *Swimming with Crocodiles: The Culture of Extreme Drinking*. London: Routledge.

Mayo, E. & Nairn, A. (2009) *Consumer Kids: How Big Business is Grooming Our Children for Profit*. London: Constable.

Mayzlin, D. (2006) Promotional chat on the internet. *Marketing Science*, 25(2), 155–163.

McAlister, A. & Cornwell, T. B. (2010) Children's brand symbolism understanding: Links to theory of mind and executive functioning. *Psychology & Marketing*, 27(3), 203–228.

McAlister, A. & Peterson, C. (2006) Mental playmates: Siblings, executive functioning and theory of mind. *British Journal of Developmental Psychology*, 24, 733–751.

McDonald, C. & Scott, J. (2007) A brief history of advertising. In G. J. Tellis & T. Ambler (Eds.) *The Sage Handbook of Advertising*, pp. 17–34. Thousand Oaks, CA: Sage.

McNeal, J. U. (1992) *Kids as Customers*. New York: Lexington Books.

McNeal, J. U. & Yeh, C. (1993) Born to shop. *American Demographics*, 15, 6.

Mediamark Research & Intelligence (2007) Gaming is nearly ubiquitous with kids online. Available at: www.gfkmri.com/pdf/gaming%20is%20nearly%20ubiquitious%20 with%20kids%20online. Accessed 22 July 2013.

Merriam-Webster (no date) brand. Available at: www.merriam-webster.com/ dictionary/brand. Accessed 18 June 2013.

Meyer, D. E. (1970) On the representation and retrieval of stored semantic information. *Cognitive Psychology*, 1, 242–300.

Meyers-Levy, J. (1989) The influence of a brand name's association set size and word frequency on brand memory. *Journal of Consumer Research*, 16(2), 197–207.

Meyers-Levy, J. & Tybout, A. M. (1989) Schema congruity as a basis for product evaluation. *Journal of Consumer Research*, 16(1), 39–54.

Mills, C. & Keil, F. C. (2005) The development of cynicism. *Psychological Science*, 16(5), 385–390.

Millward Brown (2011, August). How should your brand capitalize on social media? Available at: www.millwardbrown.com/Libraries/MB_Knowledge_Points_ Downloads/MillwardBrown_KnowledgePoint_SocialMedia. Accessed 3 June 2013.

Moe, W. W. & Fader, P. S. (2003) Dynamic conversion behaviour at e-commerce sites. *Management Science*, 50(3), 326–335.

Montgomery, K. C. & Chester, J. (2009) Interactive food and beverage marketing: Targeting adolescents in the digital age. *Journal of Adolescent Health*, 45, S18–S29.

Montgomery, K. & Chester, J. (2011, October) *Digital Food Marketing to Children and Adolescents. Problematic Practices and Policy Interventions*. National Policy and Legal Analysis Network to Prevent Childhood Obesity. Available at: www.foodpoli tics.com/wp-content/uploads/DigitalMarketingReport_FINAL_web_20111017. Accessed 27 June 2013.

Montgomery, N. V. & Unnava, H. R. (2007) The role of consumer memory in advertising. In G. J. Tellis & T. Ambler (Eds.) *The Sage Handbook of Advertising*, pp. 105–119. Thousand Oaks, CA: Sage.

Moore, E. S. (2004) Children and the changing world of advertising. *Journal of Business Ethics*, 52(2), 161–167.

Moore, E. S. & Rideout, V. (2007) The online marketing of food to children: Is it just fun and games? *Journal of Public Policy and Marketing*, 26, 202–222.

Moore, R. L. & Moschis, G. P. (1981) The role of family communication in consumer learning. *Journal of Communications*, 31 (Autumn), 42–51.

Moreau, C. P., Markman, A. B. & Lehman, D. R. (2001) What is it? Categorization flexibility and consumers' responses to really new products. *Journal of Consumer Research*, 27 (March), 489–498.

Morris, N. (2010, 18 February) Cameron aims at 'excessive commercialisation' of childhood. *The Independent*. Available at: www.independent.co.uk/news/uk/politics/cameron-aims-at-excessive-commercialisation-of-childhood-1903869. Accessed 26 July 2013.

Morton, C. R. & Friedman, M. (2002) 'I saw it in the movies': Exploring the link between product placement beliefs and reported usage behaviour. *Journal of Current Issues & Research in Advertising*, 24(2), 33–40.

Moschis, G. P. & Churchill, G. A. Jr. (1978) Consumer socialization: A theoretical and empirical analysis. *Journal of Marketing Research*, 15 (November), 599–609.

Moschis, G. P. & Moore, R. L. (1979) Decision making among the young: A socialization perspective. *Journal of Consumer Research*, 6 (September), 101–112.

Moschis, G. P. & Moore, R. L. (1980) Purchasing behaviour of adolescent consumers. *Proceedings of the American Marketing Association*, 45, 89–92.

Moschis, G. P., Moore, R. L. & Stanley, T. J. (1984) An exploratory study of brand loyalty development. *Advances in Consumer Research*, Vol. 11, pp. 412–417.

Moses, L. J. & Baldwin, D. A. (2005) What can the study of cognitive development reveal about children's ability to appreciate and cope with advertising? *Journal of Public Policy and Marketing*, 24, 186–201.

Mothers' Union (2010, September) *Bye Buy Childhood: A Report into the Commercialisation of Childhood*. London: Mothers' Union.

Mudambi, S. M. & Schuff, D. (2010) What makes a helpful online review? A study of customer reviews on Amazon.com. *MIS Quarterly*, 34(1), 185–200.

Muniz, A. M. & O'Guinn, T. C. (2001) Brand community. *Journal of Consumer Research*, 27(4), 412–432.

Naik, P. A. (2007) Integrated marketing communications: Provenance, practice and principles. In G. J. Tellis & T. Ambler (Eds.) *The Sage Handbook of Advertising*, pp. 35–53. Los Angeles, CA: Sage.

Nairn, A. & Hang, H. (2012, December) *Advergames: It's Not Child's Play. A Review of Research*. London: The Family and Parenting Institute. Available at: www.familyandparenting.org. Accessed 12 June 2013.

Nash, A. S. (2002, August) *Children's Responses to Alcohol Advertising on Television: A Summary of Recent Research. Report to the Office of Communications*, Department of Psychology, University of Hertfordshire, Hatfield.

Nash, A. S., Pine, K. J. & Lutz, R. J. (2000) TV alcohol advertising and children – A longitudinal study: Analysis of the first data collection. Paper presented at the British Psychological Society Development Conference, Brighton, England.

Nash, A. S., Pine, K. J. & Messer, D. J. (2009) Television alcohol advertising: Do children really mean what they say? *British Journal of Developmental Psychology*, 27, 85–104.

Nelson, M. R. (2002) Recall of brand placements in computer/video games. *Journal of Advertising Research*, 42(2), 80–92.

Nelson, M. R. (2005) Exploring consumer response to 'Advergaming'. In C. P. Haugvedt, K. A. Machelt & R. F. Yalch (Eds.) *Online Consumer Psychology: Understanding and Influencing Consumer Behavior in the Virtual World*, pp. 167–194. Mahwah, NJ: Lawrence Erlbaum Associates.

Nelson, M. R., Keum, H. & Yaros, R. A. (2004) Advertainment or advercreep? Game players' attitudes towards advertising and product placement in computer games. *Journal of Interactive Advertising*, 4(3), 1–30.

Nelson, M. R. & McLeod, L. E. (2005) Adolescent brand consciousness and product placements: Awareness, liking and perceived effects on self and others. *International Journal of Consumer Studies*, 29(6), 515–528.

Nelson, M. R., Yaros, R. A. & Keum, H. (2006) Examining the influence of telepresence on spectator and player processing of real and fictitious brands in a computer game. *Journal of Advertising*, 35, 87–99.

Nevitt, T. R. (1982) *Advertising in Britain: A History*. London: William Heinemann Ltd.

Newell, J., Salmon, C. T. & Chang, S. (2006) The hidden history of product placement. *Journal of Broadcasting & Electronic Media*, 50(4), 575–594.

News Bureau, University of Missouri (2008, 1 October). Advergames: Theme of game is secret to success. Available at: www.munews.missouri.edu/news-releases/2008/1001-wise-advergames.php. Accessed 24 June 2013.

Nieburg, O. (2013, 11 January) Top 20 candy brands on Facebook. Available at: www.confectionerynews.com/Markets/Top-20-candy-brands-on-Facebook. Accessed 27 June 2013.

Nielsen (2011) How social media impacts brand marketing. Nielsen Newswire. Available at: www.nielsen.com/us/en/newswire/2011/how-social-media-impacts-brand-marketing. Accessed 2 June 2013.

Norris, V. P. (1981) Advertising history – according to the textbooks. *Journal of Advertising History*, 9(3), 3–11.

Oates, C., Blades, M. & Gunter, B. (2002) Children and television advertising: When do they understand persuasive intent? *Journal of Consumer Research*, 1, 238–245.

Oates, C., Blades, M., Gunter, B. & Don, J. (2003) Children's understanding of television advertising: A qualitative approach. *Journal of Marketing Communications*, 9, 59–71.

O'Brien, P. (2012, 12 June). Should you let your child play at Habbo Hotel? Available at: www.channel4.com/news/should-you-let-your-child-play-in-Habbo-Hotel. Accessed 14 June 2013.

Ofcom (2010) *New Rules to Govern TV Product Placement*. London: Office of Communications. Available at: www.ofcom.org.uk/2010/12/news-rules-to-govern-product-placement. Accessed 26 June 2013.

Ofcom (2011) *Product Placement on TV*. London: Office of Communications. Available at: www.consumers/ofcom.org.uk/2011/02/product-placement-on-tv. Accessed 26 July 2013.

Ogden, C. L., Carroll, M. D. & Flegal, K. M. (2008) High body mass index for age among US children and adolescents. *Journal of the American Media Association*, 299, 2401–2405.

O'Guinn, T. C., Allen, C. T. & Semenik, R. J. (2009) *Advertising and Integrated Brand Promotion*. Mason, OH: South-Western Cengage Learning.

Opree, S. J., Buijzen, M., van Reijmersdal, E. A. & Valkenburg, P. M. (2013) Children's advertising exposure, advertised product desire and materialism: A longitudinal study. *Communication Research*, 40, 1–19.

Otnes, C., Kim. Y. C. & Kim, K. (1994) All I want for Christmas: An analysis of children's brand requests to Santa Claus. *Journal of Popular Culture*, 27 (Spring), 183–194.

Owen, L., Lewis, C., Auty, S. & Buijzen, M. (2012) Is children's understanding of non-traditional advertising comparable with their understanding of television advertising? *Journal of Public Policy and Marketing*, published online at: www.journals. marketingpower.com/toc/jppm/0/ja. Accessed 14 June 2013.

Oyserman, D. (2007) Social identity and self-regulation. In A. W. Kruglanski & E. T. Higgins (Eds.) *Social Psychology: Handbook of Basic Principles*, pp. 432–453. New York: Guilford Press.

Page, R. M. & Brewster, A. (2007) Emotional and rational product appeals in televised food advertisements for children: Analysis of commercials shown on US broadcast networks. *Journal of Child Health Care*, 11, 323–340.

Page, R. M. & Brewster, A. (2009) Depiction of food as having drug-like properties in televised food advertisements directed at children: Portrayals as pleasure enhancing and addictive. *Journal of Pediatric Health Care*, 23, 150–157.

Palmer, A. & Koenig-Lewis, N. (2009) An experiential, social network-based approach to direct marketing. *Direct Marketing: An International Journal*, 3(3), 162–176.

Palmer, S. (2006) *Toxic Childhood*. London: Orion.

Panic, K., Cauberghe, V. & De Pelsmacker, P. (2013) Comparing TV ads and advergames targeting children: The impact of persuasion knowledge on behavioural responses. *Journal of Advertising*, 42(2–3), 264–273.

Papadopoulos, L., (2010), *Sexualisation of Young People*. London: Home Office.

Park, J. & Hastak, M. (1994) Memory-based product judgements: Effects of involvement at encoding and retrieval. *Journal of Consumer Research*, 21 (December), 534–547.

Parrotta, A. & George, M. (2008) The future of advergames. *Casual Connect*, Fall. Available at: www.firsthillmedia.com. Accessed 12 June 2013.

Peracchio, L. A. & Myers-Levy, J. (1997) Evaluating persuasion-enhancing techniques from a resource-matching perspective. *Journal of Consumer Research*, 24, 178–191.

Percy, A., Wilson, J., McCartan, C. & McCrystal, P. (2011, February) *Teenage Drinking Cultures*. York: Joseph Rowntree Foundation. Available at: www.jrf.org. uk. Accessed 8 August 2013.

Peskin, J. (1992) Ruse and representations: On children's ability to conceal information. *Developmental Psychology*, 28, 84–87.

Peters, S. & Leshner, G. (2013) Get in the game: The effects of game-product congruity and product placement proximity on game players' processing of brands embedded in advergames. *Journal of Advertising*, 42(2–3), 113–130.

Pettey, C. (2008) Gartner says social networks are attracting too much traffic for retailers to ignore. *Gartner Research*. Available at: www.gartner.com/it/page.jsp?id=1. Accessed 8 August 2013.

Petty, R. E. & Cacioppo, J. T. (1979) Issue involvement can increase or decrease persuasion by enhancing message relevant cognitive responses. *Journal of Personality and Social Psychology*, 37, 1915–1926.

Petty, R. E. & Cacioppo, J. T. (1981) *Attitudes and Persuasion: Classic and Contemporary Approaches*. Dubuque, IA: W. C. Brown.

Petty, R. E. & Cacioppo, J. T. (1986) *Communication and Persuasion: Central and Peripheral Routes to Attitude Change*. New York: Springer/Verlag.

Petty, R. E., Cacioppo, J. T. & Schumann, D. (1983) Central and peripheral routes to advertising effectiveness: The moderating role of consumer involvement. *Journal of Consumer Research*, 10, 135–146.

Phelps, J. E. & Hoy, M. G. (1996) The Aad-Ab-PI relationship in children: The impact of brand similarity and measurement timing. *Psychology & Marketing*, 13, 77–105.

Piaget, J. (1970) Piaget's theory. In P. H. Mussen (Ed.) *Carmichael's Manual of Child Psychology*, pp. 703–732. New York: Wiley.

Piaget, J. (1972) Intellectual evolution from adolescence to adulthood. *Human Development*, 15, 1–12.

Piaget, J. & Inhelder, B. (1956). *The Child's Conception of Space*. London: Routledge & Kegan Paul.

Piccalo, G. (2004, 17 November) TiVo will no longer skip past advertisers. *Los Angeles Times*. Available at: www.latimes.com/business/la-et-tivo17nov17,4464624,print. story?coll-la-home-headlines. Accessed 24 June 2013.

Pincott, G. (2009) *The Keys to Brand Success*. Millward Brown: Point of View. Available at: www.millwardbrown.com/Libraries/MB_POV_Downloads/MillwardBrown_POV_KeysToBrandSuccess. Accessed 23 July 2013.

Powell, L. M., Szczypka, G., Chaloupka F. J. (2007) Exposure to food advertising on television among US children. *Archives of Pediatric and Adolescent Medicine*, 161(6), 553–560.

Powell, L. M., Szczypka, G., Chaloupka F. J. (2010) Trends in exposure to television food advertisements among children and adolescents in the US *Archives of Pediatric and Adolescent Medicine*, 164(9), 794–802.

Prasad, V. K., Rao, T. R. & Sheikh, A. A. (1978) Mother vs commercial. *Journal of Communication*, 28, 91–96.

PR Week (no date) Kids Brand Index 2011. Available at: www.prweek.com/uk/go/kidsbrandindex. Accessed 4 July 2013.

Purswani, G. (2010) Advergames, their use and potential regulation. *Asian Pacific Public Relations Journal*, 11, 57–63.

Quilliam, E. T., Lee, M., Cole, R. T. & Kim, M. (2011) The impetus for (and limited power of) business self-regulation: The example of advergames. *Journal of Consumer Affairs*, 24, 224–247.

Randrup, L. & Lac, K. T. (2000) Children and TV commercials. Research Paper No.1, Department of Marketing, Copenhagen Business School.

Raney, A. A. (2004) Expanding disposition theory: Reconnecting character liking, moral evaluations and enjoyment. *Communication Theory*, 14(4), 348–369.

Raney, A., Arpan, L. M., Pashupati, K. & Brill, D. A. (2003) At the movies, on the net: An investigation of the effects of entertaining and interactive web content on site and brand evaluations. *Journal of Interactive Marketing*, 17(4), 38–53.

Reeves, R. (1960) *Reality in Advertising*. New York: Alfred Knopf.

Rheingold, H. (1993) *The Virtual Community: Homesteading on the Electronic Frontier*. New York: Harper Collins.

Richardson, T. & Harris, H. (2011) Food marketing and social media: Findings from Fast Food FACTS and Sugary Drinks FACTS. Paper presented at the American University Digital Food Marketing Conference, 5 November. Available at: www.uconnruddcenter.org/resources/upload/docs/what/reports/FoodMarketingSocialMedia_AmericanUniversity_11.11 Accessed 12 March 2015.

Richardson-Klavehn, A. & Bjork, R. A. (1988) Measures of memory. *Annual Review of Psychology*, 39, 475–543.

Richins, M. L. & Dawson, S. (1992) A consumer values orientation for materialism and its measurement: Scale development and validation. *Journal of Consumer Research*, 19 (December), 303–316.

Rideout, V. J., Foehr, U. G. & Roberts, D. (2010) *Generation M2: Media in the Lives of 8 to 18 Year Olds*. Menlo park, CA: Kaiser Family Foundation. Available at: www.kff.org/other/poll-finding/report-generation-m2/media-in-the-lives. Accessed 13 June 2013.

Roberts, D. F. (1983) Children and commercials: Issues, evidence, interventions. In J. Sprafkin, C. Swift & R. Hess (Eds.) *Rx Television: Enhancing the Preventive Impact of TV*, pp. 19–36. New York: Haworth Press.

Roberts, D. F., Christenson, P., Gibson, W. A. et al. (1980) Developing discriminating consumers. *Journal of Communication*, 30, 94–105.

Robertson, T. S. & Rossiter, J. R. (1974) Children and commercial persuasion: An attribution theory analysis. *Journal of Consumer Research*, 1, 13–20.

Robinson, T. N., Borzekowski, D. L. G., Matheson, D. M. & Kraemer, H. C. (2007) Effects of fast food branding on young children's taste preferences. *Archives of Pediatric and Adolescent Medicine*, 161(8), 792–797.

Robinson, T. H., Saphir, M. N., Kraemer, H. C. et al. (2001) Effects of reducing television viewing on children's requests for toys: A randomized controlled trial. *Developmental & Behavioural Pediatrics*, 22(3), 179–184.

Roedder, D. (1981) Age differences in children's responses to television advertising: An information processing approach. *Journal of Consumer Research*, 8 (September), 144–153.

Roediger, H. L. & McDermott, K. B. (1995) Creating false memories: Remembering words not presented in lists. *Journal of Experimental Psychology: Learning, Memory and Cognition*, 21, 803–814.

Roediger, H. L., Wixted, J. H. & DeSoto, K. A. (2012) The curious complexity between confidence and accuracy in reports from memory. In L. Nadel and W. P. Sinnott-Armstrong (Eds.) *Memory and Law*, pp. 84–118. Oxford: Oxford University Press.

Rogers, D. (2002, 14 November). Media Smart tells kids 'be sceptics'. *Marketing*, p. 4.

Roper, S. & Shah, B. (2007) Vulnerable consumers: The social impact of branding on children. *Equal Opportunities International*, 26(7), 712–728.

Ross, J. & Harradine, R. (2004) I'm not eating that! Branding and young children. *Journal of Fashion Marketing and Management*, 8(1), 11–26.

Rossiter, J. R. (1976) Visual and verbal memory in children's product information utilization. In B. B. Anderson (Ed.) *Advances in Consumer Research*, Vol. 3, pp. 572–576. Ann Arbor, MI: Association for Consumer Research.

Rozendaal, E., Buijzen, M. & Valkenburg, P. M. (2009) Do children's cognitive defenses reduce their desire for advertised products? *Communications: The European Journal of Communication Research*, 34, 287–303.

Rozendaal, E., Buijzen, M. & Valkenburg, P. M. (2010) Comparing children's and adults' cognitive advertising competences in the Netherlands. *Journal of Children and Media*, 4(1), 77–89.

Rozendaal, E., Buijzen, M. & Valkenburg, P. M. (2011) Children's understanding of advertisers' persuasive tactics. *International Journal of Advertising*, 30(2), 329–350.

Rozendaal, E., Lapierre, M. A., van Reijmersdal, E. A. & Buijzen, M. (2013) Reconsidering advertising literacy as a defense against advertising effects. *Media Psychology*, 14(4), 333–354.

Rozendaal, E., Slot, N., van Reijmersdal, E. A. & Buijzen, M. (2013) Children's responses to advertising in social games. *Journal of Advertising*, 42(2–3), 142–154.

Russell, C. A. (2002) Investigating the effectiveness of product placements in television shows: The role of modality and plot connection congruence on brand memory and attitude. *Journal of Consumer Research*, 29(3), 306–318.

Russell, C. A., Norman, A. T. & Heckler, S. E. (2004) The consumption of television programming: Development and validation of the connectedness scale. *Journal of Consumer Research*, 31(2), 150–161.

Russell, C. A. & Puto, C. P. (1999) Rethinking television audience measures: An exploration into the construct of audience connectedness, *Marketing Letters*, 10(4), 387–401.

Russell, C. A. & Stern, B. B. (2006) Consumers, characters, and products: A balance model of sitcom product placement effects. *Journal of Advertising*, 35(1), 7–21.

Safko, L. & Brake, D. (2009) *The Social Media Bible*. New Jersey: John Wiley & Sons.

Saunders, J. R., Samli, A. C. & Tozier, E. F. (1973) Congruence and conflict in buying decisions of mothers and daughters. *Journal of Retailing*, 49, 3–18.

Schachter, D. L. (1987) Implicit memory: History and current status. *Journal of Experimental Psychology: Learning, Memory and Cognition*, 13 (July), 501–518.

Schachter, D. L., Norman, K. A. & Koustaal, W. (1998) The cognitive neuroscience of constructive memory. *Annual Review of Psychology*, 49, 289–318.

Schlosser, A. E. (2003) Experiencing products in the virtual world: The role of goal and imagery in influencing attitudes versus purchase intentions. *Journal of Consumer Research*, 30(2), 184–198.

Schneider, W. & Pressley, M. (1997) *Memory Development Between Two and Twenty*. 2nd edn. Mahwah, NJ: Lawrence Erlbaum Associates.

Scott-Thomas, C. (2010, 8 December) Study reveals social media brand marketing potential. Available at: www.foodnavigator-use.com/Suppliers2/Study-reveals-social-media-brand-marketing-potential. Accessed 6 July 2013.

Seaman, P. & Ikegwuonu, T. (2010, November), *Drinking to Belong: Understanding Young Adults' Alcohol Use With Social Networks*. Joseph Rowntree Foundation. Available at: www.jrf.org.uk. Accessed 26 June 2013.

Seifert, R. (2012, 12 June) Striptease and cyber sex: My stay at Habbo Hotel. Available at: www.channel4.com/news/striptease-and-cyber-sex-my-stay-at-habbo-hotel. Accessed 14 June 2013.

Selman, R. L. (1980) *The Growth of Interpersonal Understanding*. New York: Academic Press.

Shamdasani, P. N., Stanaland, A. J. & Tan, J. (2001) Location, location, location: Insights for advertising placement on the web. *Journal of Advertising Research*, 41(4), 7–21.

Shapiro, S. & Krishnan, H. S. (2001) Memory-based measures for assessing advertising effects: A comparison of explicit and implicit memory effects. *Journal of Advertising*, 30(3), 1–14.

Sherry, J. L., Lucas, K., Greenberg, B. S. & Lachlan, K. (2006) Video game uses and gratifications as predictors of use and game preference. In P. Vorderer & J. Bryant (Eds.) *Playing Computer Games: Motives, Responses and Consequences*, pp. 213–224. Mahwah, NJ: Lawrence Erlbaum Associates.

Shrum, L. J. (2004) (Ed.) *The Psychology of Entertainment Media: Blurring the Lines Between Entertainment and Persuasion*. Mahwah, NJ: Lawrence Erlbaum Associates.

Siegel, M. (1997) *Knowing Children: Experiments in Conversation and Cognition*. 2nd edn. Hove, East Sussex: Psychology Press.

Siegler, R. S. (1998) *Children's Thinking*. 3rd edn. Englewood Cliffs, NJ: Prentice Hall.

Sigman, A. (2010, 5 January). Product placement's threat to children. *The Guardian*. Available at: www.guardian.co.uk/commentisfree/2010/jan/05/product-placement-tv-children. Accessed 26 June 2013.

Sirgy, M. J. (1982) Self-concept in consumer behaviour: A critical review. *Journal of Consumer Research*, 9 (December), 287–300.

Skaar, H. (2009) Branded selves: How children in Norway relate to marketing on a social network site. *Journal of Children and Media*, 3(3), 249–267.

Slater, M. D., Rouner, D., Domenech-Rodriguez, M. et al. (1997) Adolescent responses to TV beer advertisements and sports content/context: Gender and ethnic differences. *Journalism and Mass Communications Quarterly*, 74, 108–122.

Slavin, A. (2009) Crashing the party. *Best's Review*, 109(10), 24–27.

Smith, C. (2013, 5 June). Why do consumers follow brands on Facebook? *Business Insider*. Available at: www.businessinsider.com/brands-on-facebook-win-with-promotions-2013-06. Accessed 28 June 2013.

Smith, E. E., Shoben, E. J. & Rips, L. J. (1974) Structures and process in semantic memory: A factual model for semantic decision. *Psychological Review*, 81, 214–241.

Smith, L. (1980) Development of classification: The use of similarity and dimensional relations. *Journal of Experimental Child Psychology*, 36, 150–178.

Smith, L. (1989) A model of perceptual classification in children and adults. *Psychological Review*, 96, 125–144.

Smith, P. K., Cowie, H. & Blades, M. (2003) *Understanding Children's Development*, 4th edn. Oxford: Blackwell.

Smith, R. A. & Houston, M. J. (1985) A psychometric assessment of measures of scripts in consumer memory. *Journal of Consumer Research*, 12 (September), 214–224.

Socialbakers.com (2011) Brazil Facebook statistics. Available at: www.socialbakers.com/facebook-statistics/brazil. Accessed 23 July 2013.

Socialbakers.com (2011) India Facebook statistics, penetration, demography. Available at: www.socialbakers.com/facebook-statistics/india#chart-intervals. Accessed 23 July 2013.

Solberg, E. G., Diener, E. & Robinson, M. D. (2004) Why are materialists less satisfied? In T. Kasser and A. D. Kanner (Eds.) *Psychology and Consumer Culture*, pp. 29–48. Washington, DC: American Psychological Association.

Solomon, M. (1983) The role of products as social stimuli: A symbolic interactionism perspective. *Journal of Consumer Research*, 10 (December), 319–329.

Speers, S. E., Harris, J. L. & Schwartz, M. B. (2011) Child and adolescent exposure to food and beverage brand appearances during prime-time television programming. *American Journal of Preventive Medicine*, 41(3), 291–296.

Steuer, J. (1992) Defining virtual reality: Dimensions determining telepresence. *Journal of Communication*, 42, 73–93.

Stewart, D. W., Morris, J. & Grover, A. (2007) Emotions in advertising. In G. J. Tellis and T. Ambler (Eds.) *The Sage Handbook of Advertising*, pp. 120–134. Thousand Oaks, CA: Sage.

Stewart-Knox, B. J., Sittlington, J., Rugkasa, J. et al. (2005) Smoking and peer groups: Results from a longitudinal qualitative study of young people in Northern Ireland. *British Journal of Social Psychology*, 44, 397–414.

Stokes, J. (2011, 9 February) Social media case study – Wrigley's Extra versus Polo Mints. Available at: www.freshnetworks.com/blog/2011/02/social-media-case-study-wrigleys-extra-v-polo-mints. Accessed 4 July 2013.

Stoneman, Z. & Brody, G. H. (1982) The indirect impact of child-oriented advertisements on mother–child interactions. *Journal of Applied Developmental Psychology*, 2, 369–376.

Stratman, J. (2010, 12 August) Social media case study: Cadbury spots versus stripes campaign. Available at: www.freshnetworks.com/blog/2010/08/social-media-case-study-cadbury-spots-versus-stripes-campaign. Accessed 4 July 2013.

Suh, K. S. & Chang, S. (2006) user interfaces and consumer perceptions of online stores: The role of telepresence. *Behaviour and Information Technology*, 25(2), 99–113.

Sujan, M. & Bettman, J. R. (1989) The effects of brand positioning strategies on consumers' brand and category perceptions: Some insights from schema research. *Journal of Marketing Research*, 26(4), 454–467.

Sulake.com (2012) Habbo Hotel – where else? Available at: www.sulake.com/habbo. Accessed 24 July 2013.

Suntornpithug, N. & Khamalah, J. (2010) Machine and person interactivity: The driving forces behind influences on consumers' willingness to purchase online. *Journal of Electronic Commerce Research*, 11(4), 299–308.

Sutherland, L. A., MacKenzie, T., Purvis, L. A. & Dalton, M. (2010) Prevalence of food and beverage brands in movies: 1996–2005, *Pediatrics*, 125(3), 469–474.

Sutter, J. (2009) Tutorial: Introduction to web 2.0. *Communications of the Association for Information Systems*, 25(1), 40.

Symantec (2009) Norton Online Living Report 09. Available at: www.us.norton.com/content/en/us/home_homeoffice/media/pdf/nofr/NOLR_Report_09. Accessed 3 March 2013.

Tan, D. 2010 Success factors in establishing your brand. Franchising and Licensing Association. Available at: www.flasingapore.org/info_branding.php. Accessed 3 March 2013.

Taylor, R. (1999) A six-segment message strategy wheel. *Journal of Advertising Research*, 39(6), 7–17.

Tellis, G. J. (1998) *Advertising and Sales Promotion Strategy*. Reading, MA: Addison-Wesley.

Terlutter, R. & Capella, M. L. (2013) The gamification of advertising anlaysis and research directions of in-game advertising, advergames and social network games. *Journal of Advertising*, 42 (2–3), 95–112.

Thomson, D. (2010) Marshmallow power and frooty treasures: Disciplining the child consumer through online cereal advergaming. *Critical Studies in Media Communication*, 27(5), 438–454.

Tinson, J. & Nancarrow, C. (2007) 'GROw'ing up: Tweenagers' involvement in family decision making. *Journal of Consumer Marketing*, 24(3), 160–170.

Tobin, J (2013, 30 May). Top 50 brands rocking Facebook marketing. Ignite. Available at: www.ignitesocialmedia.com/facebook-marketing/top-50-brands-rocking-facebook-marketing-2013. Accessed 28 June 2013.

Tulving, E. (1972) Episodic and semantic memory. In E. Tulving & W. Donaldson (Eds.) *Organization and Memory*, pp. 382–406. New York: Academic Press.

Tulving, E., Schachter, D. L. & Stark, H. A. (1982) Priming effects in word-fragment completion are independent of recognition memory. *Journal of Experimental Psychology: Learning, Memory and Cognition*, 8 (July), 336–342.

Turnipseed T. R. I. & Rask, A. (2007, 14 November) *Children's Health and Advergaming: A Theoretical Study of Advertisement Driven Video Games, Product Placement and Integrated Marketing Communication*. Chicago, IL: NCA 93 Annual Convention.

Underwood, R. L. (2003) The communicative power of product packaging: Creating brand identity via live and mediated experience. *Journal of Marketing Theory and Practice*, 11(1), 620–676.

Urban, G. L., Hauser, J. R., Qualls, W. J. et al. (1997) Information acceleration: Validation and lessons from the field. *Journal of Marketing Research*, 34(1), 143–153.

Valkenburg, P. M. & Buijzen, M. (2005) Identifying determinants of young children's brand awareness: Television, parents and peers. *Applied Developmental Psychology*, 26, 456–468.

Valkenburg, P. M. & Cantor, J. (2001) The development of child into a consumer. *Journal of Applied Developmental Psychology*, 22, 61–72.

Van Reijmersdal, E. A., Jansz, J., Peters, O. & van Noort, G. (2010) The effects of interactive brand placements in offline games on children's cognitive, affective and conative brand responses. *Computers in Human Behavior*, 26(6), 1787–1794.

Van Reijmersadal, E. A., Rozendaal, E. & Buijzen, M. (2012) Effects of prominence, involvement, and persuasion knowledge on children's cognitive and affective responses to advergames. *Journal of Interactive Marketing*, 26(1), 33–42.

Vaughn, R. (1980) How advertising works: A planning model. *Journal of Advertising Research*, 20(5), 27–33.

Verhellen, Y., Oates, C., De Pelsmacker, P. & Dens, N. (2014) Children's responses to traditional versus hybrid advertising formats: The moderating role of persuasion knowledge. *Journal of Consumer Policy*, 37(2), 235–255.

Vollmer, C. & Precourt, G. (2008) *Always On: Advertising, Marketing and Media in an Era of Consumer Control*. New York: McGraw-Hill.

Voorveld, H. A. M., Neijens, P. C. & Smit, E. G. (2009) Consumers' responses to brand websites: An interdisciplinary review. *Internet Research*, 19, 535–565.

Voorveld, H. A. M., Neijens, P. C. & Smit, E. G. (2010) The perceived interactivity of top global brand websites and its determinants. In R. Terlutter, S., Diehl & S. Okazaki (Eds.) *Advances in Advertising Research 1: Cutting Edge International Research*, pp. 217–234. Wiesbaden: Verlag.

Waiguny, M. & Terlutter, R. (2011) Differences in children's processing of advergames and TV commercials. In S. Oakzaki (Ed.) *Advances in Advertising Research: Breaking New Ground in Theory and Practice*, Vol. 2, pp. 35–51. Wiesbaden: Gabler.

Waiters, E., Treno, A. J. & Grube, J. W. (2001) Alcohol advertising and youth: A focus group analysis of what young people find appealing in alcohol advertising. *Contemporary Drug Problems*, 28, 695–718.

Walker, D. (2013) Change the conversation: How to use social media to co-create brand success. Available at: www.greenbooks.org/marketing-research-cfm/how-to-use-social-media-to-co-create-brand-success. Accessed 11 June 2013.

Wallendorf, M. & Arnould, E. J. (1988) My favourite things: A cross-cultural inquiry into object attachment, possessiveness and social linkage. *Journal of Consumer Research*, 14, 531–547.

Ward, S. (1974) Consumer socialization. *Journal of Consumer Research*, 1, 2–14.

Ward, S. & Wackman, D. (1973) Children's information processing of television advertising. In P. Clarke (Ed.) *New Models for Mass Communication Research*. Beverly Hills, CA: Sage.

Ward, S. Wackman, D. & Wartella, E. (1975) *Children Learning to Buy: The Development of Consumer Information Processing Skills*. Cambridge, MA: Marketing Science Institute.

Ward, S., Wackman, D. & Wartella, E. (1977) *How Children Learn to Buy*. Beverly Hills, CA: Sage.

Warren, R., Wicks, R. H., Fosu, I. & Chung, D. (2008) Food and beverage advertising on US television: A comparison of child-targeted versus general audience commercials. *Journal of Broadcasting & Electronic Media*, 52, 231–246.

Wartella, E. (1980) Individual differences in children's responses to television advertising. In E. L. Palmer and A. Dorr (Eds.) *Children and the Faces of Television: Teaching, Violence, Selling*. pp. 307–322. New York: Academic Press.

Wartella, E. (1982) Changing conceptual views of children's consumer information processing. In A. A. Mitchell (Ed.) *Advances in Consumer Research*, Vol. 9, pp. 144–146. Ann Arbor, MI: Association for Consumer Research.

Wartella, E. & Ettema, J. (1974) A cognitive developmental study of children's attention to television commercials. *Communication Research*, 1, 46–69.

Weber, K., Story, M. & Harnack, L. (2006) Internet food marketing strategies aimed at children and adolescents: A content analysis of food and beverage brand websites. *Journal of the American Dietetic Association*, 106, 1463–1466.

Weinberg, B. & Pehlivan, E. (2011) Social spending: managing the social media mix. *Business Horizons*, 54, 275–282.

Weiss, D. M. & Sachs, J. (1991) Persuasive strategies used by pre-school children. *Discourse Processes*, 14, 55–72.

Weston, R. (2008) 7 *social networking strategies*. Available at: www.entrepreneur.com/article/191312. Accessed 23 April 2013.

Wiles, M. A. & Danielova, A. (2009) The worth of product placement in successful films: An event study analysis. *Journal of Marketing*, 73, 44–63.

Williams, K. T. (2009, 7 Feb) Case study: Dell hell. Available at: www.docstoc.com. Accessed 23 April 2013.

Williams, R. B. & Clippinger, C. A. (2002) Aggression, competition, and computer games: Computer and human opponents. *Computers in Human Behavior*, 18, 495–506.

Wilson, B. J. & Weiss, A. J. (1992) Developmental differences in children's reactions to a toy advertisement linked to a toy-based cartoon. *Journal of Broadcasting & Electronic Media*, 36(4), 371–394.

Winkler, T. & Buckner, K. (2006) Receptiveness of gamers to embedded brand messages in advergames: Attitudes towards product placement. *Journal of Interactive Advertising*, 7(1), 37–46.

Wintour, P. (2011, 3 June) Cameron-backed report to protect children from commercialisation. *The Guardian*. Available at: www.guardian.co.uk/politics/2011/jun/03/cameron-backed-report-commercialisation-childhood. Accessed 26 July 2013.

Wise, K., Bolls, P., Kim, H. et al. (2008) Enjoyment of advergames and brand attitudes: The impact of thematic relevance. *The Journal of Interactive Marketing*, 9(1), 27–36.

Woolfolk, M. E., Castellan, W., Brooks P. I. (1983) Pepsi versus Coke: Labels not tastes prevail. *Psychological Reports*, 52, 185–186.

Wright, P. (2002) Marketplace metacognition and social intelligence. *Journal of Consumer Research*, 28, 677–682.

Wright, P., Friestad, M. & Boush, D. M. (2005) The development of marketplace persuasion knowledge in children, adolescents and young adults. *Journal of Public Policy & Marketing*, 24(2), 222–233.

Wyllie, A., Casswell, S. & Stewart, J. (1989) The response of New Zealand boys to corporate and sponsorship alcohol advertising in television. *British Journal of Addiction*, 84(6), 639–646.

Wyllie, A., Zhang, J. F. & Casswell, S. (1998) Responses to televised alcohol advertisements associated with drinking behaviour of 10–17 year olds. *Addiction*, 93, 361–371.

Yang, H. L. & Wang, C. S. (2008) Product placement of computer games in cyberspace. *Cyberpsychology and Behaviour*, 11(4), 399–404.

Yang, M., Roskos-Ewoldsen, D. R., Dinu, L. & Arpan, L. M. (2006) The effectiveness of 'in-game' advertising. *Journal of Advertising*, 35(4), 143–152.

Yeu, M., Yoon, H-S., Taylor, C. R. & Lee, D-H. (2013) Are banner advertisements in online games effective? *Journal of Advertising*, 42(2–3), 241–250.

Yoo, C. Y. (2008) Unconscious processing of web advertising: Effects on implicit memory, attitude toward the brand, and consideration set. *Journal of Interactive Marketing*, 22(2), 2–18.

Yoon, H-S., and Lee, D-H. (2007) The effects of consistent ad series on consumer evaluations: A test of repetition-variation hypothesis in a South Korean context. *International Journal of Advertising*, 28, 105–123.

Youn, S. & Lee, M. (2004) Advergame playing motivations and effectiveness: A 'uses and gratifications' perspective. In M. R. Stanford & R. J. Faber (Eds.) *Advertising, Promotion, and New Media*, pp. 320–347. Armunk: M. E. Sharpe.

Young, B. (1990) *Children and Television Advertising*. Oxford: Clarendon Press.

Zelazo, P. D. & Reznick, J. S. (1991) Age-related asynchrony of knowledge and action. *Child Development*, 62, 719–735.

Zimmerman, B. J. (2000) Self-efficacy: An essential motive to learn. *Contemporary Educational Psychology*, 25 (January), 82–91.

Zuckerman, P., Ziegler, M. E. & Stevenson, H. W. (1978) Children's viewing of television and recognition memory for commercials. *Child Development*, 49, 96–104.

Zufryden, F. (1996) Linking advertising to box office performance of new film releases – a marketing planning model. *Journal of Advertising Research*, 36, 29–41.

Index